Economies of Network Industries

Network industries, such as railways, telecommunications and new media, are a world apart from other more traditional organizations. Rather than being based on a model of perfect competition, network industries are characterized by a differentiation of products, shorter life cycles of products and the essential nature of innovation.

This comprehensive study of the economics of network industries covers such themes as:

- technology adoption;
- competition and market power;
- strategic alliances, mergers and acquisitions;
- the economics of the Internet.

The author's accessible writing style and knowledgeable research should make the book absolutely recommended reading for all those interested in industrial, innovation and micro policy economics.

Hans-Werner Gottinger is Professor of Economics at Kwansei Gakuin University, Kobe-Sanda, Japan and at the Institute of Management Science, the University of Maastricht, the Netherlands.

Routledge Studies in Business Organizations and Networks

Economies of Network Industries

Hans-Werner Gottinger

Routledge
Taylor & Francis Group

LONDON AND NEW YORK

First published 2003
by Routledge
11 New Fetter Lane, London EC4P 4EE

Simultaneously published in the USA and Canada
by Routledge
29 West 35th Street, New York, NY 10001

Routledge is an imprint of the Taylor & Francis Group

© 2003 Hans-Werner Gottinger

Typeset in Times New Roman by
Newgen Imaging Systems (P) Ltd, Chennai, India
Printed and bound in Great Britain by
MPG Books Ltd, Bodmin

British Library Cataloguing in Publication Data
A catalogue record for this book is available
from the British Library

Library of Congress Cataloging in Publication Data
Gottinger, Hans-Werner.
    Economies of network industries / Hans-Werner Gottinger.
        p. cm. – (Routledge studies in business organizations and networks ; 24)
    Includes bibliographical references and index.
    1. Business networks. 2. Strategic alliances (Business) I. Title. II. Routledge studies in
business organization and networks ; 24.

    HD69 .S8 G68 2003
    338.8–dc21   2002036912

ISBN 0–415–27740–X

In many ways the economy has been remade. Now some fear that the new economy, which fuelled the boom, could also deepen a bust.

Wall Street Journal, January 5, 2001

Contents

Figures

Tables

Preface

The new industrial organization theory emerging over the past twenty-five years has recognized that particular industries have been dominated by networks either in terms of physical layouts (identifying infra-structural links and nodes) or as virtual features through the provision of complementary products and services. Examples include computer hardware and software, video cassettes and cassette recorders, and compact disks and disk players.

A major feature of network industries is that they show network externalities. A network externality has been defined, generally, as a change in the benefit, or surplus, that (economic) agents derive from a product when the number of other agents consuming the same kind of product changes. As communication devices, such as fax machines, increase in popularity, for example, every additional fax machine becomes increasingly valuable because there is an ever greater use of it. In principle, the value received by agents can be separated into two distinct parts. Every product has a 'stand-alone' value that is generated by the product even if there are no other users. A 'stand-alone' computer may be such a product. It may also (or only) have a network value, that is the added value, derived from being able to interact (or share) with other users of the product. There are particular strategic characteristics that come with network externalities (effects) and which are usually identified with network industries.

These are, for example:

Interconnection and Bundling   Microsoft (MS) controls the operating environment of which a Web browser is but one component. Netscape's browser needs to work in conjunction with MS's operating system. Interconnection arises in network industries such as telecommunications, railroads, airlines, and computer industries. Conversely, bundling creates a barrier for a single product like the Netscape browser to proliferate, for example, MS Office bundles together a word processor, a spreadsheet, a browser, and a presentation tool.

Compatibility and the creation of standards

If standards fuel a positive feedback cycle to launch a new technology, they can easily cannibalize sales from an older technology.

Costs of information production   Information is costly to produce but cheap to reproduce.

Commoditization of information   Competition among sellers of commodity information pushes prices to zero.

Demand side economies of scale   This is an element of the network effect in the industry reinforcing the market leader's dominance (Microsoft).

Differential pricing   Prices aimed at locked-in customers may not appeal to new buyers. Differential pricing is the solution.

Increasing returns   Positive Feedbacks are facilitated through network externalities, standardization, lock-in effects, reinforced through demand side and supply side economies of scale which could form the backbone of the New Economy with fast-growing network industries and highly profitable monopolistic or oligopolistic companies in a highly intense technological racing environment.

Lock-ins and switching costs   For a chosen technology switching could be very expensive on the consumer's and producer's side: LP vs CD, MAC vs MS/DOS, CDMA vs GSM.

Network market's battle of systems   Digital Wireless Phones, 56 K Modems, Broadband Access: XDSL.

Network externalities (positive/negative)   Metcalf's Law: the value of a network is the square of its nodes. The addition of any new member in the network benefits each user – to obtain a critical mass and creating a bandwagon effect.

Open standards   Contributes to network effects (Unix, Java, Adobe).

Positive feedback by growth of the network   In its extreme form positive feedback can lead to a winner-take-all market.

Performance vs *compatibility*   It is a trade-off between the evolution strategy of compatability and the revolution strategy of performance. Improve performance at the cost of increasing customer switching resistance or of high compatibility with limited performance improvement (CD vs DAT). Network externalities reinforce the switch to the negative or positive dimension.

Staying ahead   Being ahead in the technological race but keeping control of standard setting (IBM and the PC). Keep would-be competitors at bay through licensing, control the process by drawing rivals into the process by R & D acquisitions.

Standardization   The availability of standardized protocols for menus/ browsers and e-mail drove the commercialization of the Internet.

Winner-take all market   Gaining a leading edge in the network, network externalities make the strong stronger and the weak weaker, therefore it leads to dominant positions.

Zero reproduction/distribution costs   Digital technology allows sharply lower reproduction and distribution costs.

Network effects are endemic to new, high technology industries, those now constituting the 'New Economy', and they experience problems that are different to ordinary commodities in conventional markets. Even beyond those high technology industries one could envision more conventional industries to play out networking for utilizing 'increasing returns' in a boom cycle though being increasingly vulnerable in a bust cycle.

This book emphasizes policy-level analysis and strategic considerations at the microstructure of industry and its aggregate effects on economic growth, factor productivity, and the business cycle. Industries with important network features have long been a concern of public policy in developed economies. Railroads and utilities form the earliest industries that belong to an archetypal network industry. Those public policy concerns continue today not only for railroads and utilities but for many other industries with important network elements: telephone, broadcasting, cable television, water pipelines, oil and natural gas pipelines, road and highway systems, airlines, ocean shipping, postal service, retailing, bank automated teller machine systems, credit card systems, bank check and payment clearance systems, multiple listing services, and the Internet. The long-standing public policy concerns over network industries are systemic because those industries often embody two major and widely recognized forms of potential market failure: significant economies of scale, with the potential for monopoly, and externalities. Yet, policy measures to address those concerns, in particular in the antitrust domain in view of dynamic competition and innovation, have often been misguided, with the result that we have inefficient and anti-competitive regulation and even government ownership of network industries.

Chapters 1–3 identify the main features of a network economy. Chapter 4 stresses dynamic competition among network firms and exhibits a model of technological racing in network industries. Chapters 5 and 6 deal with competitive opportunities and risks emanating from a network economy, and how regulators and the courts need to cope in view of inducing fair competition and antitrust policies. Chapter 7 considers market structure, strategy, and quality choice in network markets, and how companies may position themselves in preserving and growing market share.

Chapters 8 and 9 cover the Internet technology as a special facilitator of the network economy in two major ways to enhance network industry capabilities. That is, first to strengthen the information economy in terms of speed, scale, and scope, and second to implement a service economy through e-commerce activities. Chapter 10 addresses the possible impact of the aggregate of network economies, the so-called new economy, as regards its impact on productivity growth, business cycles, and economic welfare.

This book has been written during my time visiting the Fondazione Salernitana and the University of Salerno, Italy, and has been completed during my tenure at Kwansei Gakuin University, Kobe-Sanda, Japan. My thanks go to the economics faculty of the University of Salerno, in particular, Professors Pagano and Jupelli, for their hospitality, and to Lia Ambrosio for secretarial assistance. Also my thanks go to Professor DelMonte from the University of Naples, and Professor Scandizzo, University of Rome, for very fruitful discussions on some of the topics of the book. I am grateful to comments by Professors Deissenberg (University of Aix-Marseille), Kutschker (Catholic University Eichstaett), van Bemmel (Free University of Amsterdam), Glynn (Europe Economics) and, in particular, to Makoto Takashima (Nagasaki University) who is a coauthor of Appendix A, as well as to Celia Umali. For all remaining errors the responsibility is mine.

Hans-Werner Gottinger

1 Network economics

Introduction

In traditional industries the economic model conventionally used to estimate the market function is perfect competition. Perfect competition theory assumes that individual economic agents have no market power. The agents in the economy are price takers. It is generally believed that competition will drive the market price down to the competitive level (equal to the marginal costs) and consumer welfare is improved through allocative and production efficiencies. The perfect competition or nearly perfect market is premised on the assumption that in a market containing many equally efficient firms each firm in the market faces a perfectly horizontal demand curve for a homogeneous product, and that firms freely enter or exit the industry.

It is against this benchmark that network industries are a world apart. In their markets products are heterogeneous, differentiation in products is common, the life cycles of products are short, sunk cost is significant, innovation is essential and sometimes 'only the paranoid survive' (Grove, 1996). In some industries only a handful of participants are in the market and the dominant firms may easily raise the barriers of market entry to exclude competitors. In other words, in network industries, markets usually involve enormous capital and highly risky investment, economies of scale, intensive and interdependent technologies owned by different market players, network externalities of products, and tendency of product standardization. In view of this, market failures in those industries appear significant.

In this chapter, I give a fairly extensive characterization of network industries and discuss some of the policy conclusions which surface again in more detail in subsequent chapters.

Networks and network industries

In conventional terms empirical examples of network industries embrace electricity supply, telecommunications, and railroads. Network industries can be defined as those where the firm or its product consists of many interconnected nodes, where a node is a unit of the firm or its product, and where the connections among the nodes define the character of commerce in the industry.

Railroads, for example, are a network industry. The nodes of a railroad (its tracks, rolling stock, switches, depots) are scattered across a geographic area, and the configuration of the nodes determines where, when, to whom, how much, and how quickly goods can be transported. Like the railroads, the entire transportation sector can be analysed as a network industry. Be it airlines, trucks, or ships, each mode of transport has its network of nodes. Other network industries include utilities, telecommunications, broadcasting, computers, and information and financial services. The nodes of these industries are units like electricity lines, phone sets, personal computers, and information platforms. The number of nodes and connected consumers may grow in tandem, but a distinction exists between an additional node on the network and an additional consumer. A node is a capital addition. This distinction is of some importance for the analysis of positive, negative, or negligible externalities in a later section.

Star networks   A star network (Figure 1.1) has a collection of nodes clustered around some central resource. Movement of resources or products from one node to another must always pass through this central node. A simple example of a star network is a local telephone exchange, a call from any node (phone) must be transmitted through the central switch.

The figure illustrates the central resource CR with N denoting network nodes.

Tree networks   In a tree network (Figure 1.2), the purpose of the infrastructure is movement between the central resource and the nodes. Flow among the nodes

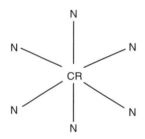

Figure 1.1 Star network.

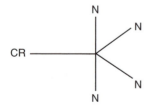

Figure 1.2 Tree network.

is not part of the system design. Examples of systems like this include the distribution of public utilities such as water, electricity, and natural gas. In each of these systems, resources flow from a central area to many outlying points.

Tree-structured networks can be considered one-way networks because resources flow in only one direction. On the other hand, if the system is defined broadly enough, tree-structured networks can also move resources in both directions. Consider, for example, a combined water and sewage system. Water flows out from the central resource to the nodes along a tree structure, and sewage returns from the nodes to the central receiving area through the same structure.

Crystal networks   A crystal network (Figure 1.3) occurs when the central resources are distributed among connected star networks. Like a star network, movement can occur from any point on the network to any other point. Unlike the star network, that movement will not always traverse a single central point. Movement from one star to the next will involve both central connections, while movement within a star will require only one. An example of a crystal network is the long-distance telephone network which is really the connection of many local networks through medium- and long-distance lines.

Web networks   In a web network (Figure 1.4), each node is connected to many other nodes. Paths between the points on the network multiply as the interconnections increase, and the network assumes a distributed character, no network centre can be identified. There are two salient features to a network with a web

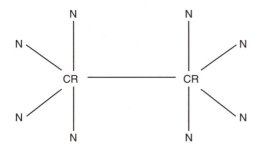

Figure 1.3 Crystal structure.

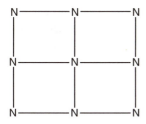

Figure 1.4 Web structure.

structure. First, the resources distributed via a network with a web structure are located in the nodes. This means that as the number of nodes increases, the resources to be distributed throughout the network also increase. Second, the distributed nature of a web network makes the system less vulnerable to the failure of any part. This feature was a key attraction of networked computing projects evolving into today's Internet.

Here each node is connected to four nodes around it, and a lattice or grid emerges. That is, if you pick any two points between which data should travel, the failure of any one point in the lattice (as long as it is not the origin or destination of the data) will not interrupt communication. This is not the case with the other structures presented here. In a star network, for example, failure of the central node disables the rest of the system.

Network characteristics   Beyond the various structures of networks, there are also a few characteristics of networks that can influence their economics. Two of the most common characteristics made about networks concern their directionality and spatial character. Most networks carry their loads to and from all the nodes on the network, traffic is reciprocal. Transportation networks and the telephone system are like this, and reciprocal networks are probably what most people imagine if they think about networks. One-way networks, however, also exist. Most of the tree structured networks, electricity, water, natural gas, deliver from a central resource to homes, but not vice versa. A communications example of a one-way network is the cellular paging system, though the introduction of two-way pagers and cellular phones shows that a transformation of that network is already underway. A spatial network is one that is fixed geographically, a railroad network is a typical example. As a spatial network, the existing track layout determines, for example, who can be served by the railroad and where goods can be delivered. A non-spatial network like the Internet, is free of these geographic constraints.

In the context proposed we define a network as a group of firms connected to each other through strategic alliances. The gains to entering into a network range from the direct benefits obtained from entering into an alliance to the indirect benefits from being part of the network. Direct benefits may take the form of access to knowledge resources, competencies, and cost economies. On the other hand, indirect benefits generally refer to greater access to information flows and control benefits from being strategically positioned in the network.

A way to measure those indirect benefits has been proposed in Appendix B.

A description of networks would not be complete if we leave out gateways or converters. They would create the possibility to have different types of (incompatible) networks communicate and work together. Gateways always impose some loss of efficiency on a system because they use resources as they connect incompatible systems. They incur costs of translation or manipulation or the opportunity costs of the gateway itself.

A case in point is the compatibility of computer systems. At some theoretical level all computers are fundamentally compatible, they just manipulate binary numbers, however, at some functional level we all observe and appreciate the standards problems that plague electronic systems. Gateways solve such problems in different ways and with different levels of success. Two of the most important ways in which gateways differ are the degree and the direction of compatibility they establish between systems. Although there are examples where networks or systems are either wholly compatible or incompatible, compatibility should be conceptualized as a continuum. Gateways can also vary in the direction of compatibility. When gateways link incompatible systems, some allow each system access to its complement, while others grant access from one system to a second, but not vice versa. The former are called two-way, or reciprocal, gateways; the latter are one-way gateways. Both reciprocal and one-way gateways are common to software systems. Import and export commands in database or word-processing programs, for instance, are examples of reciprocal gateways. The relative ease with which people can now write documents in Microsoft Word and then send those documents to WordPerfect users (and vice versa) demonstrates a two-way connection. Both users gain access to otherwise incompatible networks. In contrast, some program upgrades include a one-directional gateway: users of new software versions can access old version files, but old version users cannot work with files created by the program upgrade.

Gateways allow previously unattainable network externalities to be captured, and, in some cases, they can prevent or mitigate product 'lock-ins' to occur, in others, previously unpredictable technology development could be biased toward eventual adoption.

High-risk investments and sunk costs

A network industry company survives in the market only by maintaining rapid innovation, relying on intensive, large-scale research and development projects to develop new products or processes.

On the other hand, sizeable financial commitments receive no guarantee of profits or success, as a recent survey on the New Economy (*The Economist*, 2000) appears to substantiate. Accordingly, these tremendous sunk costs make entry and exit to market relatively difficult. Such a company, therefore, inevitably requires large, irreversible investment. Further, rapid innovation shortens the product's life cycle and leads to non-price competition. The costs of new products, hence, usually increase rather than decrease. Today's semiconductor industry illustrates this dilemma. The cost of staying at the cutting edge of semiconductor technology is horrendous. In addition to the large investment on the supply-side, customer's investment can also be enormous and irreversible. Because today's technologies are complicated, sophisticated, and complementary as well as compatible, customers must commit to a generation of equipment, where personal training, ancillary facilities, applications software, or other ongoing expenses are tied to the particular technologies. This means the investments of customer and their switching costs are very high (Choi, 1994).

Economies of scale

In network industries, the fixed costs are tremendous in proportion to its total costs of the products. The returns to size of the firms are not constant. The average total cost lowers as the total output increases.

The effect of economies of scale is commonly seen in every stage. The most important assets of network industries are knowledge or information. The costs of research and development of new products or new processes are prohibitively high. Nevertheless, once it has been developed, a product (book, software) can be produced with almost zero marginal costs. This is illustrated in the computer software industry where virtually all of the costs of production are in the design of the program of software. Once it is developed, the incremental costs of reproducing software, that means, the costs of copying a disk, are negligible. In other words, the production costs of software are almost totally independent of the quantity sold and consequently, the marginal cost of production is almost zero. At the same time, unlike in other industries, the increasing returns may be of no ending. One of the characteristics of computer software industries is that there is no natural point of exhaustion at which marginal costs begin to exceed marginal revenues and at which it becomes uneconomical to increase production. That is to say, in this industry there is always the case that the more products produced the lower the costs per product. Large-scale production is generally required in order to achieve minimum per unit cost rapidly when the descending learning curve, termed 'learning by doing' effects, are significant. The increasing returns to scale arise because increasing experiences foster the improvement of production technologies, and allows the managers and workers to specialize in their tasks. As a result, the unit costs fall as workers and operators learn by doing. This is particularly evident in the semiconductor industry or computer assembly industry. In those industries, very often than not, shadow costs lie below current-period costs because the presence of a learning curve allows firms to lower their unit costs tomorrow by acquiring production experiences today.

Figure 1.5 shows the learning curve (LC) of semiconductor manufacturing and Figure 1.6 the economies of scale effect connected with the LC advance.

Moreover, in some industries where price discrimination is possible, the learning curve effect leads to a dynamic process whereby differential pricing increases

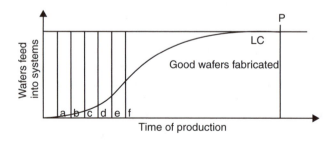

Figure 1.5 Learning curve of wafer production.

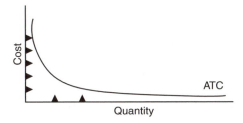

Figure 1.6 Economies of scale effect. ATC = Average total cost.

the volume of output and expanded output results in declining costs, thereby allowing new customers to be served. The presence of learning curve economies is particularly important from a public policy perspective. If there are increasing returns, then it is more economically advantageous to have one large firm producing than have many small firms.

On the other hand, the increasing returns, at the same time, handicap small-scale entry. For example, the introduction of competition into the telecommunications market generally has two phases. The first phase allows new suppliers in the areas of value-added services. The next phase introduces competition into core areas of local, trunk (long-distance), and international services. However, in practice, high capital costs and economies of scale limit the development of competition in local services.

So far we have observed economies of scale effects from the supply side, those are reinforced by equally strong effects from the demand side which are facilitated through 'network externalities'. Also those reinforcing effects could easily lead to overwhelming market dominance and winner-take-all situations (Shapiro and Varian, 1999).

Network externalities

One of the most striking economic aspects of networks is how they create externalities. Network externalities occur in both the demand and supply of the network. The textbook externality is a supply externality. For example, as a negative byproduct of a factory's production, pollution spews into the air or water. Demand externalities, on the other hand, may exist for non-network goods, but they are not usually considered important enough to merit attention. For example, economists typically do not factor demand externalities into consumers' demand functions. Many models of consumer behaviour assume that the average consumer's demand for potatoes, lettuce, corn, etc., for example, are formed without any reference to how many other people are purchasing these products. Certainly the number of consumers in a given market affects demand and therefore price, but an individual's demand is independent – it does not depend directly on a product's popularity in most models. Such effects are assumed away as insignificant.

Besides the supply-side economies of scale the demand-side economies of scale are commonly seen in the communications and computer industries among others. For some goods and services, a person's demand depends on the demands of other people, or the number of other people who have purchased the same good may affect a person's demand. For example, the buyer of a telephone or fax machine would have not bought it if there were no one else who had purchased or would have purchased it. When more people have purchased it the more value of a telephone or fax machine the buyer would have obtained. This is a positive network externality based on an 'actual' or 'physical' network. Moreover, for some goods, such as Microsoft Office, the individual demand for that good inherently exists but enormously increases when other people buy the same good. In an actual network, products have very little or no value when alone, they generate value or more value when combined with others (example: fax machine). In a virtual network, hardware/software network products have value even if they exist alone. However, they are more valuable when there are more complementary goods, and also there will be more complementary goods when more people use the products. Application software developers are likely to write for the platform of the operating system that most people favour. Conversely, the operating system that more application software writes on are favoured by more people. The operating system with a larger market share will provide a bigger market for the application programs. At the same time, the availability of a broader array of application programs will reinforce the popularity of an operating system which in turn will make investment in application programs compatible with that operating system more desirable than investment in application programs compatible with other less popular systems. As a result, the operating system with a larger installed base attracts more buyers whereas the small and later entrant with a smaller installed base with equal or even superior quality finds it difficult to compete. As more users are attracted to a network, the size of the network grows and confers greater value to the network users. Network effects directly challenge an important principle of classical economic theory, which posits decreasing (and eventually negative) returns to scale in most markets. Also this theory basically deals with increasing returns problems in case of supply side economies of scale but ignores cases of demand side economies of scale brought about by increasing value of existing users through increased demand, that is, through network externalities. That is, network markets offer increasing returns over a large portion of the demand curve or even the entire demand curve. Markets with increasing returns imply that bigger is better and consumers deriving more value as the number of users grows. The flip side of this situation in terms of market structure is that the strong grow stronger and the weak become weaker.

Hence, network markets provide potentially fruitful returns to firms that can make their own products as standards in markets or in aftermarkets for complementary goods. This presents the possibility of substantial first-mover advantages: being the first seller in a market may confer an important strategic advantage over later entrants because a first mover's technology may become locked in as a standard (Katz and Shapiro, 1986; Arthur, 1989). That is to say, the first technology that is introduced into the market may gain excess momentum when many early users join in anticipation of other users hopping on the band-wagon at a later date. This strong expectation is critical to network expansion (Choi, 1997). In the end consumers already belonging to an existing network will not likely switch to a new technology, even if it is better (Economides, 1996).

The switching costs associated with transferring to an incompatible but superior technology create 'excess inertia' to consumers. That means consumers will not adopt a new superior technology not only because of the sunk costs they have already put in but also because values from network externalities may be lost if they switch. Network effects, therefore, could stifle innovation.

In a traditional market, where network effects are negligible or non-existent, competition turns primarily upon price, quality, and service considerations. In contrast, in those markets in which network effects are significant, competition plays out in other dimensions as well: particularly in strategies to establish, maintain, and control standards for the industry. The computer industry hence suggests that network effects have played an important role in shaping the market structure and the margins on which competition occurs.

Also, increasing returns raise the possibility of leveraging a monopoly power from one market to another. Because users may be reluctant to commit to any given system unless they believe it will be adopted by many others, the 'network owner' may engage in a variety of strategies to discourage potential buyers from buying a smaller network regardless whether or not it is superior. Strategies include expanding the system to include complementary products, offering a wide variety of complementary products at very attractive prices, or through bundling. At the same time, leveraging is able to raise rivals' economic costs of competing in the marketplace.

For example, in its effort to be adopted as the next generation standard, the owner of one element of a system may enter complementary markets by engaging in alliances as part of a strategy of attracting users to its network. Consequently, rival operating systems need to ensure the provision of substantial complementary products in the market, otherwise very few buyers will try its system. As a result, the follow-on improved or complementary products markets become very difficult.

Strong network effects are therefore themselves barriers to entry, even though it is sometimes unclear whether entry into the market ought to be encouraged. Since the increasing return deters the incentive of new entrants and increases the costs of new entrants. Such a blunting of incentives can occur if the leveraging practice is undertaken, not primarily as part of a vigorous competitive strategy, but in part to decrease the likelihood of competitor entry, so that the dominant firm will continue to be dominant in competition for the next market. This has clearly be shown for the Japanese telecommunications market (Gottinger and Takashima, 2000). The unlikelihood of success for new entrants will reduce the incentives of other competitors to innovate to the extent that these competitors perceive that the opportunities to profit from their innovations are hindered. All of this is particularly significant because markets in which there is rapid technological progress are often markets in which switching costs are high, in which users find it costly to switch to a new technology that is not fully compatible with the older technology. The result is an increase in entry barriers.

From what follows the definition of a network externality is given by the value of a network created by the number of its nodes. Also, network externalities can exist both for the supply and demand side of the economic equation. And networks can generate negative, positive, or no externalities. Negative network externality networks are those that decrease in value when the number of nodes increases. More 'traditional' network industries fit into this category negative network externalities. The key to the negative externality is that in many tree-structures networks, resources are concentrated in a central location. For the electricity grid, that location is the main power plant, for the water system, the central resource is usually a reservoir. The utility network exists to connect consumers to the central resource. When new nodes are added to the network, the number of consumers with access to the resource increases but the potential resource to be distributed remains the same. Thus adding nodes to the network divides a fixed resource among more consumers, meaning less of the resource for each user on average. One can see examples of this in developing countries when, for example, new electricity consumer demand is not met with increased power-generating ability and brown-out results. One can then clearly see the negative network externalities of an electrical grid. In contrast, networks may also exhibit no significant demand externalities. One may consider, for example, the many large and important broadcast networks (i.e. television, radio) that exist in the world today. Adding nodes (television sets, radio receivers) to these networks creates little or no demand externalities: the average consumer considering purchasing a television or radio does not care what percentage of other consumers own these products. Value in these networks is created centrally, and the nature of television and radio broadcasts is such that reception by one instrument has no impact on others' reception. Finally, many of the high technology networks flourishing today embody positive externalities. Networks like these increase in value for the consumer as nodes are added and the system expands. One of the best examples of these kinds of networks is the telephone system. What makes the difference between negative or no-externality networks and positive externality systems? The key resides in the location of resources. Where the electricity grid or the water pipelines or the radio broadcasts are built around a valuable central resource, the telephone network is used to bring highly distributed resources together. When a new phone is added to the network it makes demands on the central resources of the network (switching, for example), but it also adds the resources of the newly connected people to the network. Even more striking is the example of the World Wide Web. New servers (nodes) on the World Wide Web bring with them new web users who bring new information with them. The attraction of the World Wide Web only grows as more people make more information available.

Complementarity, compatibility, and standardization

In network industries, many products have very little or no individual value, but produce value only when combined with other products. Since a product involves lots of technologies, or is made of different components, or a product system combines several goods and services, the demand of those technologies or intermediate goods or services are thus often interrelated. That is to say, they are strongly complementary, although they need not be consumed in fixed proportions. Those complementary products are usually described as forming systems, which refer to a collection of two or more components together with an interface that allows these components to work together. Nevertheless those components, products, or services are usually provided by different manufacturers. The products, components, or services need to be compatible with each other in order to combine the components into operable systems. By the same token, other manufacturers can market their individual products only when the products are compatible with other products. This is easily illustrated in computer assembly, software industries, and elsewhere. In many cases, these strongly complementary components purchased for a single system are spread over time. If the components or products of different brands are incompatible, the customers need to make their purchase decision on the total system. Besides the complementary components, a system may include the future stream of ancillary products and services over the life of a primary product. In other words, rational buyers should take into consideration availability, price, and quality of the components that they would be buying in the future. As a result, customers' costs in purchasing network products are not limited to the price of the product but more importantly, also include the customer's large investment in complementary equipment or training for employees when they use the product. Likewise, whenever consumers become accustomed to the products of particular manufacturers, they do not shift to other products quickly not only because they are unfamiliar with the new products to operate with but also because the complementary equipment or system is sometimes incompatible. In short, the incumbent users switching to a new technology would lose existing network benefits and would have to replace not only the durable goods themselves, but also any sunk investment in complementary assets. It thus provides opportunities for the existing system to exploit the customers and deter competition from the rivals. Compatibility is crucial to gain the benefits in network industries. Network effects will be workable in products of different manufacturers only when their products have the same protocol or bridging technologies allowing them to communicate with each other. Even in the computer software industry, although the product will allow even a single user to perform a variety of functions, whether or not others own the software, the value of a given software program grows considerably as the number of additional purchasers increase. This means that network effects will be unavailable in the software of different manufacturers, which are not compatible, unless converters exist in the interface, if the technology allows (Farrell and Saloner, 1992). Standards, especially interface standards, therefore play an important role in network industries. Without standardization networks would be confined to those users who purchased the products made by the same manufacturer if products made by different manufacturers are incompatible. The standardization of computer software hence facilitates the formation and operation of computer networks, the transfer of files among users and across applications, and savings in training costs. When standards are established, entry, competition, and innovation may be easier to handle if a competitor needs only produce a single better product which can then hook up to the market range of complementary products, than if each innovator must develop an entire 'system'. Compatibility standards thus allow networks to grow, providing pre-competitive benefits by creating 'networks' of compatible products.

Further, because of the standard, economies of scale drive prices down, and the network becomes more attractive and grows. The benefits to society as a whole are greater when standardization allows for product compatibility among all users (Besen and Farrell, 1994). On the other hand, standardization may carry costs of their own. First, there may be a loss of variety, reducing the flow of services generated by the product. Second, the costs of each technology may vary between and among consumers, so that if only one technology is offered, some consumers are forced to purchase what is for them the more expensive technology. Third, and most important, is that despite their advantages for innovation, networks can also retard innovation.

Some economists argue, once standardization is achieved, it can be hard to break out of that standard and move to another, even if the original is no longer the most suitable (Farrell and Saloner, 1992). It can be hard for users or vendors to coordinate a switch from an old standard to a new one, even if all would like to do so.

Moreover, some users may have invested a considerable amount in training themselves to use the existing standard. They will be reluctant to abandon that investment even if new technology is better and a switch would be desirable for the sake of efficiency. New users must choose between the benefits of compatibility and the benefits of the new technology, and often compatibility wins the game because of the effects of 'excess inertia', even if it should not. This is a socially undesirable failure to adopt an improved technology or facilitate improved innovation.

The rationale of strategic alliances

To do business in an international or globalized context more and more network companies decide to form strategic alliances instead of other interfirm transactions such as acquisitions or transactional arrangements.

Strategic alliances of that sort rely on sharing the risks, synthesizing complementary skills or assets, and attaining economies of scale and scope. More importantly, this quasi-integration arrangement can provide participants closer long-term relationships that arms-length market-transactions and short-term contracts can not offer. In network industries, strategic alliances are formed to share the costs of research and development, to complement technologies when producing new products, or to combine resources when entering new markets. Strategic alliances coordinate divergent strengths of research capacities to facilitate an efficient exchange of knowledge or a pooling of skills. More often than not the introduction of a new product, process or improving the quality of the product is possible only when these insights combine together, insights which would have been otherwise closely held as trade secrets by individuals while acting alone. Diverse skills can be brought together in a manner that creates economies of scale in product or process innovation. In addition, when the minimum efficient scale of research and development is too large relative to production and marketing, sometimes it can be performed economically only if two or more firms join together.

Setting standards

Standardization is a natural tendency in network markets, particularly in system markets where strong positive feedback enables one system to pull away the popularity from its rivals once it has gained an initial edge. This de facto standardization generated through market competition in network industries confers on the winner the full value of the standard and not just the value of his contribution. This result is inefficient in social benefits, however. Network effects, which posit incremental benefits to existing users from network growth, suggest that network goods should be optimally priced as low as possible to allow widespread adoption of the standard. Nevertheless, just as a monopolist maximizes its revenue by raising prices above a competitive level, a single company winning and owning a propriety standard can set whatever price it wants. This is not the best way to benefit consumer welfare. A proprietary standard also seems unnecessary as it is used to encourage the production of future works of intellectual property. While the intellectual property regime posits incentives of innovation, the winner of the standards competition may receive a windfall that is far greater than what an intellectual property regime normally provides. Of course, in order to resolve the problem of de facto standardization, a central government authority may simply decree a standard. This strategy is not likely to be effective. The government organization is not market-oriented, and is very likely technologically less efficient. If they choose an inefficient standard, it will be hard to surpass. Private standard setting organizations are more efficient. If they choose the wrong standard it may be leapfrogged by a new standard. At the same time the innovating firm may believe that it can be advantageous from allowing, indeed encouraging, other firms to attach to its new product. In this case, strategic alliances including licensing and joint ventures provide a direct and explicit way to make its product standard. At the same time, if people can switch back and forth between competing systems of what essentially is the same standard, perhaps society can seize the benefits of competition without wasteful duplication of efforts and without stranding consumers who make the wrong choice. A possible solution is to make competing standards interoperable. One approach to achieving interoperable standards is for a private industry organization open to all members to adopt a single standard.

If the members of such a group collectively have a significant market share, their adoption of a standard may produce a 'tipping' effect, bringing the rest of the industry into line. That is to say, the group standard setting may trade off first-round competition (to set the de facto standard) for competition within the standard in later periods. Cooperation is therefore extremely attractive in the setting of standards in the network industry because compatible systems are almost unavoidable in this field. Private group standard-setting through strategic alliances or joint ventures will be more efficient than both by government organization and de facto standardization. Since having multiple companies participating in a standard means that those companies can compete to offer products incorporating the standard after it is selected, thus expanding output and lowering prices. Group standard setting may also promote competition in the development of improvements to the standard, since each of the competitors may seek an advantage over the others by improving the design in ways compatible with the basic interface specifications. Such group standard-setting is common in the computer and telecommunications hardware industry. It has especially been known as the computer industry reaches maturity that the open system plays an essential role. An illustrative example is the market for digital videodiscs (DVD) where two major industry groups, such as Sony–Philips and Toshiba–Matsushita, competed offering incompatible standards for several years and once agreed to use a single compatible format incorporating elements from both products. The agreement is splinted at last not because advantages of compatibility are underestimated but gross profits and possibilities of controlling next generation technology by the winning system are dominant.

Some difficulties are usually found in forming the alliances to set up a standard. The first obstacle is that, since a standard must be chosen for the long term, participants want to get it right. Thus even if all interested parties had identical interests, there would be some delays. The second obstacle is vested interest. Unless discussions are in advance of market decisions, if different vendors have different installed bases neither of them may want to agree on the other's standard. This bargaining problem can cause serious delay.

References

Arthur, W. (1989) 'Competing Technologies, Increasing Returns, and Lock-in by Historical events', *Economic Journal* 99: 116–131

Besen, S. M. and J. Farrell (1994) 'Choosing How to Compete: Strategies and Tactics in Standardization', *Journal of Economic Perspectives* 8: 117–131

Choi, J. P. (1994) 'Irreversible Choice of Uncertain Technologies with Network Externalities', *Rand Journal of Economics* 25 (3): 382–401

—— (1997) 'Herd Behavior, the "Penguin Effect", and the Suppression of Informational Diffusion: An Analysis of Informational Externalities and Payoff Interdependency', *Rand Journal of Economics* 28 (3): 407–425

David, P. (1985) 'CLIO and the Economics of QWERTY', *American Economic Review* PP 75, 332–337

The Economist (2000) *Untangling E-Economics, a Survey of the New Economy*, Sept. 23, 5–44

Economides, N. (1996) 'The Economics of Networks', *International Journal of Industrial Organization* 14: 673–699

Farrell, J. and G. Saloner (1992) 'Converters, Compatibility and Control of Interfaces', *Journal of Industrial Economics* 15 (1): 9–35

Grove, A. (1996) *Only the Paranoid Survive*, New York: Doubleday

Gottinger, H. W. and M. Takashima (2000) 'Japanese Telecommunications and NTT Corporation: A case in Deregulation', *Inter. Jour. of Management and Decision Making* 1 (1): 68–102

Katz, M. and C. Shapiro (1986) 'Technology Adoption in the Presence of Network Externalities', *Journal of Political Economy* 94: 822–841

Shapiro, C. and H. R. Varian (1999) *Information Rules, A Strategic Guide to the Network Economy*, Cambridge, MA: Harvard Business School Press

2   Network size and value

Introduction

We examine competing assumptions about the relationship between network size and network value which are key to models involving network externalities. Network externalities have been the modelling basis for studies ranging from industrial location decisions (Arthur, 1987), to urban residential patterns (Schelling, 1978), to riot behaviour (Granovetter, 1978), and political revolutions (Kuran, 1995).

In industrial organization, economists like Economides (1996) have begun to apply the lessons of networks to industries characterized by vertical relations.

Despite the variety of economic work on networks and network externalities that has occurred in the past few years little empirical work on those topics exist. Almost all of the published work is of a theoretical nature, few papers have attempted to quantify network externalities in some meaningful way.

In many high-tech industries the centre of innovation has moved away from the large companies and towards a network of interorganizational relations. Both the computer and biotechnology industries are well-known cases of this proclivity. This increases our incentives to understand how these networks work as well as the value they engender. Firms join networks for various reasons. The literature highlights two major benefits to being part of a network, namely greater access to information flows, and control benefits from being strategically positioned in a network. How does the market value a firm's entry into a network? The benefits which arise from being part of a network result from both direct and indirect ties. The formation of direct ties through alliances will be used as the event from which to value the advantages of joining the network. The analysis focuses on relating the value derived from the formation of an alliance to the relationship between the firm and their change in position within the network.

First we discuss the motivation behind the work on network externalities relating to the academic and business worlds. Then we outline some key hypotheses on network size and economic value that should be subject to empirical testing. Later we establish a relationship to the macroeconomic debate on increasing returns industries, forming the 'new' vs the 'old' economy.

Perspectives on network externalities

We start with a useful distinction suggested by Economides (1996) in his survey of the literature, he divides the work on network externalities into what he calls macro and micro approaches. Macro investigations assume that externalities exist and then attempt to model their consequences. Micro investigations start with market and industry structures in an attempt to derive (theoretically) the source of network externalities. The later category is largely founded on case studies. Three of those are symptomatic. David's (1985) QWERTY study, Arthur's (1989) model, and the domination of VHS in the videotape recorder market combined, spurred theoretical and empirical interest in network externalities. The gist of David's QWERTY study is that inferior technologies through network externalities may be subject to 'lock-ins'. This might apply to the keyboard QWERTY as well as to the adoption of the VHS against the Betamax standard though with specific technological advantages of Betamax over VHS. In empirical support of network externalities, Gandal (1994) finds that consumers pay a premium for spreadsheets which are compatible with Lotus 1-2-3 (an industry standard for spreadsheets). In other words, consumers are willing to pay for the ability to share spreadsheet information and analysis easily with other computer users. Thus he concludes that there is strong empirical support for the existence of network externalities in the computer spreadsheet market. In another paper, Saloner and Shepard (1995) test for the existence of network externalities in the network of Automated Teller Machines (ATMs), their results support existence.

Hypotheses on network externalities

Perhaps it is not surprising that little quantitative work on network externalities has been done. Many examples of network industries embody cutting-edge technologies, given that theoretical work on network externalities is still relatively new, data collection is fragmentary, and common data sets upon which to test theories are severely limited. One particular important question emerging on network externalities is the functional relationship between the size of a network (its number of nodes) and the network's value.

Three key assumptions about the relationship between network size and network value underlie most analyses of network externalities and their effects. They relate to linear, logarithmic, and exponential assumptions.

The linear assumption postulates that, as networks grow, the marginal value of new nodes is constant. The logarithmic assumption postulates that, as a network grows, the marginal value of new nodes diminishes. Network externalities at the limit in this formulation must be either negative, zero, or of inconsequential magnitude in comparison to quantity effects on prices. In contrast, Katz and Shapiro (1986) make their assumptions explicit: network externalities are positive but diminish with development, at the limit they are zero. In any case, network effects diminish in importance in these models as a network grows. The third

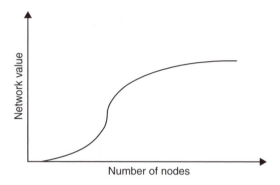

Figure 2.1 The S-hypothesis.

key assumption about the relationship between network size and value is the exponential assumption which in the popular business and technology press has been named 'Metcalfe's Law'. It embodies the idea of positive network external-ities whose marginal value increases with network size. Robert Metcalfe (1995) states the 'law' in this way: 'In a network of N users, each sees a value propor-tional to the $N-1$ others, so the total value of the network grows as $N(N-1)$, or as N squared for large N'. The validity of Metcalfe's Law is crucial to the 'increas-ing returns' debate on the New Economy, facilitated by the aggregation of positive network externalities in high-tech industries. One could also consider a mixture of hypotheses such as a combination of Metcalfe's Law and the loga-rithmic assumption, that is early additions to the network add exponentially to the value of a network, yet later additions diminish in their marginal value. The result looks like an S curve, as illustrated in Figure 2.1.

It is based on the idea that early additions to a network are extremely valuable, but at some point 'network saturation' should take place and marginal value should fall.

In summary, the industry and hence aggregate (growth) benefits can be classi-fied as follows:

(i)   industries that show an exponential growth (through strong complementarity)
(ii)   industries that show linear growth (additive benefits)
(iii) industries that show a log relationship (stable benefits).

The mixtures of those economies create the features of the New Economy. Such an economy is not immune to economic cycles, but to the extent that the network economy snowballs in an upswing period, by the same token it might also con-tract faster in a downswing period but with a better chance to stabilize quicker.

Technology adoption and network industries

We look at the main hypotheses to show how they are likely to affect the adoption process of particular network industries. The linear hypothesis is the assumption of Arthur's (1989) model subject to simulation. Given a very large number of trials, technology adoption leads (almost surely) to lock-ins. Given two technologies, *A* and *B*, further *R* and *S* agents that make adoption decisions, respectively, in Arthur's model each trial represents a random walk of an ever-increasing number of *R* and *S* agent decisions. As the number of trials increases, with symmetries in both technologies *A* and *B*, the split between *A* and *B* adoptions approach fifty-fifty. That is, either one of them will be adopted, and non-adoption will be most unlikely. In Arthur's analytical model, as the number of iteration goes to infinity, the possibility of non-adoption disappears.

Correspondingly, the average adoption time until lock-in will increase with decreasing probability (of non-adoption), in conformity with the linear hypothesis, in other words, more agents become (linearly) more convinced to adopt either way. This suggests that the network effect leaves only a neutral impact on the innovation process. Against this benchmark, when the value of network size grows logarithmically in relation to its size, the average time until lock-in occurs is extended. What appears surprising is how much the logarithmic assumption delays lock-in. That is, the logarithmic specification creates less growth prospects and greater instability by delaying (or preventing) adoption from occurring. In contrast to the logarithmic hypothesis, the exponential assumption shortens the average time until adoption occurs. The average adoption is affected just as drastically by the exponential assumption as by the logarithmic one. With the exponential assumption, however, the average adoption occurs much earlier than in the baseline case. No wonder, that on an aggregate scale across network industries, it is this network effect that lends support to 'increasing returns' by the proponents of the New Economy. It can even be reinforced by speed of transactions, for example, enabled through large-scale broadband Internet technologies. This would support a scenario of a sustained realization of an exponential assumption as even more likely. If it can be established that the Internet triggers a technology adoption process in the form of a large and broad wave ('tsunami') across key industries, sectors, regions, and countries, then increasing returns will generate exceptional growth rates for many years to come. For this to happen there should be a critical mass of network industries being established in an economy. Then an innovation-driven network economy feeds on itself with endogenous growth. It remains to be determined, empirically, which mix of sectors, with network effects with exponential, linear, and logarithmic relationships will have a sustained endogenous growth cycle.

From a slightly different perspective, it is interesting to note that the logarithmic assumption creates instability in the models. Metcalfe's Law, on the other hand, which leads to immediate adoption, creating dynamics of its own, would prevent many contemporary models from reaching equilibrium.

References

Arthur, W. (1987) 'Urban, Systems and Historical Path Dependence', in J. Ausubel and R. Herman (eds), *Cities and their Vital Systems*, Washington, DC: National Academy Press, 85–97

Arthur, W. (1989) 'Competing Technologies, Increasing Returns, and Lock-in by Historical Events', *Economic Journal* 99: 116–131

David, P. (1985) 'CLIO and the Economics of QWERTY', *American Economic Review* PP 75, 332–337

Economides, N. (1996) 'The Economics of Networks', *International Journal of Industrial Organization* 14: 673–699

Gandal, N. (1994) 'Hedonic Price Indexes for Spreadsheets and an Empirical Test for Network Externalities', *Rand Journal of Economics* 25(1): 160–170

Granovetter, Mark (1978) 'Threshold Models of Collective Behavior', *American Journal of Sociology* 83: 1420–1443

Katz, M. and Shapiro, C. (1986) 'Technology Adoption in the Presence of Network Externalities', *Journal of Political Economy* 94: 822–841

Kuran, T. (1995) *Public Truths, Private Lies: The Social Consequences of Preference Falsification*, Cambridge, MA; Harvard University Press

Metcalfe, R. (1995) 'Metcalfe's Law: Network Becomes more Valuable as it Reaches More Users', *InfoWorld* 17(40): 53

Saloner, G. and Shepard, R. (1995) 'An Empirical Examination of the Adoption of ATM', *Rand Journal of Economics* 26(3): 479–501

Schelling, T. (1978) *Micromotives and Macrobehavior*, New York: Norton

3 Technology adoption in networks

Introduction

Technology adoption in networks suggests that individually rational decisions regarding technologies can, in the presence of network externalities, generate collectively inefficient results (Arthur, 1989). Such a statement would be subject to qualifications if one incorporates adapter (converter) technologies into the adoption problem. Adapters allow previously unattainable network externalities to be captured, in some cases, adapters preclude 'lock-in' from ever occurring, in others, previously unpredictable technology adoptions can be predicted with high confidence. These issues dominated historically the late nineteenth-century rift between electric power standards and today governs the evolution of Internet standards.

Examples: present and past

Example 1 Consider two competing technologies that exhibit network externalities of some sort, such as WINTEL and Macintosh computers. In the framework of the Arthur (1989) and David (1985) models, these technologies battle for market share across several dimensions, including network size. If consumers value the size of the network (positive externalities), decisions to adopt one technology increase its subsequent attractiveness. In the classic case, market share builds on market share, and once a technology has been established a solid lead it becomes 'locked-in'. The consumer decision is plausible enough. Few people use computers just for their own sake. Most value the ability to share data electronically among co-workers, clients, friends, and family. The more data one shares the more important network compatibility becomes. In aggregate, positive network externalities drive a market towards a single standard. Now consider how the consumer decision would change if an inexpensive translating disk drive were invented that allowed PC disk and data to be read for Macintoshes and vice versa, and nothing were lost in the process. A Mac user could then completely capture the benefits of the PC network, and network size would become a trivial component of the buying decision. Assuming price and quality of the technologies remained comparable, the market would no longer drive towards one technology. Finally, consider the asymmetric situation, in which a different disk drive allows Mac users to access the PC network but did not allow PC users to access the Mac network. Given comparable prices and qualities, he attractiveness of the PC declines. The Mac would gain strength in the market. Those knowledgeable in computers will note that translating software and drives that read both Mac and PC-formatted disks have existed for a number of years, though none provides a seamless transition from one system to another. That these kinds of devices – adapters, converters, gateways – exist is not a situation unique to the Mac and PC rivalry. Gateways exist to bridge incompatible systems as diverse as railway gauges, electrical current, and computer networks. It is thus likely that the existence of gateways substantially alters the dynamics of technology adoption where positive network externalities are present.

Example 2   Another example has been noted by David (1992). It centres around the question why support for direct current (DC) power (including the one of the inventor: Thomas Edison) collapsed around the end of the nineteenth century. Until then competition between alternating current (AC) and DC systems had been fierce throughout the 1880s and neither was clearly superior at that time. DC systems, although inferior to AC in terms of transmission, led in the ability to translate electricity to mechanical power via motors. They also enjoyed an installed base of generating systems and infrastructure in the most advanced, electrified, urban areas. Moreover, DC's installed base meant that line engineers and electricians were familiar and comfortable with the system, the system was reliable and the flaws known. Support for DC power, however, dissipated as Edison withdrew from the management of Edison General Electric and the company (after merging into General Electric) began selling AC systems in the 1890s. Although DC systems continued in use over the next thirty years, they were enclipsed by the expansion of AC systems. Why after such fierce competition, did support for DC systems so suddenly evaporate?

David and Bunn (1988) find a reasonable explanation for the quick collapse of the DC system. They identify the invention of the rotary converter – a gateway that allowed AC substitutions to be attached to DC main lines – as a turning-point in the competition between the standards. It appears that the rotary converter's invention is the turning-point.

The simple mechanism of technology adoption

We consider Arthur's (1989) basic model with two agents, *R* and *S*, and two technologies *A* and *B*. Each agent makes a buying decision based upon an initial preference for the technologies and from the network externalities associated with each technology. These payoff rules can be summarized in Table 3.1 where A_R is the *R*-agent's initial preference for technology *A*, N_a is the size of the network using technology *A*, and *r* is the parameter for network valuation.

Table 3.1 Agent payoffs for technology choices

	Technology A	*Technology B*
R-agent	$A_R + rN_a$	$B_R + rN_b$
S-agent	$A_S + rN_a$	$B_S + rN_b$

The increasing returns to scale case is under consideration here, so r is always positive. The R-agent initially prefers technology A and the S-agent initially prefers technology B, therefore $A_R > B_R$ and $A_S < B_S$.

Arthur's simple model can be envisioned as a universal sales counter where all agents interested in technologies A and B must go for their purchases. The R and S agents queue, and one agent makes a purchase in each time period. In modelling terms, agent i comes to the market at time t_i, at which point he makes his decision based upon his payoff rule. Whether the i-th agent is of R or S type constitutes the stochastic element in the model. Arthur stipulates a 50 per cent probability that agent i will be of the R type. Thus the technology choice of the i-th agent is determined by a combination of three things: agent i's identity as an R or S type (determined stochastically), agent's i's initial technology preference (determined by the agent's type), and the number of previous adopters of each technology.

Arthur shows that, under these parameters, one of the two technologies will 'lock-in'. This result is easily derived from the payoffs in Table 3.1. R agents will initially prefer technology A given his preferences and no network benefits. R agents will switch to technology B, however, when

$$B_R + rN_b > A_R + rN_a. \tag{1}$$

Equation (1) can easily be rearranged into the following 'switching equation'

$$(A_R - B_R)/r < N_b - N_a. \tag{2}$$

Equation (2) and a similar one for the S agent establish 'absorbing barriers'. When the size of technology B's network exceeds A's network by some arbitrary amount, as determined by initial preferences and the r value, technology B will lock-in as the de facto standard. Intuitively, the R agent will abandon technology A when the size differential of technology B's network is so large that the benefits of B's outweigh the R's agent's initial technology preferences. Because at that point both R and S agents will purchase only technology B, the network for technology A will not grow further.

This analysis can be captured by a simple graphic (see Figure 3.1).

The horizontal axis represents the progression of time and the subsequent agent technology adoptions. The horizontal axis represents the right-hand side of equation (2), that is, the difference between the sizes of technology A's network and technology B's network.

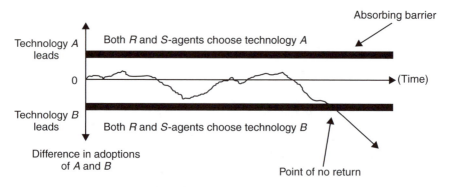

Figure 3.1 Product lock-ins under increasing returns.

Table 3.2 Agent payoff with converters

	Technology A	Technology B
R-agent	$A_R + rN_a + krN_b$	$B_R + rN_b + crN_a$
S-agent	$A_S + rN_a + krN_b$	$B_S + rN_b + crN_a$

This model formulation makes several simplifying assumptions. First, it assumes that agent choices are 'stationary in time' – once the agent has chosen a technology, the agent remains with that type. Second, the model presumes technologies are unsponsored (i.e. not subject to strategic manipulation by firms).

This simplifies by eliminating prices. Third, the model equates the two-part payoff equations (initial preference plus network benefit) with the net present value of the technology types available. In other words, the value of a technology choice is determined by past, not future agent choices. We will attempt to mitigate those assumptions by introducing converter technologies in the next sections.

Compatibility through bridging technology

Adding converter technology to achieve compatibility produces some interesting changes to Arthur's model. Consider the addition of parameters k and c, assuming values from zero to one, which represent the compatibility of technology A with technology B and the reciprocal compatibility of B with A, respectively.

A parameter equal to 1 denotes a converter that is perfectly compatible and a zero value would indicate complete incompatibility.

The payoffs for this model appear in Table 3.2. Note that the model can be collapsed to Arthur's formulation by the assumption that $k = c = 0$ which is the absence of the need of any converter.

(*a*) *Partial, reciprocal converter*   As a derivation of the model we can state: the introduction of a partial, two-way gateway will, ceteris paribus, prolong the time required for technological lock-in to occur. Assume the introduction of a bridging technology that is compatible in both directions, that is, $k = c$. The *R*-agent will switch preference to technology *B* when

$$(A_R - B_R)/r < (1 - k)(N_b - N_a). \tag{3}$$

At the introduction of a gateway, the distance between network parity and the absorbing barriers will be multiplied by $1/(1 - k)$. If the bridging technology were 50 per cent compatible, the difference between N_b and N_a would have to be twice as large to persuade the *R*-agent to switch to technology *B*. This proposition is illustrated in Figure 3.2. Note that the stochastic nature of the modelling process does not guarantee that introducing a converter will prolong the adoption process. On average, however, adoption will take longer in systems with partial, reciprocal converters.

(*b*) *Perfect, reciprocal converter*   The presence of a perfect, two-way gateway will prevent any technology from emerging as the standard. In the case where $k = 1$ (which technically makes no sense but is nevertheless instructive), equation (3) reduces to stating that *R*-agents will switch to technology *B* when $A_R < B_R$. Because initial preferences assume that $A_R > B_R$, the existence of a perfectly compatible gateway will assure agents abide by their initial preferences. This is logically consistent, because network externalities have effectively been eliminated from the situation. It is illustrated in Figure 3.3.

(*c*) *Partial, one-way converter*   The introduction of a partial, one-way converter will likely bias technological lock-in towards the favoured technology. The favoured technology is the one which has access to its counterpart network (in this case, technology *A*). The unfavoured technology has no such benefit. In a Mac/PC analogy, a partial, one-way converter might allow PC users to access the Mac

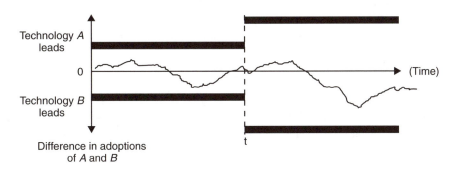

Figure 3.2 Introduction of a partially compatible converter.

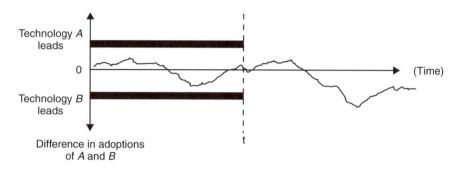

Figure 3.3 Perfectly compatible converter.

network while Mac users had no such advantage in the PC realm. To create this scenario within the model, assume that $c = 0$ and $0 < k < 1$. Users of technology A now have a partial compatibility with technology B's network, but users of technology B find the A network perfectly compatible. In this scenario, the R-agent with initial preference for technology A will switch to technology B when

$$(A_R - B_R)/r < (1 - k)N_b - N_a. \tag{4}$$

Moreover, the introduction of this partial, one-way technology will cause S-agents to switch to technology A when

$$(B_S - A_S)/s < N_a - (1 - k) N_b. \tag{5}$$

Not only does the absorbing barrier for technology B become $1/(1 - k)$ times as far away from network parity, the absorbing barrier for technology A becomes even closer. Figure 3.4 illustrates this result.

  (*d*) *Perfect, one-way converter*   If a perfect one-way converter is introduced, the standard will inevitably converge to the favoured technology. To model the case where A is perfectly compatible with B, but technology B is perfectly incompatible with A, set $k = 1$ and $c = 0$. The R-agent will then convert to technology B when

$$(A_R - B_R)/r < - N_a. \tag{6}$$

Because the left-hand side of equation (6) is always positive, the R-agent will never adopt technology B. The S-agent will stay with technology B as long as

$$(B_S - A_S)/s > N_a. \tag{7}$$

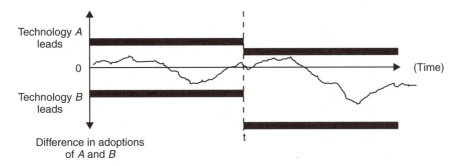

Figure 3.4 One-way partially compatible converter.

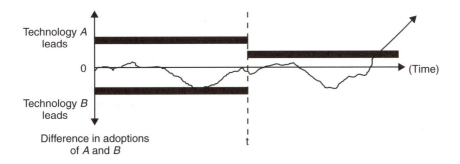

Figure 3.5 One-way perfectly compatible converter.

As the number of adopters increases $n \rightarrow \infty$, however, equation (7) will no longer hold, and the *S*-agent will switch to technology *A*. Technology *A* will become the standard. This is reflected in Figure 3.5.

Resolving empirical puzzles

As referred to in the section on 'Examples: present and past' the empirical puzzle of technology adoption relates to the question: why was it logical for Thomas Edison and Edison General Electric suddenly to stop their active support of DC power after such intense competition in the 1880s? At that time the Westinghouse company and other AC supporters, though becoming strong competitors, were far from demonstrating clear technological superiority of the AC system.

The AC system then faced substantial engineering problems related to the higher voltages it used: greater insulation and better grounding were required to protect against the higher risks of electrical shock inherent to the AC system. Because of the reasoning behind using bridging technologies to reconcile different standards a logical reason to abandon DC power could be seen in the invention of a gateway between AC and DC power systems emerging in the late 1880s. In 1888 C. S. Bradley invented the 'rotary converter', a device which allowed AC power to be converted to DC power. With this device, local DC sub-stations could be attached to high-voltage AC transmission lines from regional generators. The reverse was not true. The rotary converter was a one-way gateway favouring AC power systems. As we derived in the previous section, a one-way gateway will bias lock-in toward the favoured technology. The favoured technology gains (on average) because its users can appropriate the network externalities of its competitor technology while the reverse is not true. This scenario played itself out in the 'battle of the systems'. To visualize the transition from a contested market to AC dominance (and the role of the gateway), imagine the buying decision of an electric station owner. Stations bought equipment and/or electricity from Edison and Westinghouse and delivered service to local customers. As new stations were built, owners faced this choice: gamble on the DC system, or choose a system that could operate regardless of which standard prevailed.

Review of related work

The various models suggested in the section on 'The simple mechanism of technology adoption' build upon and extend previous work on the economics of technology adoption, standards, and compatibility in network industries.

The topic on using bridging technologies in extending network externalities has been formalized only rarely. The economics of standards and compatibility recognizes that the introduction of high or low cost gateways will have varying effects. Farrell and Saloner (1986) close their article on standards, compatibility, and innovation with a list of interesting future research topics – one being firms' strategic manipulation of network externalities through the creation of one-way gateways. Katz and Shapiro (1986) considered the significance of 'adapters'. Their work analyses the private and social incentives leading to the construction of a gateway. Similarly, Farrell and Saloner (1992) investigate primarily the provision of 'converters' under different regimes of market power. Choi's research (1994, 1997) is similar to that presented here in that he focuses on the effects of gateways. Choi, however, has directed his attention primarily to the role of gateways in the transition from one wave of technology to the next.

The model suggested contextualizes Arthur's (1989) seminal work on technology adoption. Arthur's two most surprising conclusions are: (1) that, given two competing technologies that exhibit positive network externalities, it is impossible to predict which one will be adopted by the market, and (2) that it is therefore possible for an inferior technology to be 'locked-in' by historical accident. The range of applicability for both of these results is restricted when gateways are introduced to the analysis.

A major criticism of Arthur's (1987, 1989) and similar models of technology adoption is that they consider 'unsponsored' technologies or standards. Firms in these models cannot foster a technology's chances for success. To compensate for this weakness is to incorporate prices into a dynamic model of technology adoption.

Two main approaches exist for incorporating sponsorship into the technology adoption problem. One approach to analysing the effects of technology sponsorship has employed a static equilibrium framework. Katz and Shapiro (1986) and Farrell and Saloner (1986, 1992) treat technology sponsorship in this way.

The model that Farell and Saloner (1992) use assumes that there are two technologies and that consumers make purchasing decisions based upon some preference for the technology itself and also for the size of that technology's network. The model also assumes that the initial preference for the technology varies from complete allegiance to technology *A* to complete allegiance to technology *B*. The model allows to investigate the impact of network externalities and converter costs in the standardization process. It describes the combinations of the underlying variables that produce regions of incompatibility, standardization, and conversion. Moreover, they investigate how changes in market structure (e.g. monopoly and duopoly) affect the incentives to convert or standardize.

By analysing changes in market structure, Farrell and Saloner begin to explore sponsored technologies. They explicitly incorporate prices into their model and allow prices to vary from the marginal cost of production for the technologies and thereby derive the interesting result that converters both reduce the private and social welfare losses of not standardizing. Although this is a significant step forward from previous models that do not include prices, it also has some considerable weaknesses. First, the largely static nature of the model does not allow for analysis of strategic pricing. Also the dynamic change from one wave of technology to the next is an important topic not addressable within this framework.

Several authors have approached the sponsorship question within a more dynamic framework. For example, J. P. Choi (1994) includes the role of sponsorship among the variables he includes in the standardization process. He varies sponsorship not as price variable, but as a variable measuring the riskiness of a firm's research and development activities. Then the conclusion emerges that the sponsor of an emerging technology may choose too conservative a research strategy, but it does not address the question of strategic pricing.

Arthur and Ruszcynski (1992), on the other hand, directly examine strategic pricing by modelling a 'switching' process where consumers choose over time to remain with the technology they currently own or to abandon that technology in favour of its competition. Arthur and Ruszcynski allow sponsoring firms to influence consumer decisions through price-setting, subject to the constraint that prices cannot be less than zero. Within this framework, they create a stochastic duopoly game where firms maximize their expected discounted rewards. They find that, around a critical discount rate in contested markets, firms use zero prices in an attempt to gain market share. Once a firm has a market share greater than 50 per cent, it begins to raise its price in an attempt to exploit its market dominance. They also find that when firms' discount rates are high, strategic pricing plays less of a role and market shares stabilize. Similarly, when firms' discount rates are low, strategic pricing plays a greater role and market shares polarize. As a result, when strategic pricing is possible and positive network externalities exist, prices are extremely sensitive to market conditions.

All this recent work increases understanding of positive network externalities systems and how they affect the formation of standards, yet there is substantial unexplored territory. Despite the work of Choi (1994–7) on gateways and Arthur's (1992) model on strategic pricing there has been no integrated model on technology adoption with gateways and strategic pricing. Moreover, all the cited papers assume perfect foresight for the agents of their models. Choi (1994) and Arthur and Ruszcynski (1992) complicate their analysis somewhat by introducing either increasing uncertainty in outcomes or 'myopia', in the form of stronger time preferences, but these models are still philosophically rooted in perfect foresight. Models incorporating imperfect foresight have yet to be explored. Also these models overlook the observation that asymmetric resources may play a role in strategic pricing and in technology adoption. Particularly, with the rise of enormously successful network companies like Microsoft (and its recurring discussions with the US Justice Department over antitrust allegations), investigating the effects of asymmetric financial resources could yield intriguing results.

A coordination game

One issue that shapes the discussions of standards and compatibility is the social welfare implications of various states of compatibility of technology policies.

Social welfare issues command such attention because standards and compatibility situations can create a coordination game where players are in conflict over dividing the gains from standardization. Because converters affect the degree of compatibility in any meta-system, it is unsurprising to learn that converters also impact social welfare. Social welfare could be derived from the perspective of a (fictional) social planner: it is the total benefits derived by the users of a system of technologies. For ease of analysis, the social welfare implications of the model presented in the section on 'Examples: present and past' can be examined by using the standard two-by-two matrix of a coordination game. Here all the R-agents and S-agents play the coordination game together, it is as if there is only one R- or S-agent in a sequence of rounds. The returns to that agent can be computed by summing the preference for the employed technology with the value attached to network size.

Figure 3.6 shows the general form of the two-by-two game. Such a format would support all previously obtained results on the use of converter technology. Arthur's model concerning lock-ins can also be produced given that $k = c = 0$. To play the coordination game we would have to assign parameter values to the various entries in Figure 3.6, thus for illustrative purposes only, assign the values 4 to A_R, B_S, 2 to B_R, B_S, 3 to r, and N_a, N_b could range from 0 to 2. For k and c likewise we assume three levels of equal ks and cs.

Some of the social welfare implications of converters can be seen in Figure 3.7, which combines the assumed parameter values with the form of the game as set up in Figure 3.6. There will be a best outcome in form of an equilibrium value (Nash equilibrium) of the game indicated in the upper-right corner of the matrix in Figure 3.7, provided k and c are greater than 1/3.

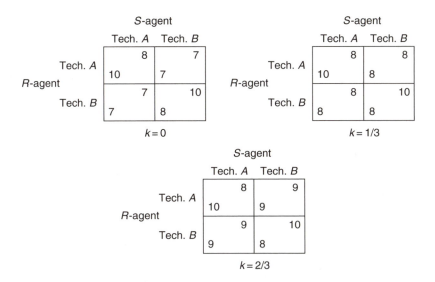

S-agent

	Tech. *A*	Tech. *B*
Tech. *A*	As + rNa + krNb	Bs + rNb + crNa
R-agent	Ar + rNa + krNb	Ar + rNa + krNb
Tech. *B*	As + rNa + krNb	Bs + rNb + crNa
	Br + rNb + crNa	Br + rNb + crNa

Figure 3.6 Social welfare game.

S-agent

	Tech. *A*	Tech. *B*
Tech. *A*	8 / 10	7 / 7
Tech. *B*	7 / 7	10 / 8

R-agent

$k = 0$

S-agent

	Tech. *A*	Tech. *B*
Tech. *A*	8 / 10	8 / 8
Tech. *B*	8 / 8	10 / 8

R-agent

$k = 1/3$

S-agent

	Tech. *A*	Tech. *B*
Tech. *A*	8 / 10	9 / 9
Tech. *B*	9 / 9	10 / 8

R-agent

$k = 2/3$

Figure 3.7 Coordination game.

One of the most interesting implications of this matrix is that, without knowledge of technology preferences, network value and converter efficiency, a social planner would not know whether the introduction of a two-way converter would increase, decrease, or have no effect on social welfare. Figure 3.7 shows that when $k = 2/3$, the move to the Nash equilibrium from either an all *A*-technology network (the upper-left corner) or an all *B*-technology network (the bottom-right corner) leaves social welfare unchanged. When k and c are greater than one-third yet less than two-thirds, the move to the mixed technology network Nash equilibrium decreases social welfare. On the other hand, when converter efficiency increases about the two-thirds level, the move to the mixed network increases social efficiency. At the extreme, a perfect two-way converter ($k = c = 1$) makes the switch to a mixed-technology network better off (Pareto improving). Coordination game analysis indicates that above a certain minimum efficiency threshold, the introduction of a two-way converter will prelude lock-in from any standard. Moreover, the efficiency of the converter will directly determine whether the move away from a single standard technology will improve, worsen, or be neutral to social welfare.

A second interesting point raised by the analysis of Figure 3.7 is that two-way converters have equity implications. Standardization as either an *A*-technology network or an all *B*-technology network results in identical overall welfares, but distribution is skewed towards the user group whose preferred technology becomes the standard. The introduction of a two-way converter of sufficient efficiency (here k and c must be greater than 1/3), however, eliminates the unequal distribution of benefits in these examples. It is possible, therefore, that converters' ability to increase equity is one reason converters may play a role in network evolution.

Antitrust policy

The widely published antitrust case against Microsoft has led to continuing debates whether control of a network constitutes monopoly power in a market.

Also the economics profession is split in their judgement (Kwoka and White, 1999). Arthur (1996) points out that there are pros and cons of antitrust regulation for increasing returns industries, and he argues that when lock-in occurs with a technologically inferior product, it is in the interest of technological progress that regulators intervene. The logic of the argument is simply that when lock-in occurs, a user may be reluctant to abandon the network externalities of a standard, even if a superior technology surfaces. In this situation a company can 'unnaturally' prolong its control over a market.

Such an argument is much less convincing in the presence of effective converters, because their very existence has severed the benefits of the network from the control of the technology provider. Thus, if an effective two-way converter exists between a dominant player's network and smaller networks, regulators need to be less concerned about market power derived from that area of business.

Unfortunately, regulators face several difficulties in considering converter impact on industries and market power. First, deciding whether a converter is effective may not be an easy matter. In the case of Microsoft, there is no doubt that Macintosh operating system users have access to some of the network externalities created by Windows users. But what percentage of the externalities are actually available? The question of whether converters have kept Microsoft from gaining excessive market power through its network still remains. Also, even where converters exist, legal barriers may limit or deny others' access to a network. We have previously shown in this chapter that the introduction of a converter may promote product diversity while decreasing social welfare. Regulators motivated by the social planner perspective must consider this possibility when writing or enforcing antitrust policies.

In summary, the existence of effective converters mitigates the need for antitrust regulation in increasing returns to scale situations, but the mere existence of converters fails to resolve the question of whether networks create market power. Regulators should be aware of converters and their implications in these situations, but they will still be required to make judgements about the quality and effects of gateways on market power.

Strategic pricing

We present a model where prices are set using heuristics and sponsoring firms have limited resources. It sheds light on how gateways affect the standardization process when firms have price-setting power.

The model follows the basic form established previously. There are two agents, R and S, and two technologies, A and B. The adoption process proceeds in discrete time. In each time period, the agent type, R or S, is determined stochastically. Like the previous model the probability of selecting each agent is 50 per cent. Once an agent type is selected that agent determines which technology to adopt. The adoption decision is determined by the initial preference for the technology, the size of the network, and, in this model, the prices of the two technologies.

In addition to the assumptions that carry over from the previous model, the strategic pricing model incorporates several new conditions. First, the model assumes the existence of two firms, A and B, each sponsoring its own technology. These firms have the market power to set prices different from the marginal cost of producing the technologies. Second, positive fixed and marginal costs are associated with each technology. These costs are symmetric with respect to the technologies. Fixed costs are assessed in each period, regardless of whether a firm makes a sale. Marginal costs are assessed only when the firm sells one unit in a period. Third, each firm begins the adoption process with an initial endowment. This endowment embodies the firm's relative financial strength at the beginning of the adoption process. As a firm sells (or fails to sell) units of its technology, the endowment is incremented (or decremented). When a firm's endowment becomes negative, the firm goes bankrupt and exits the adoption process. This construction follows Shubik's model (1959) of economic survival which incorporates 'gambler's ruin'.

Gambler's ruin is the idea that perfect credit markets would supply funds to any enterprise as long as expected profits (including loan repayment) were positive, but many enterprises, though exhibiting positive expected returns, cannot secure funding sufficient to survive some early difficulties and thus go bankrupt. Gambler's ruin recognizes that credit markets are not perfect, and some projects that would be successful, especially high risk ones, fail due to lack of liquidity. Gambler's ruin is incorporated into this model through a firm's initial

Table 3.3 Agent decision payoffs for technology
          purchases with prices

	Technology A	Technology B
R-agent	$A_R + rN_a - P_A$	$B_R + rN_b - P_B$
S-agent	$A_S + rN_a - P_A$	$B_S + rN_b - P_B$

endowment. One can think of the endowment as the maximum support a large corporation has allotted to a particular product line or to the credit limit of a small firm.

The fourth major assumption recognizes the implications of gambler's ruin. Because firms can dip into their endowments to influence consumer behaviour through strategic pricing, lock-in no longer occurs when the attractiveness of a technology's network outweighs an agent's initial technology preference. Rather, lock-in occurs when one sponsoring firm is driven from the market by the depletion of its endowment. The final major addition to the model is a firm's incentive to price strategically. Once lock-in occurs, a firm has a monopoly in the market, it controls the standard. In this model, achieving monopoly power is approximated by a large payoff for driving one's competitor from the market.

Incorporating prices into the model changes the payoffs which underlie R and S agents' adoption decisions. Following the payoff decisions of the previous model. Table 3.3 shows the addition of prices to these payoffs.

P_A is the price of one unit of technology A and P_B is the price of one unit of technology B. If $P_A = P_B = 0$, the model collapses into Arthur's (1989) original formulation. We know from the previous model in the section on 'The simple mechanism of technology adoption' that the positive network externalities case is the focus of this analysis, so r is always positive. The R-agent initially prefers technology A and the S-agent initially prefers technology B, therefore $A_R > B_R$ and $A_S < B_S$.

Now the R-agent will switch to technology B when

$$[(A_R - B_R) + (P_A - P_B)]/r < N_b - N_a.$$

This inequality and the symmetric equation for the S-agent show that the consumer switching decision consists of balancing the initial technology preference and a price difference against the size of the networks. If a firm can undercut the price of its competitor substantially enough, both initial technological preferences and network effects can be pushed aside in the consumer's decision.

The most important feature of the firm's price-setting decision is the firm's lack of perfect foresight. In each time period of the adoption process, each firm uses the following algorithm to choose its price for the next period. First, each firm makes an extended Cournot assumption that its rival will continue to use its previous period price in all future periods. This naive forecast is the most simplifying heuristic that each firm uses in the price-setting decision. Logically, a firm should know that its competitor will change prices in response to its own strategic decisions, but here we assume that each firm lacks the ability to calculate all the possible moves and countermoves in a standardization process. Second, each firm looks at the financial health of its competitor. The model assumes a firm knows its competitor's current endowment, a reasonable assumption given required quarterly reports for publicly traded companies, abundant stock analyses, and the financial press. From the endowment, each company then calculates the minimum possible number of periods it would require to drive its competitor into bankruptcy. Third, each firm calculates its estimated profits for each price in the feasible price set. Because the structure of the model, with its single sale per period, does not allow the use of a normal demand function, a firm's feasible price set has been arbitrarily assigned in the model. For each price in the feasible price set, the firm calculates its estimated profit based upon the probability it will drive its competitor out of the market and reap a monopoly payoff, the probability its competitor will drive it from the market, and the probability both firms survive. The firm assumes that its competitor will not change its current price strategy for the duration of its forecast. Moreover, the firm assumes that it will maintain the price it chooses in the current period. Finally, the firm sets its price where estimated profits are highest. Each firm performs this algorithm simultaneously. The consumer decision follows. This process is repeated for each iteration of each trial.

Conclusions

There are five main conclusions from this chapter:

- Introduction of a partial, two-way gateway will, on average, delay technology adoption
- Introduction of a perfect, two-way converter will preclude technology adoption
- Introduction of a partial, one-way gateway will bias lock-in toward the favoured technology
- Introduction of a perfect, one-way converter will cause the favoured technology to be adopted
- Analysis of converters can be applied to historical examples to provide plausible explanations of outstanding empirical puzzles.

Furthermore, this chapter demonstrates three major points. First, the role of strategic pricing in models of technology adoption, especially where gateways are concerned, is an interesting one to pursue. Models derived under the assumption of unsponsored technologies show strong support for the gateway propositions in technology adoption. Through the incorporation of 'gambler's ruin', the model can also address questions of imperfect credit markets and their effect on the technology adoption process. If financial resources of two sponsoring companies are asymmetric one can show that highly advantaged firms can establish their technologies as standards but also that slightly advantaged firms may employ strategies which are too risky and result in a diminished ability to sponsor a standard. Which state of affairs (firms with comparable access to credit, slightly asymmetric access, or highly asymmetric access) results in greatest welfare has yet not been established.

References

Arthur, W. (1987) 'Urban Systems and Historical Path Dependence', in J. Ausubel and R. Herman (eds), *Cities and their Vital Systems*, Washington, DC: National Academy Press, 85–97

—— (1989) 'Competing Technologies, Increasing Returns, and Lock-in by Historical Events', *Economic Journal* 99: 116–131

—— (1996) 'Increasing Returns and the New World of Business', *Harvard Business Review* 49: 100–109

—— and Ruszcynski (1992) 'Dynamic Equilibria in Markets with a Conformity Effect', *Archives of Control Sciences* 37: 7–31

Choi, J. P. (1994) 'Irreversible Choice of Uncertain Technologies with Network Externalities', *Rand Journal of Economics* 25(3): 382–401

—— (1997) 'The Provision of (Two-way) Converters in the Transition Process to a new Incompatible Technology', *Journal of Industrial Economics* 45(2): 139–153

David, P. (1985) 'CLIO and the Economics of QWERTY', *American Economic Review*, PP 75: 332–337

—— (1992) 'Heroes, Herds, and Hysteresis in Technological History: Thomas Edison and "The Battle of the Systems" Reconsidered', *Industrial and Corporate Change* 1(1): 129–180

—— and J. A. Bunn (1988) 'The Economics of Gateway Technologies and Network Evolution: Lessons from Electricity Supply History', *Information Economics and Policy* 3: 165–202

Farrell, J. and G. Saloner (1985) 'Standardization, Compatibility, and Innovation', *Rand Journal of Economics* 16: 70–83

—— (1986) 'Standardization and Variety', *Economics Letters* 20: 71–74

—— (1992) 'Converters, Compatibility and Control of Interfaces', *Journal of Industrial Economics* 15(1): 9–35

Katz, M. and C. Shapiro (1986) 'Technology Adoption in the Presence of Network Externalities', *Journal of Political Economy* 94: 822–841

Kwoka, J. E. and L. White (1999) *The Antitrust Revolution*, 3rd edn, New York; Oxford University Press

Shubik, M. (1959) *Strategy and Market Structure: Competition, Oligopoly and the Theory of Games*, New York: Wiley

4 Technological racing in network industries

Introduction

The striking pattern that emerges in firms' innovative activities is that the firms rival for a technological leadership position in situations best described as 'races'. A 'race' is an interactive pattern characterized by firms constantly trying to get ahead of their rivals, or trying not to fall too far behind. In network industries, where customers are willing to pay a premium for advanced technology, leadership translates into increasing returns in the market. Racing in a networked, increasing returns economy means, that if some firm is in the lead chances are that it keeps the lead and that the lead enables her to get stronger vs her rival. If we reasonably assume that the innovation is equivalent to a big enough network advantage, thus if there are enough increasing returns in the market then the firm's lead gives her a dominant advantage over her rival. Each race involves only a subset of the firms in the industry, and the activity within each race appears to strongly influence the behaviour of the firms within that race. Surprisingly, the races share broad similarities. In particular, firms that fall behind in their race display a robust tendency to accelerate innovative effort in order to catch up.

Existing theory focuses on the impact of a single innovation at the firm level, or on the effect of a single 'dominant design' on an industry's evolution. Like the dominant design literature, racing behaviour is also a dynamic story of how technology unfolds in an industry. In contrast to any existing way of looking at the evolution of technology, racing behaviour recognizes the fundamental importance of strategic interactions between competing firms. Thus firms take their rivals' actions into account when formulating their own decisions. The importance of this characterization is at least twofold. At one level, racing behaviour has implications for understanding technology strategy at the level of the individual firm and for understanding the impact of policies that aim to spur technological innovation. At another level, racing behaviour embodies both traditions that previous writings have attempted to synthesize: the 'demand-pull' side emphasized by economic theorists and the 'technology-push' side emphasized by the autonomous technical evolution school. It remains an open problem how technological races can be induced endogenously, for example, by changes in economic variables (such as costs, prices, and profitability) but we already know that network externalities promote incentives for racing (Kristiansen, 1998).

Our stochastic model of a race embraces several features that resemble moving objects towards a stochastic final destination. By exploring 'hypercompetitive' patterns of racing behaviour in respective industries, we look into racing patterns of individual firms in view of their strategic responses to their racing environment. Among those features we identify is the *speed race problem*, the selection of an *optimal decision point* (t^*), to optimize a gradient trajectory (of technological evolution) and to determine the '*stopping line and the waiting region*'. Such a model would be conducive to observations on innovation races in network industries, in particular, with race-type behaviours such as leapfrogging and catching up, striking a balance between moving ahead, waiting and repositioning themselves. The model can be improved by incorporating constraints. For example, constraints on an innovation path could be given by road blocks such as a bankruptcy constraint or an R & D uncertain payoff constraint. Some of these constraints may be conceptually easy to introduce, others may be tougher such as an investment constraint if the total innovation effort en route to t^* plus the worst case would violate it. In such a case one may want to weigh the distant finishing line unproportionately.

Beyond the micro-meso level of explaining changes in industry structures the model also addresses comparable issues on the macro level of global industry change. Aggregation of racing behaviour may result in catch-up behaviour among countries that are the second subject level of our exploration.

Simple catch-up hypotheses put emphasis on the great potential of adopting unexploited technology in the early stage and the increase in the self-limiting power in the later stage. However, an actual growth path of technological trajectory of specific economy may overwhelmingly be constrained by social capability. And the capability endogenously changes as states of the economy and technology evolve. The success of economic growth due to diffusion of advanced technology or the possibility of leapfrogging is mainly attributable to how the social capability evolves, that is, which effects become more influential, growing responsiveness to competition or growing obstacles to it on account of vested interests and established positions.

The prescription and description of industrial racing patterns has to be viewed as identifying objectives for performance evaluation of firms, industries, regions, and national economies:

(*a*) A key objective is to explore and explain which type of 'racing behaviour' is prevalent in network industries, as exemplified by information technology (computer and telecommunications) industries. The pattern evolving from such racing behaviour would be benchmarked against the frontier racing type of the global technological leaders.

(*b*) Another objective is to draw policy inferences on market structure, entrepreneurship, innovation activity, industrial policy, and regulatory frameworks in promoting and hindering industry frontier races in a global industrial context.

(*c*) One could draw the statistical profile of technological evolution and innovation for respective global industries as it relates to competitive racing and rivalry among the leading firms. Among the performance criteria to be assessed are frequency of frontier pushing, technological domination period, innovations vs imitations in the race, innovation frequency when behind or ahead, nature of jumps, leapfrogging or frontier sticking, inter-jump times and jump sizes and race closeness measures.

(*d*) An empirical proliferation of racing in these global industries can be explored, comprising of datasets identifying 'relationship between technological positions (ranks) of firms in successive years' (twenty-five-year period).

This chapter proceeds as follows. We first review the state of research in the industrial economics of technological racing. Then the model framework identifies the essential elements under which racing patterns will occur. This will be complemented by empirical considerations of the complex diversity of racing patterns, and the measurement problems that emanate from them.

State of research

Economic models and observations on 'technology races' are the most direct intellectual precursor to this chapter (Tirole, 1988; Reinganum, 1989; Scherer, 1991). This follows from the tradition of investigating the varied implications of the notion, first advanced by Schumpeter, that it is the expectation of supernormal profits from the temporary monopoly position following an innovation that is the chief driver of R & D investment. The existence and prevalence of racing behaviour in a foremost sector of high technology, that is, the mainframe computer industry, has been accounted in detail by Fisher *et al.* (1983). The simplest technology race model would be as follows. A number of firms invest in R & D. Their investment results in an innovation with the time spent in R & D subject to some uncertainty (Gottinger, 1989). However, a greater investment reduces the expected time to completion of R & D. The models investigate how many firms will choose to enter such a contest, and how much they will invest.

Despite some extensive theoretical examination of technological races there have been very few empirical studies on the subject (Lerner, 1997) and virtually none in the context of major global industries, and on a comparative basis. This will be one major focus in this chapter.

Technological frontiers at the firm and industry race levels offer a powerful tool through which to view evolving technologies within an industry. By providing a roadmap that shows where an individual firm is relative to the other firms in the industry, they highlight the importance of strategic interactions in the firm's technology decisions.

Does lagging behind one's closest technological rivals cause a firm to increase its innovative effort? The term 'race' suggests that no single firm would want to fall too far behind, and that every firm would like to get ahead. If a firm tries to innovate more when it is behind than when it is ahead, then 'catch-up' behaviour will be the dominant effect. Once a firm gets far enough ahead of its rivals, then rivals will step up their efforts to catch up. The leading firm will slow down its innovative efforts until its rivals have drawn uncomfortably close or have surpassed it. This process repeats itself every time a firm gets far enough ahead of its rivals. An alternative behaviour pattern would correspond to a firm increasing its innovative effort if it gets far enough ahead, thus making catch up by the lagging firms increasingly difficult. For any of these forms there appears to be a clear link to market and industry structure, as termed 'intensity of rivalry' by Kamien and Schwartz (1980). We investigate two different kinds of races: one that is a frontier race among leaders and 'would-be' leaders and another, that is, a catch-up race among laggards and imitators.

These two forms had been applied empirically to the development of the Japanese computer industry (Gottinger, 1998), that is, a frontier race model regarding the struggle for technological leadership in the global industry between IBM and 'Japan Inc.' guided by MITI, and a catch-up race model relating to competition among the leading Japanese manufacturers as laggards.[1]

Furthermore, it is interesting to distinguish between two kinds of catch-up behaviour. A lagging firm might simply try to close the gap between itself and the technological leader at any point in time ('frontier-sticking' behaviour), or it might try to actually usurp the position of the leader by 'leapfrogging' it. When there are disproportionately large payoffs to being in the technical lead (relative to the payoffs that a firm can realize if it is simply close enough to the technical frontier), then one would expect that leapfrogging behaviour would occur more frequently than frontier-sticking behaviour (Owen and Ulph, 1994). Alternatively, racing towards the frontier creates the 'reputation' of being an innovation leader facilitating to maintain and increase market share in the future (Albach, 1997). All attempts to leapfrog the current technological leader might not be successful since many lagging firms might be attempting to leapfrog the leader simultaneously and the leader might be trying to get further ahead simultaneously. Correspondingly, one should distinguish between attempted leapfroggings and realized leapfroggings. The leapfrogging phenomenon (though dependent on industry structure) appears as the predominant behaviour pattern in the US and Japan frontier races (Brezis *et al.*, 1991), Albach (1994) cites studies for Germany that show otherwise.

Leapfrogging behaviour influenced by the expected size of payoffs as suggested by Owen and Ulph (1994) might be revised in compliance with the characteristics of industrial structure of the local (regional) markets, the amount of R & D efforts for leapfrogging and the extent of globalization of the industry. Even in the case where the payoffs of being in the technological lead is expected

---

1 A catch-up race is likely to occur when innovators fall too far behind in a frontier race or if innovators turn to imitators and follow just one or several leaders. It could also occur in markets that are saturated or technologically mature with a lack of breakthroughs. Therefore, at some point every frontier race can turn into a catch-up whereas it is more difficult to imagine that any catch-up race will turn into a frontier race.

to be disproportionately large, the lagging firms might be satisfied to remain close enough to the leader so as to gain or maintain a share in the local market. This could occur when the amount of R & D efforts (expenditures) required for leapfrogging would be too large for a lagging firm to be viable in the industry and when the local market has not been open enough for global competition: the local market might be protected for the lagging local firms under the auspices of measures of regulation by the government (e.g. government purchasing, controls on foreign capital) and the conditions preferable for these firms (e.g. language, marketing practices). When the industrial structure is composed of multi-product firms, as for example, in the Japanese computer industry, sub-frontier firms may derive spillover benefits in developing new products in other technologically related fields (e.g. communications equipment, consumer electronic products). These firms may prefer an R & D strategy just to keep up with the technological frontier level (catch up) through realizing a greater profit stream over a whole range of products.

What are the implications of the way the firms split cleanly into the two technology races, with one set of firms clearly lagging the other technologically? The trajectories of technological evolution certainly seem to suggest that firms from one frontier cannot simply jump to another trajectory. Witness, in this regards, the gradual process necessary for the firms in the Japanese frontier to catch up with the global frontier firms. There appears to be a frontier 'lock-in' in that once a firm is part of a race, the group of rivals within that same race are the ones whose actions influence the firm's strategy the most. Advancing technological capability is a cumulative process. The ability to advance to a given level of technical capability appears to be a function of existing technical capability. Given this 'path dependence', the question remains: why do some firms apparently choose a path of technological evolution that is less rapid than others? We propose two sets of possible explanations, which need not to be mutually exclusive. The first explanation hinges primarily on the expensive nature of R & D in industries like the computer industry which rely on novel scientific discovery for their advancement. Firms choosing the subfrontier will gain access to a particular technical level later than those choosing the frontier, but will do so at a lower cost. Expending fewer resources on R & D ensures a slower rate of technical evolution. The second explanation relates mainly to technological spillovers. Following the success of the frontier firms in achieving a certain performance level, this fact becomes known to the subfrontier firms. In fact, leading-edge research in the computer industry is usually reported in scientific journals and is widely disseminated throughout the industry. The hypothesis is that partial spillover of knowledge occurs to the subfrontier firms, whose task is then simplified to some extent. Notice that the subfrontier firms still need to race to be technological leaders, as evidenced by the analysis above. This implies that the spillovers are nowhere near perfect. Firm specific learning is still the norm. However, it is possible that knowing something about what research avenues have proved successful (for the frontier firms) could greatly ease the task for the firms that follow and try to match the technical level of the frontier firm.

A model framework for a simple stochastic race

The concept of a race is intrinsic to sports events, crossing the finishing line first is everything to a racer, the rewards may be immense by reaching for the gold. In general, if such a race evolves, it looks like a sequential machine (finite automaton) acting under resource and time constraints, until a winner clearly emerges. A winner may establish himself at the first trials or runs, leaving very little chance for those left behind to catch up. The situation of competitive rivalry among firms or businesses in high technology industries may resemble more complex paradigms of a race that appear more difficult to describe than a sports event. First of all, the finishing line may not be sharply defined. It could be a greater market share than any of the rivals attain, it may be a higher profitability given the share, or a higher growth potential. In terms of process, it could be even a slow race at the beginning which might accelerate to whatever the finishing line constitutes of. It may be a race that is open to new entrants along the way, in a dormant, low innovation-driven industry that brings changes to this industry. It may allow moves among rivals, unheard of in conventional races, such as 'leapfrogging', 'take a breath and recharge' or redefining a new race through mergers and acquisitions, in the course of the given one. Races may be endogenous, induced by changes in innovation patterns, market structures, and productivity cycles. All these issues of complexity may justify setting up of a racing model that captures many of the essential features. This would be a model of a stochastic race which is proposed. Let us describe the characteristics of such a race on achieving technological and market supremacy, a universal mathematical treatment is given in Gottinger (2001). A finishing line would be ahead of a present technological frontier which would be the common ground for starting the race.

Let $TF(C)$ be each racing company's technological knowledge frontier while $TF(I)$ would be the respective industry's frontier represented by the most advanced company as a benchmark. All firms engage in pushing their frontier forward which determines the extent to which movements in the individual $TF(C)$ of the racing firms translate into movements of the $TF(I)$. While a variety of situations may emerge, the extreme cases involve: either one firm may push the frontier at all times, with the others following closely behind or all firms share more or less equally in the task of advancing the $TF(I)$. The first situation corresponds to the existence of a unique technological leader for a particular race, and a number of quick followers. The other situation corresponds to the existence of multiple technological leaders. In some industries firms share the task for pushing the frontier forward more equally than in other industries. This is usually the case the more high paced and dynamic is the race in an industry. In any race of the sort 'closeness' is an important but relative attribute. The races are all close by construction, however, some might be closer than others. As a closeness measure of the race at any particular time one could define $c(t) = \sum_{0}^{N}[TF(C_i) - TF(I)]^2/N(t)$ where $N(t)$ is the number of active firms in that industry at time t. The measure thus constructed has a lowest value of 0, which corresponds to a 'perfectly close' race. Higher values of the measure correspond to races that are less close. Unlike other characteristics such as the domination period length during a race, innovation when ahead vs when behind, leapfrogging vs frontier sticking, which describe the behaviour of a particular feature of the race and of a particular firm in relation to the frontier, the closeness measure is more of an aggregate statistic of how close the various racing parties are at a point in time. The closeness measure is simply an indication of the distance to approach a benchmark, and it does not say anything about the evolution of the technological frontier. To see this, note that if none of the frontiers were evolving, the closeness measure would be 0, as it would if all the frontiers were advancing in perfect lock-step with one another.

The Problem: On an Euclidean plane let N be a set of n points (x_i, y_i); $i = 1, \ldots, n$. Let n probabilities p_i; $i = 1, \ldots, n$ be given such that $\Sigma p_i = 1$. We use the Euclidean distance on a plane because innovation characteristics (x_i, y_i); are at least two-dimensional, that is, it would apply to so-called system products that consist of at least two components. The probabilities will most likely be subjective probabilities determined by the individual firm's chances to position itself, endogenously determined by its distance to the finishing line or its proximity to the next rival in the race. They may be formed by considering the firm's own position in the race as well as depending on the stochasticity of the rivals' efforts. As a first approximation we may let the firm's R & D investment in x_i, in relation to the total investment of its rivals Σx_j, determine the probability $p_i = x_i / \Sigma x_j$. Let a starting point, the current state of system products, point (x_0, y_0) or (point 0) also be given; let $c(S)$; $S \geq 0$ be a function such that

$$c(0) = 0, \tag{1}$$

$$c(S) > 0; \qquad \text{for all } S > 0, \tag{2}$$

$$c(S + \varepsilon) \geq c(S); \quad \text{for all } S, \varepsilon > 0, \tag{3}$$

and such that except for $S = 0$, $c(S)$ is (not necessarily strictly) convex and represents the cost of racing at speed S; let $F > 0$ be given (the fixed time value); and finally let $T > 0$ be given (the decision period). It is required to minimize the following function by choosing $t \equiv (x_t, y_t)$ and S (i.e. choose a point t, to be at T time units from now, and a speed S with which to proceed afterwards, so that the expected total cost to cross the 'finishing line' will be minimized):

$$Z(t, S) = FT + c(\mathrm{d}(0, t)/T) \, \mathrm{d}(0, t) + (c(S) + F/S) \, \Sigma p_i \, \mathrm{d}(t, i), \tag{4}$$

where $\mathrm{d}(i, j)$ is the Euclidean distance between points i and j. Thus, $Z(t, S)$ is the cost of the decision time, the decision delay in moving to a next state and the cost of speed of moving. The Euclidean distance can be seen as a metric how close the destination has been hit. The last term of equation (4) indicates the mixture of costs of speed racing and the cost of the time resource weighted by the probabilities of reaching alternative stochastic destinations.

We denote the optimal S by S^*, and similarly we have t^* and $Z^* = Z(t^*, S^*)$. Note that FT is a constant, so we can actually neglect it; the second term is the cost of getting to t during T time units, that is, at a speed of $d(0, t)/T$. Now, clearly the problem of finding S^* can be solved separately, and indeed we outline the steps toward solution.

The speed race problem

If we look at the list of stipulations for $c(S)$, equation (1) just means that we can stop and wait at zero marginal cost (which we first keep as a strict assumption to justify the flexibility of the race) equation (2) is evident, and, equation (3) is redundant, given equation (1), since if c is not monotone for $S > 0$, then it has a global minimum for that region at some S, say S_{min}, where the function assumes the value $c_{min} < c(S)$ for all $S > 0$. Now suppose we wish to move at a speed of λS_{min}; $\lambda \in (0,1]$, during T time units, thus covering a distance of λTS_{min}; then who is to prevent us from waiting $(1 - \lambda)T$ time units, and then go at S_{min} during the remaining λT time units, at a variable cost of c_{min} per distance unit? As for the convexity requirement, which we actually need from S_{min} and up only, this is not a restriction at all. Not only do all the firms we mentioned behave this way in practice generally, but even if they did not, we could use the convex support function of c as our 'real' c, by a policy, similar to the one discussed above, of moving part time at a low speed and part time at a higher one at a cost which is a linear convex combination of the respective c's. Hence, our only real assumption is that we can stop and wait at zero cost, that is, equation (1).

Lemma   let $c(S)$; $S > 0$ be any positive cost function associated with moving at speed S continuously and let equation (1) hold, then by allowing mixed speed strategies, we can obtain a function $c(S)$; $S > 0$ such that c is positive, monotone non-decreasing and convex, and reflects the real variable costs.

Now, since each time unit cost is F, and we can go S distance units during it, each distance unit's 'fair share' is F/S. To this add $f(S)$, to obtain the cost of a distance unit at a speed of S when the firm knows where it is going, and requires their fixed costs to be covered. (On the other hand, not knowing what it wants to do means that the firm has to lose the F money, or part of it.) Denote the total cost as above by $TC(S)$, or $TC(S) = c(S) + F/S$.

But, F/S is strictly convex in S, and $c(S)$ is convex too, so $TC(S)$ is strictly convex.

Choosing t optimally

Our problem is to find the point t, or the 'decision point', where we elect to be at the end of the decision period. Then, we will know with certainty what we have to do, so we will proceed at S^* to whichever point i is chosen, at a cost of $TC(S^*)d(t, i)$. Denoting $TC(S^*) = TC^*$, we may rewrite equation (4) as follows:

$$Z(t) = FT + c(d(0, t)/T) \, d(0, t) + TC^* \sum p_i \, d(t, i). \qquad (5)$$

Theorem $Z(t)$ is strictly convex in t.

Proof Clearly FT is a constant so it is convex. Let $h(w) = c(w/T)w$, hence our second term, $c(d(0, t)/T) d(0, t)$ is $h(d(0, t))$. By differentiation we can show that $h(w)$ is strictly convex, monotone increasing and non-negative. $d(0, t)$ is convex (being a norm), and it follows that $h(d(0, t))$ is strictly convex as well (see Theorem 5.1 in Rockafellar (1970), for instance), As for the third term it is clearly convex (since $\{p_i\}_{i=1,\ldots,n}$ are non-negative probabilities), and our result follows for the sum.

The stopping line and the waiting region

For $T \geq T^*$, we obtain $S = S_{min}$, and by $W(S) = c(S) + Sc'(S)$ it follows that $W(S) = c_{min}$, that is, the overall costs of speed of moving next state should satisfy a minimum level. For $G(t^*) = W(S)$ we have

$$G(t^*) = c_{min}. \tag{6}$$

Now, starting at different points, but such that $G(0) > c_{min}$ and $T > T^*$ as defined for them we should stop at different decision points respectively. Actually there is a locus of points satisfying (6), which we call D as follows

$$D = \{t \in E^2 | G(t) = c_{min}\}. \tag{7}$$

We call D the stopping line (although it may happen to be a point). Now denote the area within D, inclusive, as C, or

$$C = \{t \in E^2 | G(t) \leq c_{min}\}. \tag{8}$$

C is also called the waiting area, since being there during the decision period would imply waiting. Clearly $C \subseteq D$, with $C = D$ for the special case where one of the points $N \cup 0$ is the only solution for a large T. In case $C \neq D$, however, we have a non-empty set E as follows

$$E = C - D \text{ (or } C/D). \tag{9}$$

Specifically, there is a point in C, and in E if $E \neq \emptyset$, for which $G = 0$. We denote this point by t_{min}, that is,

$$G(t_{min}) = 0. \tag{10}$$

Clearly, in order to identify t_{min}, we do not need any information about the starting point or any of the costs we carry, but just the information on N and $\{pi\}$.

Statistical measurements of industrial racing patterns

By focusing on the stochastic parameters of the outlined racing model, like N, p, c and t, that involves speed racing over an uncertain path, we can establish statistically descriptive measures of racing behaviour that support the richness of the model outcomes as prescribed by the optimal process of the model outlined in the previous section.

The point of departure for a statistical analysis of industrial racing patterns is that the technological frontier is in fact a reasonable indicator of the evolving state of the knowledge (technical expertise) in the industry. At any point in time the 'industry frontier' (ITF) indicates the degree of technical sophistication of the most advanced product in the industry, in a sense described below. Firm level technology frontiers (FTF) are constructed analogously and indicate, at any point in time, the extent of the technical sophistication achieved by any firm until that point in time.

In the context of this study we define 'race' as a continual contest for technological superiority among some subset of firms within a well-defined industry (classification). Under this conceptualization a race is characterized by a number of firms whose FTF's remain 'close' together over a period (T) of, say, 10–25 years. The distinctive element is that firms engaging in a race have FTF's substantially closer together than the FTFs of any firms not in the race. A statistical analysis should reflect that a race, as defined, may or may not have different firms in the leadership position at different times. It may be a tighter race at some times than at others, and in general, may exhibit a variety of forms of industrial behaviour.

Methodology   Based on previous work on stochastic modelling of innovation races, we look for clusters of firms whose FTFs remain close enough throughout the twenty-five-year period (formal measures of closeness are defined and measured). We identify at least two races in progress in the industries throughout and up to twenty-five years of duration. One comprises the world frontier race in each of those industries, the other a subfrontier race (say, North America, Europe, East Asia) which technically would constitute a subfrontier to the world, also allowing for the subfrontier to be the frontier. Since the data set by no means exhaust the firms in the industry, it is certainly easier to accept that these are the significant technological races in progress. The technology frontier of the firms in a particular race (that is ITF) is constructed in a manner similar to the individual FTFs. Essentially, the maximal envelope of the FTFs in a particular race constitute the ITF for that race. So the ITF indicates, as a function of calendar time, the best achievable performance by any firm in the race.

Characterization of statistical indicators of industrial racing

The empirical explorations examine the features of the innovative process that are common to all the races, and those that distinguish between them. This will help us understand some of the similarities and differences between different technology strategies that the races appear to represent. A frontier is 'pushed' forward when the performance level of the technology (for the firm in case of FTF and for the racing group of firms in the case of ITF) is being enhanced. For example, to which extent are different firms in each race responsible for pushing the frontier forward (i.e. to which extent are movements in the individual FTFs of the racing firms translated into movements of the ITF)?

While a variety of situations are possible, the extremes are the following: (*a*) one firm may push the frontier at all times, with the others following closely behind, (*b*) all firms share more or less equally in the task of advancing the ITF. Extreme situation (*a*) corresponds to the existence of a unique technological leader for a particular race, and a number of quick followers. Situation (*b*), on the other hand, corresponds to the existence of multiple technological leaders.

We demonstrate those cases by using the data of major players in the global telecommunications equipment industry (TIS, 2000).

(*a*) *Assessment of frontier pushing*   The relevant statistics for the three races are given in Table 4.1 in illustrative terms.

(*b*) *Domination period statistics*   Accepting the view that a firm has greater potential to earn rents from its technological position if it is ahead of its race suggests that it would be interesting to examine the duration of time for which a firm can expect to remain ahead once it finds itself pushing its ITF. We define statistically the 'domination period' to be the duration of time for which a firm leads its particular race. It is interesting to note that the mean domination period is virtually indistinguishable for the three races, and lies between three and four years. A difference of means test cannot reject the hypothesis that the means are identical. So firms in each of the races can expect to remain ahead for approximately the same amount of time after they have propelled themselves to the front of their respective races. However, the domination period tends to be a more uncertain quantity in the world frontier race and in the EU frontier race than in the Japan frontier race (as evidenced by the lower domination period standard deviation in Table 4.2).

Table 4.1 Pushing the frontier

Firm no.	Number of times each firm pushes the frontier						Total
	1	*2*	*3*	*4*	*5*	*6*	
World frontier	6	3	2	—	—	—	11
EU subfrontier	4	1	0	2	1	2	10
Japan frontier	3	3	5	—	—	—	11

Table 4.2 Domination period statistics

	Mean (*years*)	Std. dev. (*years*)	*n*
World frontier	3.44	5.19	9
EU frontier	3.88	3.14	8
Japan frontier	3.86	2.20	8

Note
One-tailed difference of means t tests: world frontier and EU frontier: $t = 0.2$, d.f. $= 15$; world frontier and Japan frontier: $t = 0.19$, d.f. $= 15$.

(*c*) *Catch-up statistics*   If a firm tries to innovate more when it is behind than when it is ahead, then 'catch-up' behaviour will be the dominant effect. (Evidence that catch-up behaviour is the norm is also provided by data from the US and Japanese computer industry.) Extending this evidence to illustrate our innovation race statistics, we make up Table 4.3A.

For each firm, this table compares the fraction of the total innovations carried out by the firms (i.e. the fraction of the total number of times that the FTF advanced) when the firm in question was leading its race with the fraction of time that the firm actually led its race. In the absence of catch-up behaviour, or behaviour leading to a firm increasingly dominating its rivals, we would expect to see no difference in these fractions. Then the fraction of time that a firm is ahead of its race could be an unbiased estimator of the fraction of innovations that it engages in when it is ahead.

The data, however, suggest that this is not the case. Difference of means tests indicate that the fraction of time that a firm leads its race is larger than the fraction of innovations that occur when the firm is ahead, that is, more innovations occur when the firm is lagging than would be expected in the absence of catch-up or increasing dominance behaviour. Catch-up behaviour is supported by additional observations, as in Table 4.3B, that the firms make larger jumps (i.e. the FTF advances more) when they are behind than when they are leading the race.

(*d*) *Leapfrogging statistics*   From this, the distinction emerges between two kinds of catch-up. A lagging firm might simply try to close the gap between itself and the technological leader at any point in time (frontier-sticking behaviour), or it might try to actually usurp the position of the leader by 'leapfrogging' it when there are disproportional larger payoffs in being in the technical lead (relative to the payoffs that a firm can realize if it is simply close enough to the technical frontier), then one would expect that leapfrogging behaviour would occur more frequently than frontier-sticking behaviour.

Tables 4.4 and 4.5 describe the results of some analyses of this leapfrogging/frontier-sticking phenomenon. All attempts to leapfrog the current technological leader might not be successful since many lagging firms might be attempting to leapfrog the leader simultaneously. Correspondingly, we report both the attempted leapfroggings and the realized leapfroggings. It appears likely that the leapfrogging phenomenon would be more predominant in world frontier than in the EU frontier races.

(*e*) *Interfrontier distance*   How long does 'knowledge' take to spillover from frontier firms to subfrontier firms? This requires investigating 'interfrontier distance'. One measure of how much subfrontier firms' technology lags the frontier firms' technology could be graphed as 'subfrontier lag' in terms of calendar time. At each point in time, this is simply the absolute difference in the subfrontier performance time and the frontier performance time. The graph would clearly indicate that this measure has been declining or increasing more or less monotonically over the past twenty-five years to the extent that the subfrontier firms have been able/unable to catch-up with the frontier firms. A complementary measure

Table 4.3A More innovations when behind or ahead

Firms no.	World frontier			Total	EU frontier						Total	Japan frontier			Total
	1	2	3		1	2	3	4	5	6		1	2	3	
Total innovations	7	8	3	18	9	3	6	5	2	2	27	8	6	10	24
Number when ahead	3	2	0	5	2	0	1	1	0	1	5	2	2	3	7
% when ahead*	43	25	0	28	22	0	17	20	0	50	19	25	33	30	29
% of time ahead**	81	10	0	20	29	47	3	36	18	75		16	45	52	

Notes

One-tailed difference of means t test: per cent when ahead *vs* per cent of time ahead: $t = 1.62$, d.f. $= 22$, $p < 0.06$.

* Percentage of innovations occurring when firm leads its race.

** Percentage of time that a firm leads its race.

Table 4.3B Firm jump sizes larger behind or ahead?

	When ahead		When behind	
	Mean jump size	*Number of jumps*	*Mean jump size*	*Number of jumps*
World frontier	2.37	5	2.92	12
EU frontier	2.84	4	2.82	22
Japan frontier	6.41	7	8.41	17

Table 4.4 Nature of jumps: leapfrogging or frontier-sticking

Leapfrogs	*Total jumps*	*Attempted leapfrogs*	*Realized*
World frontier	18	15 (83%)	11 (61%)
EU frontier	27	13 (48%)	10 (37%)
Japan frontier	24	15 (63%)	11 (46%)

Table 4.5 Inter-jump times and jump sizes

	Inter-jump times		Jump sizes	
	Mean	*Std. dev.*	*Mean*	*Std. dev.*
Time and jump statistics summarizing all FTFs				
World frontier	3.87	3.42	2.87	2.52
EU frontier	3.59	2.76	2.95	1.94
Japan frontier	3.81	1.50	7.82	14.14
Time and jump statistics summarizing ITFs				
World frontier	2.90	2.99	2.02	1.02
EU frontier	3.11	2.02	2.14	1.36
Japan frontier	2.90	1.70	6.04	2.15

would be to assess the difficulty of bridging the lag. That is, how much longer does it take the subfrontier to reach a certain level of technical achievement after the frontier has reached that level. Thus it might very well turn out that the inter-frontier distance may be decreasing though the difficulty in bridging the gap is increasing.

(*f*) *Race closeness measure* (*RCM*)   None of the previous analyses tell us how close any of the overall races are over a period of time. The races are all close by construction. However, some might be closer than others. We define 'a measure of closeness' of a race RCM at a particular time as follows: $RCM(t) = \Sigma_0^N [f_i(t) - F(t)]^2/N(t)$ where $f_i(t)$ is the firm's FTF at time t, $F(t)$ is the ITF at time $t = \max [FTF(t)]$ and $N(t)$ is the number of active firms at time t.

The measure thus constructed has a lowest value of 0, which corresponds to a 'perfectly close' race. Higher values of the measure correspond to races that are less close. Unlike the earlier characteristics (domination period length, innovation when ahead vs when behind, leapfrogging vs frontier-sticking) which investigate the behaviour of a particular feature of the race and of a particular firm in relation to the race frontier, the RCM is more of an aggregate statistic of how close the various racing parties are at a point in time. The closeness measure is simply an indication of parity, and not one that says anything per se about the evolution of the technological frontier. To see this, note that if none of the frontiers were evolving, the closeness measure would be 0, as it would if all the frontiers were advancing in perfect lock-step with one another.

Discussion

The model sets out to examine and measure racing behaviour on technological positions among firms in network industries, as exemplified by the globally operating telecommunications and computer industries. In measuring the patterns of technological evolution in these industries we attempt to answer questions about whether and to which extent their racing patterns differ from those firms in respective industries that do not operate on a global scale. Among the key issues we want to address is the apparent inability of technology oriented corporations to maintain leadership in fields that they pioneered. There is a presumption that firms fail to remain competitive because of agency problems or other suboptimal managerial behaviour within these organizations. An alternative hypothesis is that technologically trailing firms, in symmetric competitive situations, will devote greater effort to innovation, so that a failure of technological leaders to maintain their position is an appropriate response to the competitive environment. In asymmetric situations, with entrants challenging incumbents, research could demonstrate whether startup firms show a stronger endeavour to close up to or leapfrog the competitors. Such issues would highlight the dynamics of the race within the given market structure in any of the areas concerned. We observe two different kinds of market asymmetries bearing on racing behaviour: (*a*) risk-driven and (*b*) resource-based asymmetries.

When the incumbents' profit are large enough and do not vary much with the product characteristics, the entrant is likely to choose the faster, less aggressive option in each stage as long as he has not fallen behind in the race. The incumbent's behaviour is influenced by what is known as the 'replacement effect' (Tirole, 1988). The conventional 'replacement' effect says that, in an effort to maximize the discounted value of its existing profit stream, the incumbent (monopolist) invests less in R & D than an entrant, and thus expects to be replaced by the entrant (in the case where the innovation is drastic enough that the firm with the older technology would not find it profitable to compete with the newer technology). In one of our models, when the incumbent's flow profit is large enough, the same replacement effect causes the incumbent to be replaced only temporarily (if the innovation is drastic). Subsequently, she is likely to regain a dominant position in the market since she has a superior version of the new technology.

In view of resource-based asymmetries, we observe, as a firm's stage resource endowment increases, it could use the additional resources to either choose more aggressive targets or to attempt to finish the stage quicker, or both. This hypothesis suggests two interpretations, suitable for empirical exploration: (*a*) if the demand for new products displays different elasticities for different local/regional markets, then we might expect there to be only imperfect correlation between aggressiveness and resource richness when products from different markets are grouped together, (*b*) if, however, demand for these products is not inelastic enough, then we would expect resource-rich firms to aim for both higher speed in R & D and greater aggressiveness.

A further point of exploration is whether chance leads result in greater likelihood of increasing lead, or in more catch-up behaviour. Previous work in this regard (Grossman and Shapiro, 1987; Harris and Vickers, 1987) has suggested that a firm that surges ahead of its rival increases its investment in R & D and speeds up while a lagging firm reduces its investment in R & D and slows down. Consequently, previous work suggests that the lead continues to increase. However, based on related work for the US and Japanese telecommunications industry (Gottinger, 1998) when duopoly and monopolistic competition and product system complexity for new products are accounted for, the speeding up of a leading firm occurs only under rare circumstances. For example, a firm getting far enough ahead such that the (temporary) monopoly term dominates its payoff expression, will always choose the fast strategy, while a firm that gets far enough behind will always choose the slow and aggressive approach. Then the lead is likely to continue to increase. If, on the other hand, both monopoly and duopoly profits increase substantially with increased aggressiveness then even large leads can vanish with significant probability.

Overall, this characterization highlights two forces that influence a firm's choices in the various stages: proximity to the finish line and distance between the firms. This probability of reaping monopoly profits is higher the further ahead a firm is of its rival, and even more so the closer the firm is to the finish line. If the lead firm is far from the finish line, even a sizeable lead may not translate into the dominance of the monopoly profit term, since there is plenty of time for the lead situation to be reversed and failure to finish first remains a probable outcome. In contrast, the probability that the lagging firm will get to be a monopolist becomes smaller as it falls behind the lead firm. This raises the following question. What kind of actions cause a firm to get ahead? Intuitively, one would expect that a firm that is ahead of its rival at any time *t*, in the sense of having completed more stages by time *t*, is likely to haven chosen the faster, less aggressive strategy more often. We will construct numerical estimates of the probability that a leading firm is more likely to have chosen a strategy less aggressively (faster) to verify this intuition.

Moving away from the firm-led race patterns revolving in a particular industry to a clustering of racing on an industry level is putting industry in different geoeconomic zones against each other and becoming dominant in strategic product/process technologies. Here racing patterns among industries in a relatively free trade environment could lead to competitive advantages and more wealth creating and accumulating dominance in key product/process technologies in one region at the expense of others. The question is, whether individual races on the firm level induce such like races on the industry level and if so, what controlling effects may be rendered by regional or multilateral policies on regulatory, trade, and investment matters.

Similar catch-up processes are taking place between leaders and followers within a group of industrialized countries in pursuit of higher levels of productivity. Moses Abramovitz (1986) explains the central idea of the catch-up hypothesis as the trailing countries' adopting behaviour of a 'backlog of unexploited technology'. Supposing that the level of labour productivity were governed entirely by the level of technology embodied in capital stock, one may consider that the differentials in productivities among countries are caused by the 'technological age' of the stock used by a country relative to its 'chronological age'. The technological age of capital is an age of technology at the time of investment plus years elapsing from that time. Since a leading country may be supposed to be furnished with the capital stock embodying, in each vintage, technology which was 'at the very frontier' at the time of investment, 'the technological age of the stock is, so to speak, the same as its chronological age'. While a leader is restricted in increasing its productivity by the advance of new technology, trailing countries 'have the potential to make a larger leap' as they are provided with the privilege of exploiting the backlog in addition of the newly developed technology. Hence, followers being behind with a larger gap in technology will have a stronger potential for growth in productivity. The potential, however, will be reduced as the catch-up process goes on because the unexploited stock of technology becomes smaller and smaller. This hypothesis explains the diffusion process of best-practice technology and gives the same sort of S-curve change in productivity rise of catching-up countries among a group of industrialized countries as that of followers to the leader in an industry.

Although this view can explain the tendency to convergence of productivity levels of follower countries, it fails to answer the historical puzzles why a country, the United States, has preserved the standing of the technological leader for a long time since taking over leadership from Britain around the end of the last century and why the shifts have taken place in the ranks of follower countries in their relative levels of productivity, that is, technological gaps between them and the leader. Abramovitz poses some extensions and qualifications on this simple catch-up hypothesis in the attempt to explain these facts. Among other factors than technological backwardness, he lays stress on a country's 'social capability', that is, years of education as a proxy of technical competence and its political, commercial, industrial, and financial institutions. The social capability of a country may become stronger or weaker as technological gaps close and thus, he states, the actual catch-up process 'does not lend itself to simple formulation'. This view has a common understanding to what Mancur Olson (1996) expresses to be 'public policies and institutions' as his explanation of the great differences in per capita income across countries, stating that 'any poorer countries that adopt relatively good economic policies and institutions enjoy rapid catch-up growth'. The suggestion should be taken seriously when we wish to understand the technological catching-up to American leadership by Japan, in particular, during the post-war period and explore the possibility of a shift in standing between these two countries. This consideration will directly bear on the future trend of the state of the art which exerts a crucial influence on the development of the world economy.

Steering or guiding the process of racing through the pursuit of industrial policies aiming to increase competitive advantage of respective industries, as having been practised in Japan (Gottinger, 1998), in that it stimulates catch-up races but appears to be less effective in promoting frontier racing. A deeper reason lies in the phenomenon of network externalities affecting high-technology industries. That is, racing ahead of rivals in respective industries may create external economies to the effect that such economies within dominant industries tend to improve their international market position and therefore pull ahead in competitiveness vis-à-vis their (trading) partners.

As P. Krugman (1991) observed: 'It is probably true that external economies are a more important determinant of international trade in high technology sectors than elsewhere'. The point is that racing behaviour in key network industries by generating frontier positions create cluster and network externalities pipelining through other sectors of the economy and creating competitive advantages elsewhere, as supported by the 'increasing returns' debate (Arthur, 1996). In this sense we can speak of positive externalities endogenizing growth of these economies and contributing to competitive advantage.

It is interesting to speculate on the implications of the way the firms in major network industry markets, such as telecommunications, split clearly into the two major technology races, with one set of firms clearly lagging the other technologically. The trajectories of technological evolution certainly seem to suggest that firms from one frontier cannot simply jump to another trajectory. Witness, in this regard, the gradual process necessary for the firm in the catch-up race to approach those in the frontier race. There appears to be a frontier 'lock-in' in that once a firm is part of a race, the group of rivals within that same race are the ones whose actions influence the firm's strategy the most. Advancing technological capability is a cumulative process. The ability to advance to a given level of technical capability appears to be a function of existing technical capability. Given this path dependence, the question remains: Why do some firms apparently choose a path of technological evolution that is less rapid than others? Two sets of possible explanations could be derived from our case analysis, which need not be mutually exclusive. The first explanation lingers primarily on the expensive nature of R & D in industries like telecommunications and computers which rely on novel discovery for their advancement. Firms choosing the catch-up race will gain access to a particular technical level later than those choosing the frontier, but will do so at a lower cost.

References

Abramovitz, M. (1986) 'Catching Up, Forging Ahead, and Falling Behind', *Journal of Economic History* 66: 385–406

Albach, H. (1994) 'Information, Zeit und Wettbewerb', paper presented at Jahrestagung des Vereins für Sozialpolitik, Münster 1993. Berlin: Duncker und Humblot, 113–154

—— (1997) 'Global Competition among the Few'. The Ehrenrooth Lectures, Swedish School of Economics and Business Administration, Res. Reports 40. Helsingfors

Arthur, B. (1996) 'Increasing Returns and the New World of Business', *Harvard Business Review*, July–August, 100–109

Brezis, E., Krugman, P., and Tsiddon, D. (1991) 'Leapfrogging: A Theory of Cycles in National Technological Leadership', National Bureau of Economic Research (NBER), Working Paper no. 3886

Fisher, F., McGowan, J., and Greenwood, J. (1983) *Folded, Spindled, and Mutilated: Economic Analysis and US v. IBM*, Cambridge, MA: MIT Press

Gottinger, H. W. (1989) 'Stochastics of Innovation Processes', *Journal of Economics* 49: 123–138

—— (1998) 'Technological Races', *Annual Review of Economics* (Japan) 38: 1–9

—— (2001) 'Stochastic Innovation Races', *Technological Forecasting and Social Change* 68: 1–18

Grossman, G. and C. Shapiro (1987) 'Dynamic R & D Competition', *Economic Journal* 97: 372–387

The Group of Lisbon (1995) *Limits to Competition*, Cambridge, MA: MIT Press

Harris, C. and J. Vickers (1987) 'Racing with Uncertainty', *Review of Economic Studies* 54: 305–321

Krugman, P. (1991) 'Myths and Realities of U.S. Competitiveness', *Science* 285, Nov. 8: 811–815

Kamien, M. I. and N. L. Schwartz (1980) *Market Structure and Innovation*, Cambridge: Cambridge University Press: Cambridge

Kristiansen, E. G. (1998) 'R&D in the Presence of Network Externalities: Timing and Compatibility', *The Rand Journal of Economics* 29(3): 531–547

Lerner, J. (1997) 'An Empirical Exploration of a Technology Race', *The Rand Journal of Economics* 28(2): 228–24

Olson, Jr., M. (1996) 'Big Bills Left on the Sidewalk: Why Some Nations are Rich, and Others Poor', *Journal of Economic Perspectives* 10: 3–24

Owen, R. and Ulph, D. (1994) 'Racing in Two Dimensions', *Journal of Evolutionary Economics* 4: 185–206

Reinganum, J. (1989) 'The Timing of Innovation', in R. Schmalensee and R. Willig (eds), *The Handbook of Industrial Organization*, Vol. 1, Amsterdam: North-Holland, Chapter 14

Rockafellar, R. T. (1970) *Convex Analysis*, Princeton, NJ: Princeton University Press

Scherer, F. (1991) 'International R & D Races: Theory and Evidence', in L.-G. Mattsson and B. Stymme (eds) *Corporate and Industry Strategies for Europe*, New York: Elsevier Science Publishers

J. Tirole (1988) *The Theory of Industrial Organization*, Cambridge: MIT Press

TIS (2000) *Telecommunications Industry Statistics*, www.fcc.gov./bureaus/common_ carrier/reports/, 2000

5 Networks and competition

Introduction

After privatization, liberalization, and deregulation the telecommunications service industry has increasingly focused on a competitive mode that could be circumscribed by innovation competition (a term coined by the US Federal Trade Commission (FTC)). The features of network industries that apply in this context involve (i) speed of change, (ii) complexity of products, in terms of use of knowledge, patents, and intellectual property rights, (iii) competitive racing with market leaders driving consistently ahead receiving exceptional (long-run) rewards in terms of market share and profit growth. Given the particular dynamics and uncertainty in those markets regulation would be hard to tailor to such markets. Instead it might be more appropriate to properly apply competition law (including anti-trust law) as adjustable mechanisms to cover those markets (Lang, 1996; EC, 1997; Pons, 1998).

An approach towards defining markets should take into account network effects dominant in many high-technology markets. It here depends on the location of networks of particular firms that decide about 'bottleneck' controls (upstream and downstream), the dominance of companies controlling system, network, and interface standards.

Markets in telecom services will increasingly be determined by at least three aggregate driving forces, reinforcing each other (Gottinger et al., 1997).

Technological change

The merging of telecommunication, computer, and broadcasting technologies (fostered through digitization of media) is allowing new service competitors such as computer and cable TV companies to offer new services that compete with traditional telephone companies. The merging of data processing and telecommunication functions within large corporations is generating the development of new local area networks (intranets, distributed networks) which no longer depend on telephone companies. The shift to computer-based switching technology undermines the basic network switching economics that have traditionally been a core strength of telephone companies. The development of more advanced 'digital-based' package switching technology will make obsolete the current 'circuit' switching systems and could, as a result, reduce telephone companies to 'low technology' commodity transport providers, which will resemble low value, homogeneous steel producers. A large amount of communications will then be provided through the interconnection of local area networks, potentially by non-traditional telecommunication providers. This pressure is forcing deregulation or liberalization and privatization activities which allows telecommunication firms the opportunity to diversify into new areas.

The development of new telecommunications service capabilities is also being driven by changes in the equipment infrastructure. New networks are able to support the high information transmission requirements of such services. More advanced operating systems can keep costs down and provide more customer control and security over their communication systems. New switching technologies are being developed for high speed, dynamic traffic control of digital and multimedia applications. Advances in photonics, optronics, and information processing technologies will support improved service requirements. Furthermore, there is an increasing trend toward the provision of mobile services, on voice, data, and vision, that to a large extent by-pass the traditional wireline network.

Changing market demands

The merging of traditional voice communication with digital information transfer and visual communication has the potential of revolutionizing the basic concept of the telecommunication services market and its offerings. New services will be more visual, more intelligent, and more personal than in the past. More visual services break from the past tradition of voice oriented telephony to open a whole new visual dimension. More advanced intelligent networks will be able to anticipate customer requirements and manage the distribution of telecommunication services. More personal services will be tailored to meet individual needs for personal communication systems, with greater mobility and flexibility of service. While voice communication may still account for the 90 per cent of the OECD market, it is expected to account for under 50 per cent of the market within two decades. Data communication will grow to over 35 per cent and visual communication to nearly 20 per cent. Penetration rates could be much faster depending on relative price changes.

Globalization

In response to technological and market pressures in the telecommunications services industry, and freed from restrictions by deregulation and privatization, the world's leading telecommunication companies have been rapidly expanding into the global marketplace. The recent economic downturn and excess capacity problems of the industry have slowed but not stopped the pace of market development. This global activity has changed the fundamental structure of an industry which, until the early 1980s, seldom extended outside of national boundaries or allowed competition. However, this process of deregulation or liberalization and privatization has still left many constraints on local competition that have, in fact, encouraged telecommunication firms to find opportunities outside their local markets. For example, US service providers have moved into cellular technology in foreign markets because it requires a relatively low capital investment with the potential for high returns. Priority markets have been in emerging markets where traditional telephone service is poor and limited in availability. At the same time, service providers have joined with equipment suppliers and large customers to complete such large projects. These new relationships blur the boundaries found in traditional industry analysis.

Summary and outlook

(1) Clearly the Schumpeterian force of creative destruction through technological change is at play in the telecommunication services industry. This force is affecting both market demand, deregulation, and globalization. First, service providers are being pushed to develop technological skills and competences when previously they could simply rely on the skills of equipment providers. Now as customers demand more sophisticated services and as equipment markets become more competitive, service providers must develop their own technological resources, not necessarily to develop their own equipment, but to be able to incorporate new technologies into their networks and to develop the services based on those technologies that the customer wants. Second, as telephone, computer, and video technologies continue to converge, there is continuing pressure by government regulators to open up more markets to competition, including the provision of local phone service.

(2) Deregulation/liberalization is likely to continue (Gottinger and Takashima, 2000), but it is unlikely that these markets will ever become totally free of regulation or oversight. Since basic telephone service is seen in most countries as a right, governments must continue to ensure that some level of universal service is available at a reasonable price. Furthermore, there will continue to be efforts of re-regulation. All of these telecommunications carriers say that they are willing to compete as long as the competition is 'fair' and on a 'level playing field'. Opponents argue that as long as the service providers maintain close to monopoly control over basic networks, then the government must prevent them from using monopoly power to crush competitors and thereby reduce competition. The challenge for these providers is to deal with continuing, albeit reduced, government regulation and at the same time learn to compete in an increasingly complex environment with demanding, sophisticated customers.

Issues in the telecommunications industry

The starting point here is to look at a fairly comprehensive list of issues connected with the dynamics of the telecommunications industry that were subject of an emerging telecommunications policy for a broad range of OECD countries (Laffont and Tirole, 1999).

Regulation

Regulation should not stand as an end itself but should be used to support market forces, increase the chances of fair competition, and achieve wider social, economic, and general policy objectives.

A reliance on economic incentives suggests that one should place greater reliance on the ability of market forces to ensure regulatory objectives. If this cannot be achieved in particular instances we should seek a balance between competition rules and sector-specific regulation.

Market entry and access   A particular issue is market entry in a given market structure. In this context, one might argue that where any network can potentially carry any service, public authorities should ensure that regulation does not stop this happening. Artificial restrictions on the use of networks, or to maintain monopolies where other parts are fully open to competition, may deny users access to innovative services, and create unjustified discrimination. Such an approach could be seen as running counter to the technological and market trends identified with convergence.

Types of restrictions are particularly important where competition is at an early stage or where a particular player enjoys a very strong position (e.g. over a competing network). In such cases, specific safeguards can ensure that potential competitors are not discriminated against or that there are adequate incentives for them to enter the market. According to this argument, appropriate safeguards might take the form of accounting separation or transparency requirements, structural separation or even full line-of-business restrictions. Access at either end of the transmission network will be of crucial importance. In general, the terms on which access is granted to networks, to conditional access systems, or to specific content is a matter for commercial agreement between market actors. Competition rules will continue to play a central role in resolving problems which may arise. The emerging market will consist of players of very different sizes, but as indicated above there will also be strong vertically integrated operators from the telecommunications, audiovisual (principally broadcasting) and IT/software industries building on their traditional strengths and financial resources. Issues which could arise across the different sectors include bundling of content and services, or of network capacity and services, predatory pricing, cross-subsidization of services or equipment, and discrimination in favour of own activities.

Within the telecommunications sector, the development of the Internet is raising a range of issues connected to the terms on which Internet access providers get access to current fixed and mobile networks. One issue is whether they should enjoy the same interconnection rights as other players and whether they should be able to get access to unbundled service elements, whilst another issue is whether such providers in offering a range of telecommunications services should share some of the obligations of providing telecom services.

Frequency spectrum   The provision of services (and the development of effective competition) will depend on the availability of sufficient network capacity, which for many services means access to radio spectrum. The parallel expansion of television broadcasting, mobile multimedia and voice applications, and the use of wireless technologies within fixed networks will lead to a significant growth in demand. The take up of wireless local loops and the arrival of Universal Mobile Telecommunications Services (UMTS) early in this century all point to a steady growth in demand for spectrum. Given the importance of spectrum, variations identified in between sectors with regard to how much spectrum is available and how much that spectrum will cost may have an important impact on the development of existing and new delivery channels. Though overall allocations are determined at an international and regional level, current differences across sectors to the pricing of frequency may create potential competitive distortions. One example could be where a broadcaster offering multimedia or on-line services uses spectrum obtained free or at low cost, competes with operators from the telecommunications sector who have paid a price reflecting the commercial value of the resource allocated.

From an economic standpoint, pricing spectrum may encourage its more efficient use and may help to ensure that frequency is allocated to the areas where it is most needed. Clearly, such an allocation also bears a lot of risk for the telecom operators. Frequency auctioning is favoured by many economists as the way to best ensure outcomes which are in the consumer's ultimate interest. Although others express concern about the impact of such pricing on prices charged to users.

The Internet

Two different developments in Internet service provision could be observed in an international context. One, mostly an American phenomenon, was an entrepreneurship drive to establish new companies to do e-business from the bottom up, while in Europe a top down approach emerged through established telecom carriers to launch internet service subsidiaries. Those spin-offs are now by far the largest Internet Service Providers (ISPs), and most of the smaller players rely on the services offered by the bigger players (depending on them for the supply of internet connectivity). Given this heterogeneous market structure, network effects could bias competition to the effect that if one network becomes larger through positive feedback by comparison with its competitors, those competitors may no longer be able to compete, because their subscriber base is too small to attract customers away from the dominant network. It is unable to offer the same access to subscribers. And although that may not matter when interconnection is free, any operator who becomes dominant may not be able to resist the temptation to charge others for connection to his network, thus further hampering competitors from offering any effective constraint to the dominant player's pricing. A case in point was the potential problem in deciding on the MCI Worldcom case.

Another issue is of merging internet and content providers, such as the AOL Time Warner case, or other joint ventures that are designed to improve the quality of the content on the Internet and enable customers to be charged for accessing that content.

At present the Internet is a relatively open and competitive environment, so there is a comparatively conservative task in applying the competition rules to ensure that it stays that way. But the speed of development of the Internet is such that competition issues could be raised very quickly, and therefore one needs to be vigilant when examining the sector in the context of competition law.

Internet regulation and telecoms regulation come from completely opposite directions. Telecoms regulation has been born out of the liberalization of the monopoly, single provider environment and new entrants have been introduced into the market. Internet regulation before now has been largely self-regulation, if any regulation existed at all. Now the Internet is becoming a system over which more and more business is being done, as opposed to the simple exchange and sharing of data which it used to be. This commercialization asks for a more robust regulatory system to protect users and suppliers. An important element of that protection is the assurance of the application of competition law.

There is no problem with the Internet continuing to have strong elements of self-regulation in the future. That is one of the reasons why it has developed in such a dynamic manner in the past.

One has to be wary, however, that self-regulation does not lead to private monopolistic practices that run counter to competition law.

Market access

Access (and the related issue of network interconnection) is one of the central issues in the telecommunications/media/information technology market and the way in which competition rules are applied to the players within it.

The central problem is that, given the evolving market structure, the converging sectors depend upon ensuring access to bottleneck facilities. These are essential for entering the market to reach customers.

In particular, through vertical mergers and joint ventures there is the potential danger that thresholds are exceeded at which point the concentration of market power in the whole value chain – content, distribution, cable – becomes unacceptable. This can be shown in a number of recent telecom and media cases. In these cases particular developments deserve attention such as, for example, attempts by market players to gain control: for digital TV based services in view of set-top boxes or decoders; or for Internet services in view of the browser, the server, and the access provider.

These are developments which link up critical elements of the future information infrastructure with other dominant market positions, that is, link ups between telecoms, online providers, and content providers

Backbone access The Internet is a network of interconnected networks. In order to provide a full Internet service any operator will need access to all, or at least the vast majority, of the networks connected to the Internet. Market definition in this area is difficult: the distinction between competitors to whom an operator will provide reciprocal access to its customers, and customers to whom an operator will provide access to all other Internet users appears more fluid than is the case in traditional telecommunications, such as voice telephony.

Notwithstanding these difficulties of market definition and quantification, similar concerns in relation to the power of particular networks appear to arise as with traditional telephony and interconnection. These concerns include the risks that a dominant network operator charges supra-competitive fees for network access, seeking to reinforce its position, for example, by concluding lengthy exclusive arrangements with its customers; or favouring its own operations at the expense of third parties.

Local loop

Given the commercial and technological constraints on providing competing local access mechanisms, it will be fundamentally important to ensure that competition in the local loop develops and that network operators of local loops are not at the same time the only service providers over those networks.

Of particular interest is unbundling the local loop. Unbundling entails the separate provision of access to the switch and to the copper wire: this allows alternative operators to use only the copper wire of the incumbent, to invest in their own switching equipment and thus bypass the switching infrastructure of the incumbent.

Bundling can in itself constitute an abuse under Article 86 (EC Treaty), in addition, however, refusing to unbundle where such unbundling would allow competitors to invest in infrastructure which would upgrade the narrowband copper telecommunications network to broadband capability could, depending on the circumstances, constitute a separate abuse under Article 86(b) – that of limiting production, markets, or technical development.

Competition cases

Within this new framework, competition policy is increasingly being applied to deal with antitrust and merger cases. Already some major telecom competition cases came up in recent years in the European Union. Here Article 85 (anti-competitive agreements), Article 86 (abuse of dominant positions, including issues of unfair pricing and refusing access and interconnection), and the Merger Regulation, were the basis for examining the planned mergers or alliances. Some of the cases were only acceptable from a competition point of view with sufficient remedies. Increasingly competition cases involve telecom companies and companies from neighbouring sectors, indicating the emergence of convergence.

Telecom framework

Competition policy will have an increasing role in telecoms markets and in markets with converging services. Sometimes the conclusion is therefore drawn that sector specific regulation must be gradually replaced by the application of competition law. Indeed, the application of competition rules can correct anti-competitive developments or interpret initially unforeseen challenges according to the spirit of the framework. However, competition policy will not entirely replace regulation.

The issue is not one of specific sector regulation versus competition rules, but rather which evolution of the existing regulatory framework should be envisaged. This evolution will be accompanied by competition cases based on the experience they carry.

Evaluating complex network competition cases

In view of the issues listed the public policy focus should be directed toward (i) market definition, (ii) dominance and oligopolies, (iii) allocation of frequency licences, (iv) competition rules vs sector specific regulation, (v) internet issues, and (vi) access to networks. We develop a methodology that map any of those cases to be investigated into a system complexity associated with a qualitative assessment of those issues.

For the evaluation of any of those cases, system complexities are aggregated to a case specific score reflecting the multiple aspects of each case subject to particular tradeoffs and supporting particular policy guidance.

An effective antitrust analysis is no more than an anatomy of competition effects of a particular transaction or activity (Ordover and Saloner, 1989). That means a practice or transaction will be reviewed in a sequence of competitive situations to see whether it originates in any anti-competitive or pro-competitive effects that have to be balanced against each other.

An assessment scheme could be designed to obtain the (aggregate) competition value of different modes of pro-competitive effects (enhancing economic efficiencies, reducing wasteful duplication) and anti-competitive effects (collusion, reducing innovation and rivalry, exclusion, leveraging market power, and raising rivals' costs).

Pro-competitive effects

Enhancing economic efficiencies (EEE)

There is widespread agreement that the goals of antitrust law are to promote economic efficiency and consumer welfare through competition (Brodley, 1990; Jorde and Teece, 1992) Economic efficiencies, which emphasize lower prices, cost savings, and technical innovation would be rooted in three elements: allocative efficiency, production efficiency, and innovation efficiency. In fast-paced network markets innovation efficiency is the most important because it increases social wealth most effectively. Unlike allocative efficiency (Figure 5.1) which only pushes prices close to cost and diminishes dead-weight loss, an innovation may promise consumers a new product, or new process to manufacture products or to improve existing products or processes which benefit consumers most. Second in social importance is production efficiency because it increases social

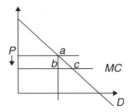

Figure 5.1 Allocative efficiency.

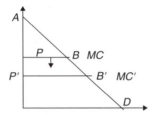

Figure 5.2 Production efficiency and consumer surplus.

wealth over the whole range of output, while allocative efficiency increases social wealth only at the margin. In addition, production efficiency (Figure 5.2) directly affects the growth of future social wealth because the gains from lower production costs are expanding, recurring, and cumulative. Allocative efficiency can be achieved through price competition. When price equals marginal cost, there is no dead-weight loss and society is better off.

Strategic alliances do not necessarily impede allocative efficiency. Although cost-reducing alliances may simultaneously enhance market power and enable the combined firms to raise prices, output may increase or remain unchanged hence satisfying allocative efficiency.

Costs of production are reduced when production processes or methods improve. Lower costs not only increase production quantity but also increase consumer surplus. Production efficiency makes costs go down, thus increasing consumer surplus.

This is particularly obvious where firms enter into strategic alliances to reach economies of scale, learning curve effects work immediately, and to lower research, production or marketing costs in short time. The costs of R & D also will dramatically be lowered since participants share the risks associated with investments that serve uncertain demand or involve uncertain technology. Economies of scale and scope in production, procurement, and logistics will be attained.

Alternatively, innovation efficiency resulting from technological improvement, economically increases consumer welfare, not merely through the lower cost, expanded production capacity, but it also increases demand and consequently consumer surplus.

In Figure 5.3, *D* is the original demand curve. When new products or new production processes are introduced into the market, the demand curve shifts to the right.

D' represents the new demand curve for new products or original products plus new products. Assuming price equals marginal cost, that is, in perfect competition, the consumer's surplus is *AFP* which is larger than the original consumer's surplus BEP. The same result occurs when output increases when innovation comes along. Figure 5.4 illustrates that consumer's surplus expands when innovation takes place. In Figure 5.4, *S* is the original supply curve. When new products or new production techniques are introduced into the market output increases. The supply curve shifts toward the right, *S'* represents the new supply curve, and price goes down to *P'*, the new price level. As a result, new consumer's surplus *ACP'* is larger than the original consumer's surplus *ABP*.

Since new products or production processes resulting from innovation often increase market demand, this results in an increase in consumer welfare. Nevertheless, the introduction of many new products or new processes could not come into being without the combination of resources owned by two or more different companies. Different firms forming strategic alliances may spread the costs of R & D and encourage the participants engaging in new innovation that an individual firm would not or could not otherwise achieve because of huge sunk costs or the lack of technologies (Jorde and Teece, 1992). Moreover, the combination of complementary technologies, the exchange of information, and circulation of technicians owned by different firms ensures for new production in the anticipated future. Synergies arise when participants sharing complementary skills or assets

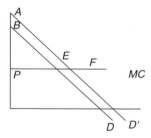

Figure 5.3 Demand-induced consumer surplus.

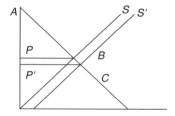

Figure 5.4 Supply-induced consumer surplus.

generate both private and social benefits. Strategic alliances between small innovative firms and large companies with the ability of mass production and marketing are often necessary for achieving technological breakthrough.

Reducing wasteful duplication (RWD)

The question of whether research and development is socially optimal or market concentration increases or decreases innovation has been controversial for a long time. There is no comprehensive theory or empirical study to support a general proposition, but there is general agreement that parallel R & D is socially undesirable. Competitors in network industries often pursue similar courses for the development of a new product or imitate their rivals' strategies while circumventing legal protection. In particular, when competitors strive to be the first in the market to win the technological race, they may in large part duplicate one another's R & D effort (Shapiro, 1985). At the same time, in such races, each rival will invest to maximize his chance of success whereas society as a whole only cares that someone succeeds. This suggests that competitive levels of R & D may be socially 'excessive'. In those situations, one may argue that integration of competitors' resources in a strategic alliance often eliminates wasteful duplication (Jorde and Teece, 1990). By combining their R & D programmes, they can avoid unnecessary duplication and the attendant social waste. The resources saved may be employed in diversifying R & D strategies and arriving at a product that maximizes innovation and expected consumer demand.

Further, R & D discoveries usually involve public good character. That means a given research finding can be used in many applications at little extra cost. A large-scale research project may be attractive only if the research finding can be used by a number of downstream producers. When the minimum efficient scale of R & D is much larger relative to the scale in production and distribution, it makes little sense for several downstream firms to each conduct similar research projects. Several downstream producers combining to fund a large-scale research project is more efficient.

Besides increasing efficiency through economies of scale and scope and the avoidance of wasteful duplications, strategic alliances provide a vehicle to jointly carry out research and development more efficiently by transferring new information they have jointly developed among themselves at marginal cost and applying that information to manufacturing. In other words, strategic alliances can internalize positive technological spillover.

Anti-competitive effects

The traditional classification into horizontal as well as vertical arrangements highlights the antitrust concerns only on the collusion effects when looking at horizontal arrangements ('cartelization'), less so on the exclusion effect when looking at vertical agreements. Nevertheless, horizontal arrangements can have exclusion effects while vertical arrangements can have the collusion effects. For example, horizontal agreements such as price fixing and market division create a collusion effect between the partners to the arrangements while group boycott and membership exclusion creates an exclusion consequence. Conversely, vertical arrangements such as tying, exclusive dealing or refusal to deal reveal an exclusion effect, resale price maintenance and non-price restraints exhibit a collusion effect (Hovenkamp, 1999). In traditional goods markets, antitrust concerns principally come from the collusion dangers that competitors can provoke through their concerted activities regardless of whether they are horizontal or vertical ones. Exclusion effects, on the contrary, are actually rare because markets are basically constant and static. In network industries, as in telecommunications, the scenario may be totally different. Where products life cycles are short, competition is not based on price but innovation, collusion seems unlikely. At the same time, if markets in these industries tend to be oligopolistic, network externalities are obvious, information is asymmetrical, and products are complementary, exclusionary strategies may be implemented more easily. The various arrangements and effects that could happen are summarized in Figure 5.5.

Collusion effects (CE)

Traditional anti-competitive concerns with respect to the formation of strategic alliances stem from the conviction that these transactions usually facilitate reducing output and fixing prices. In other words, strategic alliances are thought to be like cartels. In network industries, nonetheless, competition is based on quality features far more than prices. The collusion concerns should be put on the risk of decreasing innovation when competitors form strategic alliances.

Decreasing competition is of major concern. Partners may collude by sharing information about costs of raw materials, labour, and transportation, volumes of orders and shipments or wholesale and retail prices of current and future products. The sharing of information can encourage oligopolistic pricing and output behaviour that interferes with the efficient functioning of the market. Such a reduction of competition will occur even without any perceived conspiracy because the partners will, in a natural course, refrain from competing with

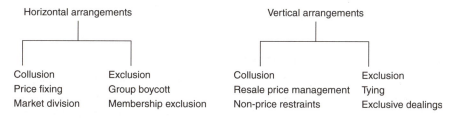

Figure 5.5 Competition effects.

an alliance in which they have a financial interest. After all, when rivals become allies, even for limited purposes, industry concentration is very likely increasing and, other things being equal, industry competition is very likely decreasing.

The diminishing competition between alliance partners does not necessarily reduce competition in the relevant market, provided that there are other competitors in the market. Sometimes, the alliance formed by smaller market participants may increase the alliance's competitiveness allowing it to compete with larger firms more effectively in the market. Strategic alliances can be used as part of the competitive strategy of parent companies within the industry, serving to increase intra-industry competition rather than decrease it (Harrigan, 1988). Furthermore, even if collaboration between partners temporarily reduces competition, alliances of partners are very often necessary to overcome market failures and to reach innovation and production efficiencies. This is also illustrated in network industries, collaboration that allows industry groups to get together may lower the costs of achieving compatibility and thus make it more likely.

Another competition concern results from the 'spillover' effects of strategic alliances. On the one hand, it is a general belief that strategic alliances should be treated more leniently than mergers because the participants of the arrangements are assumed to compete with each other outside the market in which the strategic alliances or joint ventures operate. On the other hand, unlike mergers where competition between participants no longer exists after the merger, strategic alliances or joint ventures, however, may sometimes serve as conduits for coordinating participants' market behaviour or for exchanging competitively sensitive information about other business activities.

The existence of alliances may also provide a mechanism for one partner to 'punish' the other for overly aggressive pricing in the spillover market. The existence of concern may depend on partners' competitive positions in that market, that is, whether they have market power or the hope of exercising market power through collusion. To prevent the 'spillover effect', a joint venture may include operational or procedural safeguards that substantially eliminate any risk of anti-competitive spillover effects. Examples of such safeguards include a 'Chinese Wall' to prevent the participants from exchanging unnecessary information about price, cost, and requiring the participants to make production, marketing, and pricing decisions independently. Contracts can require that certain types of competitively sensitive business information be disclosed only to neutral third parties. The use of effective safeguards may eliminate the need to conduct an elaborate structural analysis of the spillover market.

Reducing innovation and rivalry (RIR)

Some observations emphasize reducing innovation and rivalry when competitors enter strategic alliances. Empirical evidence suggests that for much R & D, the benefit to the public surpasses the private rate of return to the innovator, which would suggest that competitive levels of R & D may be socially insufficient (Gilbert and Sunshine, 1995). There is a firm belief among industrial economists that strong competition within an industry is fundamental to upgrade core skills, products, and process technologies. Horizontal collaboration may reduce diversity, deter participating firms from pursuing parallel paths to develop new technologies, and lower total research and development activities (Ordover and Willig, 1985). In particular, when intangible assets are involved in a strategic alliance and a technological edge is necessary to maintain competitiveness, forming alliances may weaken a firm's ability to innovate and respond to changes in the market. Strategic alliances involving the cross-licensing or patent pools may reduce incentives to investment in R & D and innovation significantly, especially when the pools include the existing and future patents. Even when patents are complementary, vertical combination also can have anti-competitive effects in horizontal markets. The Antitrust Division of the US Justice Department noted that industry-wide research projects involving many or all firms in a line of commerce may pose antitrust concerns (US DOJ, 1988). A single project may produce less innovation than will a variety of single and joint efforts employing alternative approaches. Parallel research projects are sometimes, not wasteful, but rather paths of new discoveries.

In general, reducing the number of separate R & D efforts may increase the cost to society of mistakes in R & D strategy because there will be fewer other businesses pursuing different and potentially successful R & D paths. If a large proportion of potential innovation in a chosen area of research participates in joint ventures, the incentive to make substantial investments in R & D may be sharply reduced. Because no member of the joint venture will risk being left behind, or can hope to get ahead of, fellow members, rivalry in the R & D may be suppressed and innovation retarded. Further, absence of innovation rivalry prevents a standard for assessing relative innovation performance and thus for monitoring managerial behaviour (Brodley, 1990). In network industries, the collaboration between dominant firms may easily form a standard that may lock-in current technology and inhibit innovation. Standards may codify existing practices and introduce substantial barriers to innovation. Because of these effects, there is an inverse relationship between R & D activity and the presence of product standards promulgated by industry. The underlying premise of this analysis is that if more R & D is undertaken more innovation will occur unless that R & D may be made more efficient by collaboration.

The danger of standard-setting activity is that innovation may be curtailed prematurely. If standardization is too early in the product life cycle, firms may reduce product innovation and compete only on the basis of process innovation. If a predominant standard is set before a technology reaches maturity, it is often economically disfavoured to radical innovation. A technology may thus be forced into 'early maturity' not because of technological limitations but rather the will of the competitors' collusion.

Exclusion effects (EE)

In network industries the market tends to be oligopolistic on account of large economies of scale and high sunk costs. The 'lock-in' effect resulting from sophisticated and compatible technologies or network externalities prevent an easy switch. All of these characteristics suggest higher barriers to entry. Also, imperfect information and externalities or other failures prevent markets from performing efficiently. In this state of affairs, both horizontal and vertical integration or restraints can be exclusionary tools that strategizing firms use to exclude competitors and diminish competition.

Anti-competitive exclusionary conducts deter competition as long as these acts frustrate the market function, since the market function assesses the relative social efficiency of market players. These conducts reduce the return to production efficiency while increasing the profitability of non-productive strategic behaviour. They avert competition not through better technologies but by raising rivals' cost, foreclose the market not by merits of products but by leveraging market power in one market onto the other market or increasing barriers to entry. Prevention of anti-competitive exclusionary practices is therefore vital to the promotion of production and innovation efficiency (Frazer and Waterson, 1994).

Scientific and technical innovation is often incremental and cumulative, that is to say, the development of new generation technologies must build upon existing technologies. Such improvements in existing technology result in a process of follow-on development that increases consumer welfare and accelerates the introduction of new products into an existing industry. Cumulative innovations, being pervasive in a network economy, increase the value of initial innovations, and diverse innovations are associated since the use of a marginal innovation implies the use of all its original inventions. Cumulative, sequential, improved, and complementary innovations therefore are not less important than their initial innovation at least (Chang, 1995).

Anti-competitive exclusionary products deter competition as long as these acts frustrate the market function, since the market function assesses the relative social efficiency of market players. These conducts reduce the return to production efficiency while increasing the profitability of (non-productive) strategic behaviour. They avert competition not through better technologies but by raising rival's costs, foreclose the market not by the merits of products but by leveraging the market power in one market onto the other market or increasing barriers to entry. Prevention of anti-competitive exclusionary practices is therefore vital to the promotion of production and innovation efficiency. In addition, exclusionary conduct hurts consumers whenever it leads to its anticipated result, that is, increased market power.

The economics of exclusionary practices is straightforward and demonstrated in Figure 5.6. It shows when innovative products are excluded by exclusionary practices, choices are reduced and consumer demand decreases. As a result welfare is worse.

Demand Curve D shifts leftward to D' when innovative products are excluded from the market. The demand of consumers shrink as choices of consumers decrease. As a result, the consumer surplus $AD*P$ is shrunk into BCP.

Exclusionary practices can be seen in the unilateral behaviour of dominant firms. It is more often seen in a strategic alliance which vertically integrates the dominant firm and its upstream input supplier or downstream manufacturer or

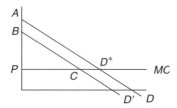

Figure 5.6 Exclusionary practice through reduced innovation.

outlet or horizontally collaborating competitors to exclude rivals. Exclusionary practices are embodied in strategic alliances, particularly in vertical strategic alliances for preventing from free riding, increasing profits or ensuring technical performance on innovation. More often than not exclusionary practices are utilized for expanding the breadth of innovation over another or future market or deterring sequential or complementary innovation.

Leveraging market power (LMP)

With the existence of some monopoly power in a major market, a particular abuse of such power in one market is of turning it into a second market. The resulting existence of monopoly power in the second market would not come from the merits of competition but through leverage (Hovenkamp, 1999). For example, in the case of a technology licence the dominant firm very likely has more information about the advantages of the products in another market than its partner does or the partner might see accommodation to the dominant firm as relatively costless. Moreover, the dominant firm bargains with its licences one at a time. Even a licensee sharing the same information and attitudes might be unwilling to deny the dominant. The licensee, standing alone, would run the risk of being cut out of the dominant's licence entirely. Only if all licensees acted concertedly could any one of the licensees confidently predict that the dominant firm could not use its power twice. Under such realistic market scenarios, leveraging may well increase the aggregate returns from monopoly.

This effect may be particularly significant in network industries where the products system is complementary and the complementary components extend over time. Sellers can indeed exploit aftermarket buyers regardless of the original equipment market being competitive if the complementary components of other manufacturers are incompatible, which is often the case. Such exploitation is possible where the seller's immediate and assured gain from aftermarket exploitation exceeds what is at most a probable loss of future sales in the original equipment or primary market. The clearest case of aftermarket exploitation without market power arises when the seller intends to abandon the primary market and thus assumes no risk of future sales loss, or where the seller for other reasons applies a high discount to future sales in the primary market. In that event the loss of future sales becomes insignificant and the prospect of more immediate gain in the aftermarket dominates the analysis.

If leveraging allows a monopolist not taking its full return in the monopolized market instead of taking a higher return in the leveraged market, the monopolist will limit pricing in the monopolized market. Consequently, by not extracting the full profits-maximizing price in that market, though still pricing above competitive price level, the monopolist currently gains a full monopoly return, part in the monopolized market and part in the leveraged market. On the other hand, as a consequence of the limit price in the monopolized market, it extends the life of monopoly by reducing the incentive to enter. Therefore, leverage may suppress innovation which is most important in network industries.

Using tying the dominant firm may manipulate to lower its monopoly profits in monopoly markets while hiding its profits in the other market. The lower profits in monopoly markets thus reduce incentives to improved innovation in that market. The dominant firm still would not lower its total profits. In network industries, the markets are often oligopolistic rather than competitive owing to the enormous irreversible costs, economies of scale, sophisticated as well as compatible technologies, and network effects. As a result, for example, in the semiconductor industry, a dominant CPU producer can enter into cross licensing or grantback agreements with other semiconductor firms to obtain the next generation microprocessor technology developed by these semiconductor firms. The dominant firm thus can easily leverage its market power in the existing CPU market into next generation's microprocessor market. This is particularly true when the market power of existing product is reinforced by the network effects. That is to say, the existing CPU has technical compatibility with a computer operating system and the applications software desired by a significant number of computer users. For a new entrant it must be very difficult to attract support from software developers who are generally unwilling to consign development resources to an unproven demand. At the same time, consumers that already have many existing software applications that were written for a particular microprocessor architecture would be reluctant to switch to a new and incompatible microprocessor architecture. Computer system manufacturers also would not risk alienating such consumers.

Alternatively, a dominant firm in the market of primary products thus can tie a complementary product to the primary product and then drive other producers of complementary products out of business, or at least foreclose them from competing in a substantial part of the market of complementary products. Through an exclusionary practice a dominant firm can create a monopoly in a second product market (Hovenkamp, 1999). As a result, a even superior complementary product may be excluded to access the market. The market function will be distorted and innovation will be suppressed. In network markets, the increasing returns from network effects also raise the possibility of effectively leveraging from a non-network market into a network market or vice versa, leveraging from a network market into a non-network market through bundling the two products. Further, a firm that controls a dominant industry standard may leverage its market power in the primary product market onto the second market of complementary products. A supplier of complementary products may provide its products to the consumer only when the complementary product is compatible with the primary product standard. A firm controlling a primary product standard could exclude competitors in complementary product markets by changing, or withholding, the key to the creation of a successful interface between the primary product and the complementary product in which it faces potentially more threatening competition.

Consequently, the incentives to innovation in complementary products will be precluded because there is no market for the complementary innovation. Theoretically, 'reverse engineering' might circumvent leveraging effects. That means analysing the dominant firm's framework system in order to arrive at a workable interface for complementary products. The interfaces needed for many of today's complementary products, such as application software, are often complex and not readily duplicated, however. Especially, where software product life cycles are short and first mover advantages are critical, reverse engineering may not provide competitors with a practical alternative. Further, reverse engineering is not an unarguably lawful alternative. Intellectual property rights today may cover many of the interfaces at issue, and the legality of accessing them for purposes of reverse engineering has been a matter of dispute.

It might be argued that monopoly profits earned in a primary market might reward the dominant firm for its innovation and legitimate business success. However, there is no basis for allowing it to reap monopoly profits in complementary markets as well. A too broad expansion of monopoly profits for the dominant firm only sacrifices the follow-on innovation. Foreclosing rivals' access to complementary markets reduces competition, product variety, and innovation in complementary markets. The complementary markets are susceptible to single-firm dominance because of the need to interface with the dominant firm's installed customer base in the primary market and because of the dominant firm's first-mover advantages derived from better and earlier access to the relevant interface. Complementary markets are the locus of the next generation of innovation. Important innovation rivalry might be lost unless the complementary products are able freely to build upon the dominant primary-market standard.

Raising rivals' costs (RRC)

If a dominant firm can negotiate with the input supplier not to deal with its rivals or deal on disadvantageous terms, the dominant firm may make it difficult for rivals to obtain the input or only obtain it at a higher cost. If the excluding firms can raise rivals' costs, they can exercise market power over the price, at least above the competitive level and up on the rival's level. It is not necessary to drive the rivals to exit the market. If a rival's costs increase, its ability of restricting market prices will proportionally decrease (Salop and Scheffman, 1983).

The strategy of raising rival's costs can be more profitable and less risky than other predatory strategies like predatory pricing. Unlike predatory pricing which involves an initial loss to the predator, which might not be recouped later, raising rival's costs leads to immediate benefits for the firm employing the strategy. This is because the higher production costs for the rival force him to reduce his output immediately, permitting the excluding firm employing the strategy to reap the benefit of higher prices or enlarged output far sooner than a predator whose strategy requires the rival's exit before any recoupment will proceed. Raising rivals' costs can be employed through several anti-competitive exclusionary practices (Ordover and Saloner, 1989). For example, the dominant firm enters into an exclusive dealing with the major input suppliers not to provide the needed inputs to its rivals. In this situation, the remaining input suppliers can easily collude to raise the price forcing the rivals' cost higher. Or, if economies of scale exist in the downstream market, the refusal to grant access to the substantial input to rivals would drive up rivals' costs. That is to say the refusal to supply input to rivals' reduces the rivals' output depriving them of scale economies. As a result, rivals would be forced out of the market. Alternatively, in an output joint venture, if the venture possesses economies of scale or other strategic advantages, it may be able to exclude or disadvantage the participants' competitors by refusing to deal with them or by demanding unfavourable terms.

Increasing barriers to entry and foreclosure

Anti-competitive exclusionary practices may raise the barriers to entry when economies of scale or other impediments forbid entry or make it more difficult. A tying arrangement may strengthen single-firm dominance or oligopoly by denying market access to more aggressive competitors or potential entrants. An exclusive dealing agreement can prevent rivals from accessing the market. For example, a dominant CPU producer may sell its product to computer makers on the condition that the computer maker must not buy the rival's compatible CPU. These exclusionary practices prevent compatible CPU producers from accessing computer makers. They also make the competitors' product more difficult to access to computer makers although the competitors' later products may be better or cheaper. As a result, follow-on improvements are never to come onto the market. Alternatively, suppose most of existing firms in an industry form an alliance to develop a standard for the industry's next generation product. Suppose also that they exclude a number of potentially significant potential entrants from the alliance and from access to technical specifications necessary for a firm to develop the new product. This restriction, in and of itself, has the anti-competitive potential of excluding output from the market.

In network industries an incumbent firm may control access to a critical standard because of network externalities that give the firm the power to make entry difficult or prevent competitors from entering the current market altogether. For example, once consumers purchase a primary good such as PC hardware or an operating system (collectively, 'framework system'), they often invest heavily in complementary products, such as peripherals and applications software. They may also develop expertise and a reserve of files usable in conjunction with the assembled system. Unless competing framework systems are compatible with the installed base's peripherals (such as printers or scanners) as well as application software, expertise, or files, the installed base may be locked into the incumbent framework system. Because switching to a competing framework entails the costs of replacing the complementary assets as well. Owing to this effect, a standard-setting body may intentionally set or manipulate a standard to exclude rival products. Standards may purposefully entrench technology that is available to few competitors because of patent protection and entry barriers.

Because adopting new technology in network industries is valuable only if others also adopt it, consumers may forgo the new technology because they are not sure what other consumers will do. The situation is exacerbated when the model takes into account the network effects of an installed base. Because early adopters of a new technology bear a higher share of transient incompatibility costs, this inhibition is more likely to occur when an installed base is large or when the new technology only attracts a small number of users. The new technology cannot offer enough network externalities and it cannot generate positive feedback unless the number of users is sufficient. It is therefore in an economic dilemma: on the one hand, the new technology would not be viable unless enough users leave the old technology, on the other hand, the new technology would not be attractive enough to draw away those users until they join. Furthermore, in computer software or semiconductor industry the markets for PC operating systems and microprocessors bear some characteristics of natural monopolies. The barriers to entry are reinforced through network effects generated by demands for interoperability and compatibility and by intellectual property rights that prevent competitors from simply copying another's work or infringing a microprocessor patent. As a result, not only does an installed base itself act as an entry barrier, but also firms producing the installed base technology may seek to buttress that barrier.

These barriers to the adoption of new technology may affect innovation at its roots. The presence of an installed base increases market risk. As with any other factor increasing market risk, an installed base may affect R & D allocation. To break up these barriers, compatible standards may therefore affect not only existing goods but possible innovations as well.

Further, because compatibility standards ensure that products made by various competitors can work together, these standards may encourage innovation in the complementary goods market. Manufacturers may enter the peripheral markets when they know their products will be widely compatible with computers.

References

Brodley, B. (1990) 'Antitrust Law and Innovation Competition', *Journal of Economic Perspectives* 4: 97–99

Chang, H. F. (1995) 'Patent Scope, Antitrust Policy and Cumulative Innovations' (1995), *Rand Journal of Economics* 26: 34–48

European Commission (1997) *Green Paper on Convergence of Telecom, Media and Information Technology Sectors*, Brussels, 3 Dec. 1997 (europa.eu.int/comm./competition/1997)

Frazer, T. and M. Waterson (1994) *Competition Law and Policy: Cases Materials, Commentary*, London: Harvester Wheatsheaf

Gilbert, R. J. and St. C. Sunshine (1995) 'Incorporating Dynamic Efficiency Concerns in Merger Analysis: The Use of Innovation Markets', *Antitrust Law Journal* 63: 569–573

Gottinger, H. W., M. Takashima, and C. Umali (1997) *Economics of global telecommunications and the Internet*, Report, University of Nagasaki, March

—— (2000) 'Deregulation in Telecommunications: the case of NTT', *International Journal of Management and Decision-Making* 1: 1–32

Harrigan, K. R. (1988) 'Joint Ventures and Competitive Strategy', *Strategic Management Journal* 9: 141–150

Hovenkamp, H. (1999) *Federal Antitrust Policy: The Law of Competition and its Practice*, St Paul, Mn.: West Publ. Comp.

Jorde, Th, and D. J. Teece (1990) 'Innovation and Cooperation: Implication for Competition and Antitrust', *Journal of Economic Perspectives* 4: 75–82

—— (1992) (eds) *Antitrust, Innovation and Competition*, Oxford University Press: New York

Katz, M. L. and C. Shapiro (1985) 'On the Licensing of Innovations', *Rand Journal of Economics* 16: 153–166

Laffont, J. J. and J. Tirole (1999) *Competition in Telecommunications*, MIT Press: Cambridge, Mass. 1999

Lang, J. T. (1996) 'European Community Antitrust Law-Innovation Markets and High Technology Industries', Fordham Capital Law Inst., NY 17/10/1996 (europa.eu.int/comm./competition/1996)

Ordover, J. and G. Saloner (1989) 'Predation, Monopolization, and Antitrust', Chap 9 in R. Schmalensee and R. D. Willig (eds), *Handbook of Industrial Organization*, Vol. I, Amsterdam: North Holland

—— and R. D. Willig (1985) 'Antitrust for High-Technology Industries', *Journal of Law and Economics* 28: 311–333

Pons, J. F. (1998) 'Application of Competition and Antitrust Policy in Media and Telecommunications in the European Union', *IBA*, 14/09/1998 (europa.eu.int/comm./competition/1998)

Salop, S. C. and David T. Scheffman (1983) 'Raising Rival's Costs', *American Economic Review* PP 73: 267–271

Shapiro, C. (1985) 'Patent Licensing and R&D Rivalry', *American Economic Review* 75: 25–32

—— and H. R. Varian (1999) *Information Rules: A Strategic Guide to the Network Economy*, Harvard Business School Press, Boston, Mass.

US Department of Justice Guide (1988) *Connecting Research Joint Ventures*, GPO, Washington, DC

6 Strategic alliances, mergers, and acquisitions

Introduction

Strategic alliances or joint ventures combine the resources of partners, integrate their operations and share profits. If the partners were competitors, they would stop competing with each other. From the viewpoint of competition, the effect can be the same as merger. Even more so in network industries, it is logical to view strategic alliances like mergers. Merger-based analysis has been taken out from traditional industrial economics. It focuses on underlying structural conditions of the market in the belief that market structure substantially influences market consequences. In a fragmented market, firms are unable to make profits by raising their prices or reducing their output because otherwise customers would easily shift to other producers. The principal anti-competitive concerns, such as price increases and output reductions, largely depend on the current production concentration in the relevant market. The anti-competitive risks of strategic alliances, as those of mergers, are closely related to competition within a highly concentrated industry or market. Given the market concentration, the relevant structural factors include the number of firms participating in the market, the participants' actual or potential share of those markets, the transaction's effects on concentration, the likelihood of entry and the ability of potential entrants to deter supra-competitive pricing. If a firm or a few firms occupy large shares of market, which means higher level of concentration, the collusion risk and supra-competitive pricing through coordinated behaviour will occur and might last over time in a certain market (McFalls, 1998).

Merger-based analysis is also adopted by antitrust agencies. The 1995 US Department of Justice and Federal Trade Commission Antitrust Guidelines for the Licensing of Intellectual Property set forth a merger-based plus efficiency analysis. Under the guidelines, the agencies define the relevant market and identify the entities that have the incentive and capability to undertake R & D closely substitutable for that to be undertaken by the venture. The agencies ordinarily will not challenge a research venture whenever there are four or more other independently controlled firms with comparable research capabilities and incentives. If there are fewer than four such firms, the agencies will consider whether the venture is likely to give the parties an incentive or ability collectively to retard the pace or scope of the R & D efforts. They will also consider the potential efficiency justifications for the venture, such as combining complementary R & D assets in a synergistic way that makes successful innovation more likely, more rapid, or less costly.

Although a merger-based market structural analysis might be a pervasive approach widely adopted by the judiciary, it collapses following the emergence of modern industrial economic analysis. First and foremost, this approach neglects the importance of economic efficiency that joint ventures are able to bring in. This is particularly substantial when the transactions engage in a concentrated market or the participants own a certain market share. For example, under the merger-based approach, joint ventures would not pass the test if the participants already have high market shares in their home markets (Brodley, 1990).

Also, the merger-based approach requires a complicated assessment of the relevant product and geographic markets, each of the partners' share of those markets, their competitors' market shares, and any increase in market concentration resulting from the transaction. Those determinations are in fact intensive and time consuming, and their outcome is difficult to predict.

This is particularly difficult in network industries. Network industry strategic alliances may make it more difficult to define the 'market' at an early stage. This is because here joint ventures may be formed to create new products that may not exist in any current product market. Furthermore, the characteristics of various forms of dynamic, non-price competition, the changing features of products over time and short product life cycles increase the difficulties of applying conventional market-definition methods, which are based primarily on price responsiveness. As a result, market definition in network industries is a very difficult process, and more easily subject to error than in conventional industries.

A large part of network industry strategic alliances are concentrated in the R & D area. The analysis of research joint ventures, or production joint ventures that begin production only after a considerable period of R & D will be difficult. It requires consideration of the effects of the transaction both on research competition and on competition in product markets in which venture participants are present competitors. Nevertheless, the market structural approach is backward looking. The assessment of relevant market and the market shares of the partners to a joint venture basically rely on present and past market records. Research joint ventures often promote long-term efficiencies and their specific impact on the relevant market will not be measurable until some time in the future. Additional complexities may arise because market delineation for R & D may often be a more uncertain exercise than in the case of output markets, and competitors in R & D markets must be evaluated on the basis of qualitative evidence of their likely future competitive significance. In a market in which innovation is emphasized the market position of incumbents changes rapidly, new entrants will appear and sometimes totally displace the incumbents. When technologies change, appropriate antitrust market conditions may change over time as well. Also, standards may quickly become obsolete, or, alternatively, the technological capital that might provide some members of the industry with a competitive advantage will turn out to afford only a short-term advantage. Attempts to employ the standard for a longer-term advantage will suffer from the general uncertainty and unpredictability of the future.

In fact, many of the analytical and evidentiary tools that are used in the delineation of output markets will have only limited use in describing research markets. Concepts such as cross elasticity of demand may be difficult to apply when the contours of the output market in which the research may come to fruition may not be clear. Evidentiary tools such as customer perceptions of the market, may lack value when customers themselves are ignorant of the likely impact of product development on their business.

Integration

The most significant economic characteristic of strategic alliances or joint ventures is the integration of separate resources to achieve the efficiencies the individual firm could not reach otherwise. Efficiency values whether an alliance is worthy of support even if it creates market power. Efficiency, however, is difficult to quantify, and even more difficult to 'trade off' against anti-competitive effects. Nevertheless, levels of integration can be proxies for efficiency. For example, a high level of integration associated with joint construction of new productive assets or substantial reorganization of existing assets generally indicates substantially more efficient operation than would occur in the absence of any joint arrangement. Also, if a joint venture can be quickly formed and quickly abandoned, the level of integration is lower. The more complicated the structure of joint ventures, the higher the level of integration of the joint venture. The more easily formed or abandoned a joint venture is, the more it is like a cartel (Hovenkamp, 1999). Some proposals have been made for an analysis of strategic alliances based on the degree of integration. They assert that integration-based analysis provides a clear picture and easy way to evaluate the joint venture. High levels of integration associated with joint construction of new productive assets or substantial reorganization of existing assets generally indicate substantially more efficient operation. They also contend that the integration-based analysis can explain some cases denying the contentions of joint ventures. For example, labelling joint ventures with no real integration of any resource, which means if no economics efficiency can be achieved to balance the restriction of competition caused by such arrangements it should be condemned automatically from an antitrust perspective (Gordon, 2002).

In addition, different business stages of arrangements usually represent different possibilities of anti-competitive risks. If a transaction engages in an upper stage of business, for instance, a joint R & D venture, which represents only a very small proportion of the input of a final product, anti-competitive risks will be very unlikely. In contrast, a downstream stage of business such as joint marketing arrangement produces likely anti-competitive risks. Other analysts, nevertheless, argue that there is no economic basis for using the degree of integration to sort anti-competitive practices from pro-competitive ones. Moreover, using the degree of integration to characterize an entity as a joint venture or a single firm for antitrust purposes would provide incentives for joint ventures to become more integrated, especially joint ventures that are interested in pursuing policies that would be subject, reasonably or not, to antitrust scrutiny. Instead, it is more sensible to develop a policy that focuses on the effects of a joint venture on competition and welfare than to try to devise a rule for determining when some joint ventures will be treated as if they were unitary firms.

Screening of market power

Notwithstanding the different approaches analysts adopted to assess strategic alliances or joint ventures they almost all agree that a market power screen is very helpful to screen out most joint ventures with no anti-competitive risk. The screen economizes on judicial resources, reduces the uncertainty of the outcome, and increases the predictability that firms face in doing business. The market power screen is based on the theory that firms without significant market power could not raise prices or reduce outputs from a competitive level without losing profits. The parties to a transaction combining no significant power could not restrain competition unreasonably in the relevant market because the consumers would suffer no harm. Similarly, strategic alliances or joint ventures of which the combined market power of participants is insignificant should have no anti-competitive risk. If the parties to a joint venture do not have substantial market power, the efficiencies the arrangements can bring in may outweigh the anti-competitive effects of the venture. In network industries, particularly given the rapidity of technological change, it is unlikely that firms forming strategic alliances without significant market power have any anti-competitive risk, their business arrangements should not be handicapped by antitrust concerns.

Traditional estimates of market power are based on three measurements. The first one is the Lerner Index. Technically, market power is a firm's ability to deviate profitably from marginal cost pricing. Hence, the Lerner Index measures the market power by ratio of market price above the marginal cost. The larger the ratio, the larger the market power.

At first sight, the Lerner Index offers an easy way to measure market power (Jacquemin, 1987). However, marginal cost and the elasticity of demand facing the firm are extraordinarily difficult to measure (Baker and Bresnahan, 1992). Further, a price largely above cost may come from a firm's superior ability to control costs on the lower level. Depending on the Lerner Index may lead the antitrust authority to condemn an efficient practice. At the same time they realize the fact that there is a positive correlation between market share and market power. This correlation of market power and market share has permitted courts to use market share as a qualified proxy for market power in antitrust cases. For a long time, the US Supreme Court had defined market power exclusively by reference to market share. Market share has long served as a surrogate for market power (Landes and Posner, 1981). The standard method of proving market share is relatively simple. It first defines a relevant product and geographic market in which to compute the defendant's market share, next computes that share, and then decides whether it is enough to support an inference of the required degree of market power. To be sure there is a bright line between those market shares that constitute monopoly power and those that do not.

While market shares greater than 65 per cent typically support a finding of market power, shares below 50 per cent generally will not. In summary, to jeopardize market performance, collusion must embrace suppliers who, in aggregate, have substantial market shares, of 60 per cent at least. Nonetheless, it is often very difficult to define the product market accurately. Most importantly, differences in supply and demand elasticity can allow two firms with totally different market shares to set prices at the same ratio above marginal costs. As a result, the market share is not an accurate proxy of market power. A Herfindahl-Hirschman Index (HHI) is used to measure horizontal merger defined as the sums of squares of the firms' market shares (Farell and Shapiro, 1990). Since this calculation will give greater weight to market shares of larger firms, it may more accurately reflect the likelihood of oligopolistic coordination in the post-merger market. Hence, a market share index of less than HHI 1800 or the presence of five or more firms in the market, is conclusive proof of the absence of market power.

Under this traditional market power screen, a strategic alliance or joint venture should be upheld when the parties' combined market shares fall below a particular percentage. When the parties to the joint ventures having market shares that are above the safe harbour threshold but below the point at which substantial market power can be inferred the regulators should balance the efficiencies of the venture against its potential anti-competitive effects. Besides the market share and concentration calculation other relevant factors should be taken into account. These factors include barriers to entry, the production stage of the strategic alliances, the relative size of competitors, the homogeneity of products, the extent of competition, and the stability of market share over time. The theory underlying antitrust in markets is that policy makers should be sceptical of concentrated markets because they can be easily cartelized. However, in network industries the probability of cartelization may not be a function of concentration. The economies of collusion are so very different in network industries, a market power determination based exclusively on numerical measures of market share ignores the indeterminacy of markets for research and future technology. In product markets, past market shares are unmeasurable and determining the number of firms in research and technology markets requires identification of potential innovators, which can be highly speculative.

Exclusion of access to alliance

Another issue involving the structure and management of strategic alliances is the exclusion of outsider access to the alliance. Basically, the participants in alliances freely choose their partners, negotiate their terms, and set up the structure for the alliances only subject to the antitrust laws limiting their scope and accumulated market power. On the contrary, very few laws will force a firm or a group of firms to share property rights with others or accept other parties (Carlton and Salop, 1996). The refusal of a member of an alliance to give the outsider access to the alliance may be based on management considerations such as inability of providing the necessary contribution, divergent goals, or insurmountable transaction obstacles. Participants in an alliance have a legitimate interest in ensuring that their partners provide valuable contributions to the alliance. Taking away the freedom of participants to exclude outsiders may force the alliance to accept incompetent partners. Mandatory access also increases the difficulty of coordinating members with different economic interests. Most importantly, the exclusionary access rules prevent free riding, thereby maintaining investment incentives. If mandatory access is required, potential partners may decide not to enter into an alliance at the outset, particularly a high-risk one, and instead opt to join the alliance when it succeeds later. The participants, however, will be required to bear the losses alone if the alliance fails. This free-rider effect creates a risk that efficiency-enhancing projects would be delayed or altogether deterred. At the same time, mandatory access may discourage excluded competitors from setting up competing ventures. As a result, mandatory access decreases the inter-venture competition.

The exclusionary access rule, on the other hand, may harm consumers by disadvantaging rivals so much that competition is adversely affected. For example, if the alliances control a major input that competitors can use to provide a better product, these competitors can be driven out of the market unless they can access the alliances, or, at least the input of alliances. Keeping competitors from the alliance excludes better products from the market or at least keeps market prices higher or prevents market prices from being factually lower than they would otherwise be. Alternatively, the exclusion rule may be used as a method to keep the monopoly profit in the alliance. It may slow innovation within a dominant system.

The mandatory access theory fundamentally results from the assumption that when joint ventures possess unique facilities, competitors could not compete with the members of joint ventures without them.

Antitrust regulators so far did not provide clear guidance to identify in what kind of circumstance the joint venture could not refuse access to competitors.

Some views rely on the structure of the market to see if there is enough room to set up alliances besides the incumbent venture. They contend that if the 'outsiders' can reasonably put together a joint venture of their own with comparable advantages, the original joint venture is justifiable in refusing to take in unwanted additional members. In practice, it means that if the joint venture itself includes parents accounting for no more than 30–40 per cent of a market, the outsiders usually can organize a comparable joint venture. Even where the original joint venture includes parents representing a higher proportion of the market, access may not be required if the minimum efficient scale of the joint venture is low enough that comparable advantages can be achieved by a smaller undertaking. Conversely, if participation in a joint venture confers a 'significant competitive advantage' and the venture itself holds a substantial market position, the law may require that competitors be allowed to participate in the joint venture or obtain the advantages of membership on reasonable and non-discriminatory terms. Other views present a more rigid approach towards membership restriction. They claim that the efficiency justification for the existence of a strategic alliance is one thing while the efficiency justification for the exclusionary access to the alliance is another. For a justification of exclusion to be valid, the efficiency benefits must result from the access restraints, not simply from the existence of the joint venture. The fact that it is efficient to permit a joint venture does not imply that every possible access restraint also is efficient. In short, there must be a reasonable connection between the exclusionary conduct and the claimed efficiency benefits.

Problems can be further complicated when involving network industries. We observe that network joint ventures are fundamentally different from non-network joint ventures. Even though the exclusionary access rule should be allowed in non-network ventures, particularly in R & D joint ventures, it needs to receive more scrutiny in network joint ventures. Note that network joint ventures generate more efficiency as more and more members join, exclusion of competitors might actually diminish the network's value by restricting the ability of the network to generate network efficiencies. Alternatively, network externalities exacerbate disadvantages of exclusion and tend to undermine intersystem competition. For example, the first mover advantage usually confers the incumbent a larger installed base, latecomers will find it very difficult to enter the market occupied by the incumbent if the new entrant could not access the existing system. Therefore, demand-side scale economies associated with networks may warrant a heightened degree of scrutiny in assessing denials of access to joint ventures. Others, however, argued that while new members increase network efficiencies, they might also reduce the returns to earlier members through competition. Further, prospective network joint venture can free ride on the investments and risk taking of existing joint venture members in exactly the same way as occurs in non-network joint ventures. Particularly, when network externalities have fallen to near zero, free-riding effects have exactly the same importance as they do for non-network joint ventures. As a result, given the existence of free riding there does not appear to be any reason to distinguish between network joint ventures and non-network joint ventures (Chang *et al.*, 1998).

The arguments basically come out from whether competition among different systems is more important than competition inside the same system. In other words, is intersystem competition promoting initial innovation more critical to society, or is intrasystem competition promoting incremental innovation more critical? Those who propose that competition rely on different systems, argue that the need to invent around other's proprietary standards stimulates innovation, so that mandating access to other's standard may reduce the development of alternative technologies and goods. Also allowing the proprietary system preserves incentives for developing resources to build an incumbent system in the first place and rewards sponsorship once the system is developed.

This may be important in network industries where marginal costs are close to zero, but the substantial fixed costs incurred in initial development must somehow be recovered. Because competition tends to drive prices down to marginal costs, admitting new rivals after the initial investment has been borne by the incumbent may not permit recovery of the fixed costs incurred in establishing the network. Moreover, it may be difficult to compensate the incumbent for the risk initially assumed alone. On the contrary, those concerned with network externalities and switching costs argue that the incumbent's potentially significant advantages from demand-side economies of scale or network externalities may make competition in different systems impossible.

If competition is to be ensured it must come from entrants with access to the interface standards necessary to make their product readily substitutable for that of the incumbent. Such compatibility reduces consumers' costs of switching to rival primary products and thus facilitates entry and competition in the primary market by promoting intrasystem competition. Whether intersystem or intrasystem competition holds priority for the consumer in any given situation depends crucially on whether the relevant market can support more than one network, and how to ultimately weigh the value of intersystem vs intrasystem competition in the particular scenario at hand. If the market has enough room to build up two or more systems the exclusion of access to the alliance system will be allowed in order to promote competition between different systems which often results in initial innovation. When there is not enough space in the market to set up a new system the exclusion rule deserves more scrutiny to prevent the deterrence of incremental innovation.

The 'essential facilities' doctrine is a better framework for bringing rationality and order to the network joint venture compulsory access issue. It has also been suggested that the essential facilities doctrine is best applied in situations where it would be impracticable or undesirable to increase competition in a given primary market, the essential-facilities doctrine provides that a regulator may require a monopolist to provide access to 'essential' resources to firms in complementary markets. This remedy maximizes efficiency by leaving the natural monopoly in place while ensuring efficiency and competition in related, complementary markets. As a result, the antitrust policy towards the exclusion of access to the alliance should depend on the facts at hand.

It will not actually matter whether the essential facilities or other theories are adopted. The question is where the line is drawn: from the most strict policy towards the exclusion access rule to the most relaxed policy, which allow the alliance to decide accepting the new member or not unless there is no room in the market for setting up a new alliance.

The confusion of drawing a distinct line for the exclusionary access rule obviously results from the fact that excluded participants can be customers of the alliance on the one hand, and competitors in output market on the other. For example, the input the alliance provides is necessary to the outsider in an output market where outsiders compete with the participants in the alliance. For input the outsider is the customer of the input the alliance produces, for output the outsider is the competitor of the member of venture. Therefore, if we can distinguish customers from real competitors the problem will be easier. After all, a refusal of an efficiency-enhancing joint venture to admit new members is economically quite distinct from a refusal by a group of non-integrated but colluding competitors to deal with a prospective customer.

To be sure, distinguishing customers from competitors is sometimes not easy. One way that can be used is to see if there is a market for the input. In other words, if there is no market for the input, but only the members of the venture and the prospective entrants, then the entrants are really the competitors and not customers. The only need of the input for the outsider is to compete with members of the alliance. The alliance should have the liberty to limit the ability of competitors to access the input unless the input constitutes a natural monopoly. That is what some commentators allege that the essential facility is the market as such.

On the contrary, if there is a market for the input and another market for the output then the 'outsider' is the customer of input in the first market even though it is the competitor of the members of alliance in other markets. The exclusionary access to the alliance should be put into severe scrutiny.

To simplify the analysis a quick look may help to review the exclusion rules. If rivals access the alliance, aggregated benefits will increase and the alliance partners will be better off, then denial should be prohibited.

If the alliance partner will be worse off, the denial should be allowed even though the benefits to the rival outweigh the losses of the alliance partners, otherwise the incentive of formation of strategic alliances will decrease. When the alliance partners and rivals are better off even if the rivals get the most of the benefit and the alliance partners get less a benefit the denial should not be allowed because economic efficiency is improved and the social welfare increased in this situation.

Discussion

In forming strategic alliances the objectives of participants in the alliance may not be totally parallel. The interests of an individual participant in the alliance may conflict with the interests of the alliance. Further, even the goals of participants can be inconsistent, different corporate cultures and management philosophies can lead to different ways of solving problems. Finally, free riding and opportunistic behaviours can destroy the alliance. Therefore, in order to operate strategic alliances or joint ventures successfully, the participants inevitably impose 'ancillary restraints' on the alliances or the participants in the alliances. These restraints may restrict participants from competing with the alliance or competing with each other in order to prevent free riding and opportunistic behaviour.

Participants may be requested to exchange certain information to cover the risks of sharing information and to prevent one firm from dumping obsolete technology into the alliance for obtaining their partner's advanced knowledge. A secrecy agreement may be imposed on the R & D of alliance to protect the technology dissemination. This is particularly important when entering strategic alliances in high-technology network markets. On the other hand, since restraints can constrain the competitors they are likely to generate concerns of deterring competition. In particular, these constraints may not give merited advantage to incumbent powerful firms over new, small entrants. From the viewpoint of competition, the importance of the ancillary restraints is no less than the alliance as such. In fact, the assessment of strategic alliances usually fall with the assessment of ancillary restraints. Ancillary restraints can be a valve for the competitive concerns of strategic alliances. That means when the alliance in itself has great anti-competitive concern ancillary constraints can be imposed to eliminate competitive risk.

Conversely when the alliance poses little or no anti-competitive concern ancillary restraints used to regulate or protect the interest of the alliance can be allowed. For example, presuming there are two companies with the ability to develop a new technology. The two companies now enter into strategic alliance to develop the technology jointly, which means they can save a lot of expenses and most importantly accelerate R & D. Because the two companies are the most likely to succeed, the alliance has great market power in the relevant market. However, the efficiency the alliance may reach is also great. Hence, the restraints the agency may impose such as prohibiting joint production and marketing when the technology developed, or non-exclusive license to other competitors of the alliance will mitigate the anti-competitive concerns of the alliance. Similarly, if the alliance has little market power, the ancillary restraints barring participants from disseminating to competitors or allocate the market may be allowed. Restraints are reasonably necessary to protect the interest of the alliance or the participants who provide the technology in the first place.

The exclusion of access to the alliance should be allowed when the exclusion only harms competitors rather than consumers or retards innovation. To be sure, the exclusion may be essential to facilitating collusion among the participants in an alliance. The main concern resulting from exclusion is, however, deterring innovation or harming the consumer. Also the exclusion rules may be necessary to maintain an efficient alliance after all. As a result, the mandatory rule of assessing should be imposed only when the access can improve innovation efficiency or consumer welfare and without harming the participants to the alliance.

Exclusionary strategies in vertical alliances

Although most literature discussing strategic alliances concentrate on the arrangements integrating horizontal partners, in fact, many more strategic alliances are entered into by vertical partners.

Discussions focusing on the horizontal strategic alliances only reflect traditional antitrust concerns of collusion effects and the re-acknowledgement of the efficiencies of strategic alliances particularly in dynamic markets, meaning primarily network industries. On the other hand, more strategic alliances are formed by firms originally in vertical production or complementary stages. In those alliances the participants provide the complementary resources such as technologies, capital, production, or marketing capabilities to integrate partners' resources vertically. At the same time participants may employ exclusionary practices to facilitate the operation of alliances or assure their profits in the transactions. These exclusionary practices include exclusive dealing arrangements, tying arrangements, grantback, and vertical integration. On the other hand, these exclusionary practices can be used to engage monopolization, or exclude a rival without merits such as lower costs, better quality, new products, or lower prices.

Competitive effects of exclusive dealing

An exclusive dealing arrangement typically involves an agreement by a distributor, dealer, or franchisee to deal exclusively in the products of a single supplier. It may arise when a licence prevents or restraints the licensee from licensing, selling, distributing, or using competing technologies. Related arrangements are requirement contracts under which the buyer agrees to purchase its entire requirements of products or services from a single seller, or agreements by a customer not to buy competing products from a competing supplier. For example, PC makers agree not to buy compatible CPUs in exchange for the dominant CPU producer's promising to provide them with technical information about new CPUs in advance of their commercial release. Such disclosure of new CPU's technical information has substantial commercial benefits for both the CPU producer and PC makers. PC makers benefit because the advance technical information enables them to develop and introduce new computer system architecture incorporating the latest microprocessor technology as early as possible. The CPU producer benefits because those customer-PC makers design their new computer systems so as to incorporate, and effectively endorse its newest microprocessor. Except as commonly defined above, exclusive dealings may feature an agreement that the dominant buyer of input requires the supplier to promise not to deal with rivals of the buyer, or only on the consent of buyer, or on a disadvantageous term.

Exclusive dealing agreements may present economic efficiencies to buyers and sellers thus providing advantage to consumers indirectly. Exclusive dealing can enhance interbrand competition. By requiring dealers to purchase products only from it and not from its competitors, a manufacturer can ensure that dealers more aggressively promote its products. Similarly, distributors whose profitability is largely dependent upon sales of a single manufacturer's products will be more likely to invest in training, promotion, and point-of-sale services that will make the products more attractive to consumers.

Exclusive dealings, however, can be anti-competitive when the arrangement forecloses a substantial amount of competition in a line of commerce. For example, in the mentioned CPU hypothesis, the exclusive dealing with the dominant producer only may prevent other compatible CPU producers from entering the market later even if their products are cheaper or superior. For example, the US Supreme Court (1949) in the case of Standard Oil, at first assessed the reasonableness of an exclusive dealing practice by considering only the extent of market foreclosure.

The Court created the 'quantitative substantiality' approach to measure the degree to which competition was foreclosed by focusing almost entirely on the percentage of the market foreclosed by the exclusive dealing arrangement.

The quantitative approach measures the degree to which competition was foreclosed by focusing almost entirely on the percentage of the market foreclosed by an exclusive dealing arrangement. A substantial lessening of competition is shown when there is 'proof that competition has been foreclosed in substantial share of the line of commerce affected'. Whether an exclusive dealing contract is unreasonable, the proper focus is on the structure of market for products or services in question. That means numbers of sellers and buyers in market, volumes of their businesses, and the ease at which buyers and sellers can redirect their purchase or sales to others. An exclusive dealing is an unreasonable restraint on trade only when sellers of services are numerous and numbers of buyers are large. Exclusive dealing arrangements of narrow scope pose no threat of adverse economic consequences. In contrast, a qualitative approach evaluates competitive effects determining the extent of market foreclosure. Courts will consider the relative strength of parties, the proportionate volume of commerce involved in relation to total volume of commerce in the relevant market area, and probable immediate and future effects which pre-emption of that share of the market might have on effective competition therein. Under the qualitative test market share continues to play a significant role in the analysis of exclusive dealing arrangements. However, it is only one factor to be considered and is probably not determinative unless the arrangement forecloses either a very large share of the market (Hovenkamp, 1994).

In applying this analysis the courts and the agencies examine a number of factors, including the percentage of the market foreclosed, the duration of the exclusive arrangement, and the 'notice of termination' period.

The competitive effects of an exclusive dealing arrangement depend, among other things, on the market power of the party imposing it, the degree of customer or input foreclosure, and the duration of the arrangement. For example, a long-term exclusive dealing arrangement between a dominant seller and most of the distributors in a market can have the effect of denying rivals sufficient outlets for exploiting their technologies and can thus be anti-competitive. Consumers cannot be adversely affected by an exclusive dealing arrangement if the parties to such arrangement lack market power. A firm without market power will be unable to 'lock up' a significant number of suppliers or customers through exclusive dealing arrangements. As a result, competitors will have access to sufficient remaining outlets to compete effectively in the relevant market.

Exclusive dealing in imperfect markets

In a perfect market, where input suppliers are ubiquitous and products are compatible, exclusive dealing arrangements will not harm competition because the rivals can easily leave for other suppliers. A supplier finding it unprofitable to grant an exclusive deal with the excluding firm may leave for other manufacturers.

In this case, only the 'excessive' duration of exclusive dealing might be relevant when assessing the anti-competitive effects. Nevertheless, in an imperfect market, exclusivity can force a new entrant to enter at both levels, thereby increasing the risk associated with new entry. In effect, a new entrant is required to have sufficient managerial expertise and experience to operate at both levels, and a failure to operate effectively at either level will likely cause both to fail. Thus the risks are cumulative, discouraging the new entry.

Furthermore, in network industries, markets are oligopolistic rather than atomistic. Let us look at the following situation in the microprocessor market. On the supply side, for example, there are only a few CPU producers in the market, when the dominant producer threatens to cut off providing technical information in advance. PC makers would not take the risk to buy the compatible CPUs from the clone producers. On the demand side, if the components buyers are only a few the suppliers of components heavily depend on a particular manufacturer to process its production. The dependence will be heightened by the fact that components might only be compatible with the manufacturer's system. The component supplier would not take the risk of losing its existing and stable customers, or its partner to deal with a new entrant with less market certainty. Losing an existing customer means there is nowhere to find another customer if the new entrant fails in the market. As a result, a component supplier, even acknowledging accepting a new entrant will increase its output and profit, would still not take the chance whenever the manufacturer can effectively detect its disloyalty. As a result, in an imperfect market, exclusive dealing arrangements can be anti-competitive even if the agreement is 'moderate in term'.

The case of the US vs Microsoft provides a case in point. The US Department of Justice (DOJ), in 1998, challenged Microsoft's licensing practices of its 'Windows' personal computer operating system to original equipment manufacturers (OEM). DOJ claimed that Microsoft maintained its monopoly over PC operating systems by using exclusionary contracts. The contracts required OEMs to pay Microsoft a royalty for each computer shipped, regardless of whether it included a Microsoft operating system. The complaint alleged that this arrangement forced an OEM to pay twice to use an alternative operating system, thereby driving up the costs of using the non-Microsoft operating system. The exclusionary effect was intensified by 'minimum commitments' contract provisions, which obligated the OEM to purchase large numbers of operating systems from Microsoft and credited unused balances to future contracts, which further decreased sales opportunities for any competitive operating system. Also found objectionable was the duration of the contracts: at minimum, it was three years, but through amendment often lasted more than five – allegedly a period of time equal to or exceeding the product life of most PC operating system products.

Microsoft and DOJ reached a consent agreement, which, as approved by the court, required Microsoft to switch to per system licences, in which the OEM would pay Microsoft only when the OEM shipped a computer that included ,a Microsoft operating system. The agreement also prohibited Microsoft from entering into any operating system licence for an initial or renewal term of longer than one year.

In industries where products are comprised of a variety of complementary components which involve different technologies and are usually produced by a large group of different firms such as automobile manufacturing, aircraft manufacturing, or other transportation equipment manufacturing industries, there exists a so-called 'satellite factories system'. That is to say, the automobile manufacturer does not make most of its parts and components itself, instead, they are supplied by a number of satellite factories. These parts and components are usually only used for the particular industry, sometimes even for the particular firm because they only complement and are compatible with each other. Accordingly, rather than entering into a purchasing agreement, instead, the automobile manufacturer and component producer are willing to maintain a closer long-term relationship to keep the supply and quality of components steady and stable. More often than not, automobile manufacturers enter into strategic alliances with their satellite factories to produce components for them. Automobile manufacturers might also provide capital, technologies, and management skills to the component producers to improve and guarantee their production. In response, the component producers promise to maintain supply. Sometimes they promise not to supply components to rival automobile manufacturers. As a result, these exclusive practices may destroy competition by providing a few firms with advantageous access to goods, markets, or customers, thereby enabling the advantaged firm to gain power over price, quality, or output (Krattenmaker and Salop, 1986).

Tying in strategic alliances

Many strategic alliances are created in order to transfer technologies from one party to the other from the research ventures jointly set by alliance partners to individual partner. Accordingly, in network industries firms are most commonly seen to enter into patent or technology licence agreements with their strategic partners or the joint venture firm to transfer the technologies.

On the other hand, in a patent licensing agreement the licensor often imposes a tying or bundling arrangement. In a tying arrangement the patentee grants its patent (tying product) on the condition that the licensee purchases or leases a separate product or service (tied product). With regard to bundling arrangements, the licensee is required to take a licence under a group of patents. As we can see today, tying arrangements have become a strategic tool in network alliances.

Tying or bundling arrangements are so common in patent licensing practice that the earliest cases of tying all involve patents licensing. A patentee or a supplier of complicated components covered by intellectual property rights might require its licensee manufacturer to obtain other related inputs from it in order to enable the licensor to control the quality of the manufacturer's product. In this case, tying is necessary for a licensor to ensure the licensing technology functions as anticipated when the quality or quantity of tied product is important to the licensing technology. Particularly, when components of a product or process are covered by different patents, the bundling licensing of a group of patents is often required. Further, when a product needs a particular technology for its effective use, ties of the technology to the product sometimes provides innovation efficiency. To be sure, a licensee may in some occasions be sophisticated enough to find the best quality of input for the efficient use of licensing technology. Where market failures preclude the licensee from choosing appropriate substitutes through the market, however, tying may eliminate the problem of imperfect information and reduce search costs.

Most commonly, proponents of tying arrangements present it as the most important tool of price discrimination. A seller or licensor can charge a lower price for tying product and charge a higher price for tied product. Thus the higher intensity of consuming the tying product pays more whereas the lower pays less if higher consumption of tied goods signals higher valuation for the tying goods (Tirole, 1988). As a result, tying not only produces one market into the other market but forecloses the second market. Particularly, where market failures exist, a monopolistic firm, which produces competitive complementary products simultaneously, can exclude competitors in the market for the complementary product through tying arrangements. Market failures usually can be economies of scale or imperfect information.

Another view rejects the leverage theory based on the assumption that the tied market has a competitive, constant-to-scale structure. However, if economies of scale exist in the production process for the tied good, tying may be an effective means for a dominant firm to foreclose the market by making continued operations unprofitable for tied-good rivals (Whinston, 1990).

In other words, by tying, the monopolist reduces the sales of its tied-good competitor, thereby lowering the output of the competitor below the level that vindicates minimum economies of scale. As a result, the competitor of tied products will exit the market because of the higher costs that result from the deficiency in scale of output. Particularly, if the sale of a tied product has cost advantage due to the effect of learning by doing and competitive producers of the tied product understand this, then no one will enter the market for the tied good.

Information imperfection will also cause foreclosure in tied good markets. The licensee may ignore the tying arrangement because the tying goods are unique or the tied goods are of no material importance to him, so that he would not object to tying arrangement even if he were knowledgeable about it. For example, when the licensee can easily shift the costs of tied products to a third party, he would not reject a tying arrangement even if he knows the higher cost of the tied product. Information imperfection also makes leveraging to increase the aggregate return from monopoly.

Tying can also be a practice that forecloses competition in network markets. Suppose, for example, that a dominant firm has a product with a current technology that is supposedly legal by its intellectual property rights. Suppose further that the firm offers to license its technology only to those firms that agree also to license that firm's complementary product, and suppose that the complementary product builds on the firm's next-generation technology. Such a tying arrangement could allow the dominant firm to create a new installed base of users of its next-generation technology in a manner that would effectively foreclose the opportunities of competing firms to offer their products in the battle for the next-generation technology. When tying does lead to exclusion of rivals, the welfare effects both for consumers and for aggregate efficiency are in general ambiguous. The loss for consumers arises because, when tied market rivals exit, prices may rise and the level of variety available in the market necessarily falls making consumers worse off (Katz, 1989).

An injury to dynamic efficiency occurs if the tying seller can foreclose a substantial percentage of the tied-product market, competing sellers of the tied product may face increased costs and be driven from the market. Barriers to entry or market penetration may also be raised. The effects on dynamic efficiency may slow the pace of welfare enhancing innovation.

Grantback provisions and cross licensing

The licensing of industrial property rights or know-how is the most common way of transferring technology between strategic partners. Entering into licensing agreements, partners may impose grantback provisions or in the form of cross licensing. Usually, grantbacks are couched in the form of a cross licence wherein each partner grants the other a non-exclusive licence. Grantback provisions oblige a licensee to transfer to the licensor any improvements in the technology represented by the licensed industrial property rights. These provisions will premise the licence upon the licensee agreeing either to assign to the licensor any improvement derived from the licensed technology or to licence the subsequently developed technology to the licensor. Cross licensing involves a mutual exchange between parties, for the parties' mutual advantage, which often helps local technological firms to form strategic alliances with foreign technological giants.

Grantback provisions may promote the dissemination of new technology, reduce bargaining costs, share risks, and reward the licensor for facilitating innovations. Also they may be advantageous to have or at least to encourage licence transaction in the first place by ensuring that the licensor is not prevented from effectively competing because it is denied access to improvements developed with the aid of its own technology.

Cross licensing is particularly important in the semiconductor and network equipment industry because the production process of chips usually involve so many patents that not any single firm can own all of them. Also most of these patents granted on technologies are incremental or entangled. Without cross licensing a semiconductor company would be unable to produce its chip without infringing others' patents. Cross licensing grants recipients with an opportunity to use technologies that it otherwise could not use. Cross licensing can be a highly effective way of resolving 'blocking patents' (which are essentially patents that cannot be used without the licensing of other patents). When firms engage in similar research or manufacturing areas, they often become involved in patent conflicts, including mutual patent infringement claims or conflict claims in patent interference. The costs associated with resolving these conflicts through litigation can often be high. Cross licensing patents in dispute provides a cost-saving, efficient way to implement their patents. Furthermore, in some industries, the pace of R & D and the market interdependencies between inventions are so high that advantages of being the first to the market make those firms cross license with their competitors.

From the standpoint of regulatory agencies, most cross licenses are, on balance, procompetitive when licensing firms with no market power, or with complementary abilities are cooperating. In addition, agencies recognize that grantback provisions may be necessary to ensure the licensors' incentives to innovate in the first place. The procompetitive effects of grantback arrangements usually outweigh the risks of reducing incentives to the licensee to improve the licensed technology. Non-exclusive grantbacks are less likely to raise antitrust issues than exclusive grantbacks, as they will allow the licensee to license any improvements in the technology to others. Although agencies acknowledge anticompetitive effects of cross licensing and grantbacks in certain circumstances, they focus on collusion concerns only. Nevertheless, these arrangements may reduce the licensee's incentive to innovate and invest in R & D by reducing the possible gains. Exclusion effects that these arrangements can bring up shall not be ignored. Cross licensing between dominant firms is very likely to suppress the competition, to deteriorate consumers' purchasing power, and to develop monopoly. Cross licensing can be used to protect the oligopoly rents by limiting the third parties' innovation. Likewise, grantback clauses when combined with other restrictions can be anti-competitive or improperly extend market power beyond that of the patent itself. Most importantly, these arrangements can provide to sustain the initial inventor's dominance and stifle sequential innovation.

Vertical integration

Firms perform vertical integration primarily by reducing transaction costs. That is to say, a firm can achieve economies by avoiding the costs of using the marketplace. Using the market can be very expensive: negotiating contract costs money, dealing with other persons involves risk because of incomplete information about each other. Consequently, if a firm can produce the product or service as cheaply as an independent producer can, then it will produce them by itself because any imperfection in the market for that product or service will make it more expensive to buy than to produce (Williamson, 1979; Demsetz, 1982).

Alternatively, vertical integration may coordinate design, production, and even marketing (including feedback from customers). This coordination is not only cost-saving but also improves quality and leads to process innovation. Asset specificity also creates a motive for vertical integration. When products are unique the use of the market will be more costly. From the viewpoint of competition policy, one may intuitively be against vertical integration that result primarily from that upstream monopolists integrating downstream competitive firms using upstream products as input, together with others, to produce a final good.

Such forward extension of monopoly power increases the monopolist's profits, which means computer prices increase. However, the relationship between vertical integration and monopoly is more complex. Vertical integration is probably used as much to reduce monopoly as to facilitate it, because the monopolist has the same strong incentive as the competitive firm does to reduce transaction costs.

For many years the conventional belief among economists was that an input monopolist had no incentive to integrate forward into a competitive final good industry. In the market of imperfection, firms know little about the costs of those with whom they deal. This is particularly true if the other firm produces or sells a variety of products. A firm just cannot know if the price other firms charge is the lowest one. When a competitive firm integrates with a monopolist, the result is higher profits for the integrating firm and a lower price for consumers if the integrating firm can produce the product as efficiently as the monopolist did. Alternatively, when the integrating firm itself is a monopolist, vertical integration can remove the downstream monopolist and make more profit, which means a lower profit-maximizing price (Vickers and Waterson, 1991).

However, conventional wisdom is only correct under conditions of fixed proportions in production at the downstream stage. Under conditions of variable proportions, when the certain input monopolist attempts to maximize its profit, the resulting price of monopoly input will lead the final good producers to use other input as a substitute for monopoly input. The high input price has adverse effects when firms are not vertically integrated. At first, the downstream firms will use less input instead of using a substitute beyond the optimal level. The substitution to other inputs maximises costs for the downstream firm, but is efficient when compared to the technology. With vertical integration, the firm can set transfer prices of the inputs that reflect their true costs. This will correct technical inefficiency and encourage more output. This behaviour creates an incentive for the monopolist to vertically integrate forward. In this case, vertical integration will tend to improve efficiency and enhance consumer welfare. Conversely, the relative size of the monopolized market is thus enlarged. As a result, allocative efficiency is likely to be reduced (Salinger, 1988).

To be sure, vertical integration may lead to monopoly in a downstream product market which was previously competitive. Thus, prices of final goods may increase as a result of monopolization of that market and a new wedge can be erected between price and marginal cost. That is to say, downstream producers may charge a higher price than marginal cost. On the other hand, integration may eliminate the wedge between the monopoly price of the input and its marginal cost, because the merged firm would not charge itself higher than the marginal cost. The effect of this is to reduce unit cost and as a result, prices of final goods. Therefore, whether the price will be lower or higher depends on which of the two effects on product price is dominant. When the elasticity of substitution for the input is greater than the elasticity of demand for the product, vertical integration would increase the product price. Conversely, vertical integration would lead to a reduction of product price.

Vertical integration may enable the monopolist to increase its returns in either static or dynamic circumstances. At first, it enables the monopolist to price discriminatorily. Nonetheless, whether or not vertical integration which achieves price discrimination should be condemned under antitrust law is questionable. On the one hand, price discrimination often results in higher output than a monopolist's non-discriminatory pricing. Perfect price discrimination provides both forms of efficiencies since price discrimination gives a monopolist incentive to increase output to the level of a competitive market, that is to say when the price equals marginal cost, the output is greatest. The increased production allows the large-scale producer to take better advantage of economies of scale, that is, to produce more efficiently. Price discrimination also enables the monopolist to match his price to the item's value, its marginal utility, to each buyer. In that way, a price-discriminating monopolist can approach allocative efficiency more closely than a single-price monopolist can do. Moreover, when a seller already has market power in a product, discriminatory pricing of the product, which permits the seller to make all sales above marginal cost, may be more efficient than forcing the seller to offer its product as its non-discriminatory, profit-maximizing price. The latter situation would restrict output, however. On the other hand, any imperfect price discrimination scheme produces a certain amount of inefficiency both from less-than-competitive output and from the cost of operating the price discrimination scheme itself.

Yet we observe some serious anti-competitive effects that come from vertical integration. One anti-competitive effect comes from the fact that vertical integration enables the monopolist to evade public regulation of prices at the monopolized level. When a natural monopoly, of which price is regulated, integrated vertically with an input firm or an output firm that is in a competitive market, the regulated firm may have an opportunity to hide profits in competitive products. At the same time, with the integration of a competitive market the price-regulated firm can cross-subsidize its competitive affiliate with returns obtained in the monopoly market. As a result, the monopolist can leverage its power into the competitive market and deter potential entrants.

The most debatable issue of vertical integration is the foreclosure effect. It is used to believe that if a monopolist takes over all or most of the downstream market, it thereafter confronts potential entrants with the need to enter at two levels rather than one. The conventional view of antitrust law condemned vertical integration primarily based on foreclosure arguments. However, the Chicago schools (see Posner, 1976; Bork, 1978) do not take the view that integration would reduce the net supply of input available to other firms. When the rivals lose access to the input supplies produced by one firm, they are likely to gain access to the input suppliers that previously supplied the integrated downstream firms. In other words, the integration only realigns purchase patterns among competing firms. Even if there are no other unintegrated firms in either market, the entrant could enter both markets simultaneously. Two-level entry is not necessarily more difficult than one-level entry. The Chicago schools assume that if upstream entry is appealing, and there are no independent barriers downstream unless the downstream market presents its own significant and independent barriers, for example, by the need for a public licence, the capital markets will support entry at both levels even though the two-level entry may require a firm to raise more capital than the one-level entry requires. If profits can be made in the market, capital will generally follow. Fundamentally, vertical integration by the monopolist will force a new entrant to integrate as well only if the vertical integration lowers the monopolist's costs. If vertical integration produces no costs savings, then the market can continue to accommodate independent input supplier and independent manufacturers or independent producers and distributors. If the vertical integration is efficient, that is, if the integrated firm has costs higher than the total costs of the upstream and downstream, independent firms will actually be encouraged to come into the market, for they will have the cost advantage. To be sure, parallel entry of new producers or distributors could delay the entry rather than prevent it.

Since the publication of the 1984 DOJ Merger Guidelines, public enforcement of the law against vertical merger has been extinguished. The 1984 Guidelines already reflected the Division's view that few vertical mergers pose a danger to competition. The vertical merger section of the 1984 Guidelines differ significantly from its 1968 predecessor. The underlying reason is that, since 1968 at least, the 'new learning' in the area of vertical integration has firmly established that in a variety of realistic market situations, vertical integration is more likely to enhance rather than to diminish allocative efficiency. The foreclosure theory is generally ignored.

Realistically viewed, any significant vertical integration by a monopolist may delay the erosion of the monopoly through entry. When the upstream market is highly concentrated, integration will reduce the non-integrated sector of the downstream market so that a few firms of efficient size can serve downstream markets. In this case, entry will be deterred because there are fewer non-integrated firms in downstream markets to be dealt with.

It is more plausible if the two levels achieve minimum efficient scale at widely different outputs. In that case, a firm seeking to enter at a level with fewer scale economies would not be able to compete unless it also entered at the other level, produced at a much higher rate there, and then had to seek a market for excess production. Even with that much of a market remaining open, prospective entrants may become discouraged because the information, talent, and experience that successful entrance requires besides capital may not be accessed. The information, talent, and experience to support entry may be blocked by vertical integration. For example, the removed suppliers might be more efficient or were perceived to be more willing to break informal supplier arrangement with the incumbent firms and to serve the entrants. Vertical integration with another supplier obviously foreclose opportunities of accessing to suppliers removed.

Either upstream or downstream foreclosure raises rivals' costs, forces rivals to increase prices and enables the newly integrated firm to enjoy increased prices. An integrated firm can place downstream rivals at a cost disadvantage in a downstream market. Other input suppliers may not take up the gap because, for example, the ability to expand is limited. The downstream price increase may harm consumers and cause the dead-weight loss because the consumers reduce purchase below the competitive level. Also the unintegrated downstream firm engages the inefficient substitution of input. Extending the integration to the monopoly downstream market also reduces competitive pressure of innovation (see, for example, Roeller and Wey, 2001).

Summary

Exclusionary practices are prevailing in network industries transactions, particularly embodied in strategic alliances. They are primarily used to enlarge the property rights of involving technologies. Consequently, they are likely to increase the incentives of initial innovation (see also Evans and Schmalensee, 2001). However, the market power of initial innovation can be inappropriately increased. By too broadly expanding, the property rights of initial innovations not only offers initial innovators a windfall but also harms the sequential or complementary innovation. Especially, when the market failures are significant in network industries, exclusionary practices can exacerbate market imperfection and deter the sequential innovation. The antitrust policy towards exclusionary practices should therefore take into account of the exclusion effect on the follow-on and complementary innovations.

International conflicts

International conflicts of antitrust laws are resulting from the overlapping of different jurisdictions, they are also partly resulting from different economic and policy concepts. In many advanced industrial countries and regions the urge of protection of intellectual property is raising to the historical height in this decade. By combining the strong market power and strengthening intellectual property protection, the dominant firms in those countries seek to make it harder for firms in developing countries to gain access to the most valuable technologies or otherwise to catch up with the global high-technology leaders. Of course, if there were no intellectual property protection the risk of suboptimal investment in technology innovation could be very high.

However, strong intellectual property tends to protect initial innovations. Overprotection of initial innovations could create legal barriers to entry. On the contrary, the small and medium-sized firms whose incremental or complementary innovations often being the real engines of economic growth can be deterred. As a result, how to reach equilibrium of initial innovation and sequential innovation is probably an essential prerequisite of the solution of international conflicts in national antitrust laws.

International strategic alliances can lower prices and promote competition in the long term. They increase the potential economies of scale for both partners and eventually allow feedback from technology importing countries' markets to affect their foreign allies' own investments in new applications and improvements at home. On the other hand, the exclusionary practices embedding in strategic alliances may inappropriately expand the market power of initial innovation in transaction. As a result, the incentives of the partner's sequential innovation are very likely retarded. The antitrust policies of technology-exporting countries tend to enlarge the market power of the initial innovation to the utmost, while technology-importing countries' policies usually favour the follow-on innovation. The policy conflicts thus cause the difficulty of international harmonization.

Conclusions

The uniform emergence of strategic alliances in network industries explains the need to form a new organizational alternative to overcome market failures in these industries. The market failures mainly stem from the characteristics in these industries: enormous sunk costs, economies of scale, network externalities, and compatible and complementary technologies and products. Market failures in network industries reflect two dimensions of competitive concerns. On the one hand, the requirement of collaboration of competitive or complementary producers in order to master market imperfections make us rethink antitrust policies. Traditional antitrust risks towards collaborative arrangements such as price fixing, output reduction, or market allocation seem unlikely in network industries or at least not so urgent as in traditional industries. If any, risks often come from the ancillary restrictions imposed on strategic alliances to decrease incentives of innovation between partners. The administrative agencies or courts can adequately correct this concern by eliminating unnecessary restraints or imposing firewalls without harming the efficiencies the alliances may bring in. On the other hand, exclusionary practices incorporated in strategic alliances are very likely to be used in exploiting market imperfections in those industries. Strategic alliances are primarily formed in order to pursue innovations. They are more likely used to expand the property rights of these innovations to another or future markets. Exclusionary practices sometimes play a necessary kick-off function to facilitate the initial innovation though they more often deter follow-on improved or complementary innovation. Accordingly, the prevailing antitrust theory aiming at collusion concerns and ignoring exclusion risks apparently may need to be adjusted.

When exploiting market failures, such as economies of scale, externality effects, and interdependent technologies, exclusionary practices including exclusive dealing, tying, grantbacks as well as cross licensing, and vertical integration may strengthen their exclusion effect. As a result, carefully distinguishing anticompetitive exclusionary practice from those really promoting efficiency and balancing benefits to initial innovation against incentives to improve innovation are primary tasks. These tasks need fact-oriented analysis and a deeper anatomy of market structure. Fortunately, modern industrial organization in combination with game theory provide advanced tools to understand the market structure of network industries. The more realistic models of competitive behaviour are ascertained, the more precise competition policy can be predicted.

In addition, most strategic alliances involve technology companies in different national territories. Overlapping jurisdictions inevitably increase costs and uncertainties of transactions for strategic alliances. Consequently, a coordination of antitrust laws becomes the task of an international legal and economic community in the next generation after successes in international trade. Greater international cooperation or harmonization will force the business community to compete on more equal terms. To attain the goal one must keep in mind that sequential and complementary innovations are not less important than initial innovations. Only when follow-on innovations have been equally weighed with initial innovations, the international harmonization can be reached. Hence, a more delicate, economic underlying antitrust policy in the international community should be accepted if high technology industries need to develop more effectively.

References

Baker, J. B. and T. Bresnahan (1992) 'Empirical Methods of Identifying and Measuring Market Power', *Antitrust Law Journal* 62: 3–9

Bork, R. (1978) *Antitrust Paradox*, New York: Basic Books

Brodley, B. (1990) 'Antitrust Law and Innovation Competition', *Journal of Economic Perspectives* 4: 97–99

Carlton, D. W. and St. Salop (1996) 'You Keep on Knocking but You Can't Come In: Evaluating Restrictions on Access to Input Joint Ventures', *Harvard Journal of Law and Technology* 9: 319–330

Chang, H. H., D. S. Evans, and R. Schmalensee (1998) 'Some Economic Principles for Guiding Antitrust Policy Towards Joint Ventures', *Columbia Business Law Review* 223–257

Demsetz, H. (1982) 'Barnes to Entry', *American Economic Review* 72: 70–79

Evans, D. S. and R. Schmalensee (2001) 'Some Economic Aspects of Antitrust Analysis in Dynamically Competitive Industries', National Bureau of Economic Research (NBER) Working Paper 8268, May (http://www.nber.org/papers/w8268)

Farrell, J. and C. Shapiro (1988) 'Dynamic Competition with Switching Costs', *Rand Journal of Economics* 19: 123–137

—— (1990) 'Horizontal Mergers: An Equilibrium Analysis', *American Economic Review* 80(1): 107–126

Gordon, R. (2002) *Antitrust Abuse in the New Economy*, Aldershot: Edward Elgar

Hovenkamp, H. (1994) *Federal Antitrust Policy: The Law of Competition and its Practices*, St. Paul, Mn.: West Publ. Comp.

—— (1999) *Antitrust*, St. Paul, Mn.: West Publ. Comp.

Jacquemin, A. (1987) *The New Industrial Organization, Market Forces and Strategic Behavior*, Cambridge, Ma.: MIT Press

—— and M. E. Slade (1989) 'Cartel, Collusion and Horizontal Merger', Chap. 7 in R. Schmalensee, and R. D. Willig (eds), *Handbook of Industrial Organization*, Vol. I, Amsterdam: North Holland

Katz, M. (1989) 'Vertical Contractual Relations' in R. Schmalensee and R. D. Willig (eds), *Handbook of Industrial Organization*, Vol. I, Amsterdam: North Holland

Krattenmaker, T. G. and S. C. Salop (1986) 'Competition and Cooperation in the Market for Exclusionary Rights', *American Economic Review* 76: 109–113

Landes, W. M. and R. Posner (1981) 'Market Power in Antitrust Cases, *Harvard Law Review* 94: 937–942

McFalls, M. S. (1998) 'The Role and Assessment of Classical Market Power in Joint Venture Analysis', *Antitrust Law Journal* 66: 651–659

Nouel, G. L. (2001) 'Competition Assessment of Vertical Mergers and Vertical Arrangements in the New Economy', http://europa.eu.int/comm/enterprise/lib_competition/doc/merger_agreement_study pdf

Roeller, L.-H. and C. Wey (2000) 'International Competition Policy in the New Economy', Wissenschaftszentrum Berlin: Yearbook

Posner, R. (ed.) (1976) *Antitrust Law: An Economic Perspective*, University of Chicago Press: Chicago

Salinger, M. A. (1988) 'Vertical Merger and Market Foreclosure', *Quarterly Journal of Economics* 103: 345–354

Tirole, J. (1988) *Theory of Industrial Organization*, Cambridge, Ma.: MIT Press

US Department of Justice (1998) *Horizontal Merger Guidelines*, Washington, DC: GPO, §1.51

Vickers, J. and M. Waterson (1991) 'Vertical Relationship: An Introduction', *Journal of Industrial Economics* 39: 445–446

Whinston, M. D. (1990) 'Tying, Foreclosure, and Exclusion', *American Economic Review* 80: 838–843

Williamson, O. E. (1979) 'Transaction-Cost Economics: The Governance of Contractual Relations', *Journal of Law and Economics* 22: 233–235

7 Standards, compatibility, market share, competition, and quality

Introduction

The intent of this chapter is to explain, largely through case-based analysis, how a company in a network economy can improve its product and actually lose market share. The model assumes that one of two firms is given the option to make its product potentially compatible with its competitor's product. Therefore, consumers who purchase the potentially compatible product have the option to purchase compatibility. If a consumer purchases compatibility, she earns the benefits from both firms' products. The products are differentiated along a linear model, and the interpretation of the line is that consumers located to the right of a given point between the products can be thought of as businesses who may purchase computers while consumers located to the left of the point can be thought of as schools or homes. In addition, the left endpoint can be interpreted as a finite market. For instance, Apple personal computers already sell in both the home and school markets. Therefore, if Apple is to gain market share, they may need to do so in the business world.

The potentially compatible product is offered only if profits increase, and in equilibrium, the firm loses market share if it is located relatively close to the left endpoint. The added benefits from compatibility have an effect which increases market share. Thus the competitor is forced to decrease its price to avoid losing too many consumers in the contested market. As a result, the potentially compatible firm increases its market share in the contested market, but the decrease in prices by the competitor significantly increases the number of products sold in the competitor's uncontested market. If the uncontested market of the potentially compatible firm is not saturated and at least one consumer purchases compatibility, its market share always increases. However, if the uncontested market is saturated, the growth of the potentially compatible firm's market is limited, and the firm may actually lose market share in equilibrium. Regardless of the effect on market share, social welfare is strictly improved if at least one consumer purchases compatibility, and the price of the competing firm always decreases. This problem relates to the following case in the computer industry.

In 1994 Apple computers launched a new line of computers based on the PowerPC processor chip. The creation of the new chip was a joint venture between Apple Computers, IBM, and Motorola, and because the new chip was capable of being compatible with the market leading Intel chip, it was marketed as a major breakthrough in computer technology. If emulation software was purchased by a consumer, the consumer could run both software made for Apple computers and software made for Intel PCs on the same Apple machine. The machine was even being called a PC with a free Mac inside.

Apple computers had controlled about 8–10 per cent of the personal computer market since 1984, and recently it had been struggling financially. Those at Apple hoped that compatibility with the Intel-based PC and its 85 per cent market share would dramatically increase the market share of Apple computers.

The results from the introduction of the new product were not everything Apple had predicted or had hoped for. The increased competition from the PowerPC chip forced Intel to slash the price of their Pentium chips by 40 per cent. Thus Apple did not live up to its promise of cheaper computers. The result of Intel's slash in prices following the introduction of Apple's new chip was that Apple's market share decreased. Apple's market share early 1994 was 9.4 per cent, but at the end of the year it was down to 8.1 per cent (Carlton, 1995), and going further down ever since. The compatibility actually hurt Apple in its drive for increased market share. Although Apple lost market share, it did earn record profits the same year while it suffered steep losses the year before which could be explained that it sacrificed market share in the interest of profitability.

Networks and industrial organization: a review

A network externality occurs when either a firm or consumer derives not only 'stand-alone' benefits from a good but also 'network benefits'. In other words, a consumer cares about the number of people who have purchased the same product, or a firm prefers additional competition that could increase the market size of its products.

As we learned in the previous chapters (Chapters 1–3), the field of network externalities is relatively young, starting in the mid-1980s with seminal papers by Katz and Shapiro (1985) and Farrell and Saloner (1985). Since then the field has branched off in several directions.

They cover indirect network externalities, supply side externalities, demand externalities, compatibility between products, and the quality of a good involving network externalities. In the case of indirect network externalities and supply side network effects we encounter situations in specific markets in which a competitor may prefer the entry of an additional firm when the indirect supply side network externality is significant. Another case explores the effect of a firm's compatibility decision on market share. The model presented demonstrates that a firm may actually lose market share when the firm profitably increases compatibility. Finally and third, we look at the effect the level of competition has on the quality of a product in the presence of a network externality and degree of compatibility, the quality of the product may be greater under either a monopoly or a duopoly.

The competition effect is caused by firms competing for a limited number of consumers who have purchased a converter. The heavy competition in prices for these consumers has an effect which decreases profits. However, the more firms (and thus locations) that offer alternative hardware, the more likely consumers are to purchase the converter which enables them to purchase the alternative (preferred) hardware sold by the firms. This is the network effect which tends to increase profits. Which of the two effects dominates is shown to depend on the difference in the marginal costs of the standard and alternative hardwares. When the cost of the alternative hardware is not much lower than the standard, firms prefer the additional competition, but when the alternative hardware gets significantly less, each firm prefers to be a monopolist in the alternative hardware.

The two opposing effects on a firm's profits are the key elements to supply side network externalities.

Katz and Shapiro (1985) and Farrell and Saloner (1985) were the first to recognize that a firm may actually prefer competition to being a monopolist. Economides (1996) derives similar results when exploring a firm's incentive to license its product. However, each of these papers assumes a network externality among consumers. Chou and Shy (1990), Church and Gandal (1992), and Desruelle *et al.* (1996) derive models in which consumers prefer a variety of software for their hardware, but no network externality is assumed. In Church's and Gandal's model, the software firms experience both the competition and network effect because they want the hardware they use to be more attractive but they do not want the additional competition for consumers on their hardware.

In another case we present a model which attempts to explain why a firm may rationally offer a product which is potentially compatible to its competitor's product but loses market share. Compatibility between products is a prominent issue within the network externality literature. Katz and Shapiro (1985, 1986) have recognized its importance. In each of these papers, the firms must decide whether or not to make their product compatible with another firm's product. However, throughout much of the literature, the degree of compatibility between products is assumed to be exogenous. For instance, Chou and Shy (1993) present a model in which an increase in compatibility of a firm's product with another firm's product causes the initial firm's product to lose market share. In Chou's and Shy's model the increase in compatibility is exogenous, so the firm may or may not want to increase compatibility in the first place. In contrast, the model presented here allows for endogenous compatibility, so the choice of compatibility must be beneficial when the firm loses market share. In the more recent literature, Choi (1994a) presents a model with an endogenous compatibility decision. In the model, a monopolist must decide whether or not to make its product compatible across periods. The monopolist must choose between having consumers make repeat purchases and increase the value of the good to future consumers through compatibility. We examine the effect of competition on the compatibility decision.

Often to isolate the importance of compatibility, the network externality is ignored. Matutes and Regibeau (1988, 1992) and Economides (1989) are a few of the early papers addressing compatibility between products. In each of these papers the incentives of a firm to make the components of its product compatible with another firm's components are analysed. The decision is endogenous, and compatibility is shown to increase the amount of product differentiation. Matutes and Regibeau explore two competing firms' decisions of whether or not to offer compatible products. In their model each firm sells component x and component y to be used together as a complete product. If the components are compatible across firms, a consumer can buy component x and component y to be used together as a complete product. If the components are compatible across firms, a consumer can buy component x and component y from either firm, but if the products are incompatible, the components must be purchased from the same firm. Their model predicts an increase in the demand for a firm's products under compatibility due to the decrease in travel costs. The increase in demand softens price competition, so profits increase. However, there is no clear-cut welfare analysis. In our model, compatibility is one way, so competition in prices is intensified. In addition, social welfare increases when compatibility is purchased by at least one consumer. In their models, compatibility increases the price of the products by increasing demand but in our case compatibility decreases prices due to an increase in competition caused by one-way compatibility.

The compatibility decision always stops with the firms. In many cases, the consumer must decide whether or not to purchase a converter in order to achieve compatibility between products. Farrell and Saloner (1992) and Choi (1994a, 1996) model the consumer's decision concerning the purchase of a converter to be used with potentially compatible products. Farrell and Saloner (1992) and Choi (1994a, 1996) model the consumer's decision concerning the purchase of a converter to be used with potentially compatible products. They show that too many consumers may purchase a converter when compatibility works both ways, and Choi's models demonstrate that it is often the case that the wrong consumers purchase a converter. Our model presented demonstrates that too few consumers purchase a converter in equilibrium when compatibility is one-way, but when at least one consumer purchases a converter, social welfare increases under compatibility.

More specifically, one of two firms is given the option to make its product potentially compatible with its competitor's product. Then consumers who purchase the potentially compatible product have the option to purchase compatibility. If a consumer purchases compatibility, he or she earns the benefits from both firms' products. The model demonstrates that if the potentially compatible firm's uncontested market is not saturated the market share of the firm offering compatibility always increases. However, if the potentially compatible firm's uncontested market is saturated, it becomes possible that the firm's market share decreases. Intuitively, potential compatibility has an effect which increases the market size of the potentially compatible firm in both its contested and uncontested markets. However, potential compatibility also forces the competitor to decrease its price to avoid losing too many consumers in the contested market. The decrease in the competitor's price significantly increases the number of products sold in its uncontested market. When the potentially compatible firm's uncontested market is limited in size, the competitor's gain in market from its price cut may reduce the potentially compatible firm's market share in equilibrium.

In a third case, firms choose the quality of their product. The quality of the product is assumed to be independent of the number of consumers purchasing the product. Throughout most of the literature, the quality of each good is assumed to be exogenous. Esser and Leruth (1988) argue that firms could compete in both network size and quality.

In their model, firms were found to differentiate the quality of their products in order to lessen competition. Later, Choi (1994a) explores a monopolist's decision as to the level of quality in the absence of competition. It is shown that a relatively large quality acts as a commitment to compatibility across periods. The model has similar cost and utility functions. Choi (1994b) and Kristiansen (1996) explore the degree of risk in R & D for quality undertaken by firms competing for consumers in a multi-period model. Choi assumes only the entrant in the second period can select its quality. Choi demonstrates that the social optimum is for the entrant to choose the largest degree of risk possible. This is consistent with Kristiansen's model. In his model, both the incumbent and entrant choose the degree of risk in R & D for the quality of their product. The incumbent chooses too risky of an R & D project, and the entrant chooses too little risk. In our model the choice of quality is compared under different levels of competition. It is shown that the magnitude of the network externality function and the degree of compatibility determine which level of competition creates the greatest quality.

More precisely, the model used allows for heterogeneous consumers, and the firms choose both their quality and network size using Cournot conjectures. The framework of the model is similar to that used in Katz and Shapiro (1985) and Economides (1996). The firms take consumer expectations about the network size as given when determining their own output, but consumer expectations are fulfilled in equilibrium. When either the network externality function or the degree of compatibility is small, it is shown that the monopolist produces a greater quality product than a duopolist. However, if both the network externality function and degree of compatibility are significantly large, quality is greater under a duopoly. In addition, it is shown that social welfare is greater under a duopoly whenever quality is greater under a duopoly despite the fact that each firm must pay both the fixed entry cost and the cost of quality, but social welfare may be greater under a monopoly when the network size is greater under a duopoly.

Intuitively, the average cost of quality is decreasing in output size. When the magnitude of the network externality is small, the output of the monopolist is much greater than that of a duopolist. Thus the monopolist chooses a greater quality. However, when the magnitude of the network externality is large and the goods under a duopoly are relatively compatible, the demand for the duopolist's product becomes relatively large, so the quality of the good is greater under a duopoly. When the quality is greater under a duopoly, the fixed cost such that social welfare is greater under a monopoly is greater than the fixed cost such that a duopoly is profitable. Thus, whenever quality is greater under a duopoly, social welfare is greater under a duopoly as well.

The model

There exist two firms in the sale of heterogeneous goods. Firm 1 is located one unit to the right of the left endpoint, and Firm 2 is located one unit to the right of Firm 1. Consumer's tastes are uniformly distributed between each integer and spread throughout the interval $[0, \infty)$. Initially, Firm 1 offers good a and Firm 2 offers good c. Good a and good c are not compatible. Alternatively, Firm 1 sells good b which is identical to good a except that compatibility can be purchased for use with good b. Compatibility is sold independently of Firm 1 and Firm 2 at a constant price, and it allows the consumer to receive the benefits from both good b and good c.

Each consumer has the option to buy a good from either firm, or she may not buy a good at all. Consumer preferences are assumed to be quasi-linear in location and prices. More precisely, if consumer x (located at point x on the line) buys good a or good b from Firm 1, the utility of the consumer is $d - |x - 1| - p^i$. If the same consumer decides to purchase compatibility with good b, her utility is $2d - |x - 1| - |x - 2| - p^b - k$. And, if the consumer decides to purchase good c, her utility is $d - |2 - x| - p^c$ where p^i is the price of good i, d is the benefit parameter of each good, and k is the cost of purchasing compatibility.

We can frame the situation as a game. The game is played in two steps. First Firms 1 and 2 simultaneously set prices in good a and good c or in good b and good c. Next, consumers decide whether or not to purchase a good, and if so, which type of good to purchase. Consumers who purchase good b also decide whether or not to buy compatibility.

Because Firm 1 is the only firm with the potential to offer the new good, the outcome is determined by Firm 1's decision whether or not to offer good b. Firm 1 only offers good b if its profits increase compared to its profits from selling good a. Firm 2 has no decision to make other than setting the optimal price of good c given Firm 1's choice as to which good to offer.

Examples Two representative examples are given before the results are presented. The first example demonstrates a case in which good b is offered, and Firm 1's market share increases. The second example demonstrates another case in which good b is offered, but this time Firm 1's market share decreases.

Example 1 Market share increases. When good b is offered, the cost of a converter is such that $p^c < p^b$, and because the consumers who purchase a good on the far left do not buy compatibility, the higher price of good b has an effect which decreases Firm 1's market share. However, even though good b is more expensive, it is a more valuable good when compatibility is purchased. Thus, the consumer who is indifferent between good b and good c is located to the right of the consumer who was indifferent between good a and good c. This has an effect which increases Firm 1's market share. As it turns out, because d is relatively small, the effect of good b being the superior product outweighs the effect on market share from $p^c < p^b$, so the market share of Firm 1 increases.

Example 2 Market share decreases. When good b is offered, the cost of a converter is such that $p^c < p^b$, just as in Example 1. However, the lower price of good c has an effect which decreases Firm 1's market share even more than before. This is because the boundary at the left endpoint is forcing Firm 1 to supply less consumers with good b than it would without a constraining boundary. Just as before, the consumer who is different between good b and good c is located to the right of the consumer who was indifferent between good a and good c. This has an effect which increases Firm 1's market share. However, the presence of the boundary has altered Firm 1's behaviour, so the price of good b is greater than it would be if the boundary did not exist. Thus for a relatively large d, the market share of Firm 1 decreases. The key to Firm 1's market share decreasing when good b is offered is that Firm 2's price for good c always decreases due to the intense competition caused by the potential compatibility of good b. The lower price of good c encourages more consumers to the right of Firm 2 to purchase a good. In addition, the boundary on the left alters Firm 1's behaviour so that the price of good b increases and becomes closer to the price of good a as d increases. This effect decreases Firm 1's market share. However, as d increases, the left boundary eventually shrinks Firm 1's market share under good a below one-half. Thus it becomes more difficult for Firm 1's market share to decrease when d increases. For d relatively large, it is no longer possible for Firm 1's market share to decrease because Firm 1 eventually decreases the price of good b such that the consumer located at the left endpoint earns positive surplus.

Competition and market share

Exploring the effects of offering a potentially compatible good for arbitrary benefits and compatibility costs, we assume for ease of demonstration, but without restricting generality, that the range of benefits lies between $1 < d \leq 2$ and the cost of compatibility is limited to $k \leq 0.5$.

The assumption $d > 1$ implies that the marginal consumer located between the two firms receives a positive utility from purchasing a good. This assumption avoids the complications of multiple equilibria, and it implies that a consumer who is indifferent between the two goods being offered strictly prefers either good to no good at all (see Salop, 1979). The assumption $d \leq 2$ implies that the left boundary does not affect Firm 1's strategic behaviour when choosing a price for good a while competing against Firm 2. When $d > 2$, good a is purchased by all consumers to the left of Firm 1.

The circumstances in which good b is offered in place of good a can be determined, given the parameters, by comparing the actual profits of each of the outcomes.

The equilibrium outcome is uniquely subgame perfect (see Fudenberg and Tirole, 1989), and in equilibrium, good b is offered when the cost of compatibility is small relative to the benefits of good a and good c.

As the benefits (d) of good a and good c increase or the cost of compatibility (k) decreases, good b becomes more valuable to the consumers relative to both good a and good c. Because of this, the profits obtained from good b increase more rapidly than the profits from good a as benefits increase and the cost of compatibility decreases. Thus good b is offered in equilibrium for relatively large benefits and small compatibility costs.

The circumstances in which good b is offered and Firm 1's market share decreases follow from subsequent observations.

As the cost of compatibility increases, the market share of Firm 1 decreases if either the benefits or the costs of compatibility are relatively large. However, as the cost of compatibility increases, good b is less likely to be offered in equilibrium. When good b is offered, it is always the case that $p^c < p^b$. Thus the number of consumers to the right of Firm 2 purchasing good c has increased more than the number of consumers to the left of Firm 1 buying good b. However, because good b is more valuable than good c, when compatibility is purchased, more consumers between Firm 1 and Firm 2 are purchasing a good from Firm 1. As it turns out, when the left boundary is not binding, Firm 1's market share always increases when good b is offered regardless of the cost of compatibility. When the left boundary becomes binding, the number of consumers purchasing good b is limited. As a result, Firm 1 charges a higher price, so fewer consumers located between the two firms purchase good b than when the boundary is not binding. Thus when the boundary is binding, it is possible that the market share of Firm 1 decreases when good b is offered.

The lower boundary on the cost of compatibility simply states the condition such that market share decreases when good b is offered. The upper boundary borrows from the first statement that good b is offered, and states when good b is offered in equilibrium. The lower boundary decreases with the size of the benefits, but it is always greater than or equal to the cost of compatibility such that the boundary is binding. However, the cost of compatibility such that good b is offered does not exceed the cost of compatibility such that the boundary is binding until the benefits are relatively large. Thus in order for Firm 1's market share to decrease when good b is offered, benefits must be even larger than required for the consumer at the left endpoint to own good b in equilibrium.

Social welfare

Social welfare is defined as the sum of consumer surplus and total profits. The social planner can choose both which good is to be offered and the prices at which the goods are to be sold. However, the consumers still choose whether or not to purchase a good and which good to purchase. We will obtain the following results.

1   Social welfare is always greater under good b if at least one consumer purchases compatibility when either firms choose prices competitively or the social planner chooses the optimal prices.

2   When good *b* is offered in equilibrium, too few consumers are purchasing good *b* with compatibility instead of good *c* relative to the socially optimal outcome.

3   Those consumers who purchase good *b* at the competitive price make the same decision whether or not to purchase compatibility as they would under the socially optimal prices.

4   Too few consumers are purchasing goods under either equilibrium relative to the socially optimal outcome.

Under competition, good *c* is always cheaper when good *b* is offered, so consumers who purchase good *c* must be strictly better off when good *b* is offered. However, the price of good *b* may be more expensive than the price of good *a*. As a result, all consumers who purchase good *b* without compatibility, some who purchase no good, and some who purchase good *b* with compatibility may be worse off. Thus to make any welfare conclusions, the benefits to both those that purchase good *b* with compatibility and those that purchase good *c* at a lower price must be weighed against the costs to both those that purchase good *b* without compatibility at a higher price and those that now purchase no good at all. As it turns out, the additional benefits from compatibility and the lower price of good *c* are greater than the costs to the others from the increase in the price for good *b* whenever compatibility is purchased by at least one consumer.

If a consumer decides to purchase a good, the price charged for the good is simply a transfer payment between the consumer and the firm. The social welfare is not affected if a consumer pays a higher price for a good. However, if the price of a good is greater than zero, some consumers choose to not purchase either firm's product.

Thus the socially optimal prices are $p^a = p^b = p^c = 0$, and good *b* is preferred under the socially optimal outcome if at least one consumer purchases compatibility with good *b* ($0.5 \leq d - k$). When good *a* is offered in equilibrium, consumers who purchase a good are making the same purchase decisions between good *a* and good *c* as when the socially optimal outcome is good *a* due to the symmetry of the problem. However, because the competitive prices are larger than the socially optimal prices, too few consumers are buying a good at the competitive prices. When good *b* is offered in equilibrium, Firm 1 is charging too high a price relative to Firm 2. Thus too few consumers are choosing to purchase good *b* instead of good *c* relative to the socially optimal outcome. As under good *a*, the competitive prices for both good *b* and good *c* are larger than the socially optimal prices, so too few consumers are buying a good.

Assessment of profits

The solution derived must be checked to see if either firm has an incentive to deviate by capturing the opponent's entire market. However, this is more complex than when good *a* is being offered. Firm 1 can offer a price

$p^b < \min\{p^c - 1, 2p^c - k - 1\}$. This would entice all consumers to buy good b whether they buy compatibility or not. Similarly, Firm 2 can offer a price $p^c < p^b - 1$. This entices all consumers who have bought good b without compatibility to buy good c, and some of the consumers who bought good b with compatibility to buy good c. Without compatibility, all consumers to the left of Firm 1 would pay the additional transaction cost of one unit to switch to good c.

Therefore, they would all make the same decision as to which good to purchase if a good is purchased by the consumer at all. However, when compatibility exists, consumers to the left of Firm 1 may make different decisions. This is due to the fact that if compatibility is purchased, the transaction cost of both good b and good c must be paid. The purchasing good b with compatibility requires an additional transaction cost of $(1 - x)$ which varies for each consumer. As it turns out, each of the payoffs derived are potential equilibrium outcomes for the given range assumed for d. Let D_1, D_2 be market demand for goods a, b, respectively.

Market share decreases if $D_1^b/(D_1^b + D_2^b) < D_1^a/(D_1^a + D_2^a)$ and $\pi_1^b > \pi_1^a$. When the equilibrium is such that $1 + k \leq p^b$, Firm 1's market share only decreases if $(8d - 1)/5 < k$. However, a necessary condition such that $1 + k \leq p^b$ is $k \leq (2d - 3)/4$, so given this equilibrium, Firm 1's market share does not decrease. When the equilibrium is such that $d - 1 < p^b \leq 1 + k$, Firm 1's market share does not decrease. When the equilibrium is such that $d - 1 < p^b \leq 1 + k$, Firm 1's market share decreases only if $(2d - 1)/2 < k$. However, compatibility is purchased by some consumers only if $k < (2d - 1)/2$, so given this equilibrium, Firm 1's market share does not decrease. As it turns out, given the range on d assumed, market share can only decrease in equilibrium when good b is consumed by all consumers to the left of Firm 1.

Wrapping up we could come to a calculation of social welfare. Under good a social welfare is defined as follows:

$$W(p^a, p^c) = \pi_1^a + \pi_2 + \int V^a(x, d, p^a)dx + \int V^c(x, d, p^c)dx.$$

Under good b, social welfare is defined as follows:

If $p^b \leq 1 + k$,

$$W(p^b, p^c) = \pi_1^b + \pi_2 + \int V^b(x, d, p^b)dx + \int V_k^b(x, d, k, p^b)dx$$

$$+ \int V^c(x, d, p^c)dx.$$

If $1 + k \leq p^b$,

$$W(p^b, p^c) = \pi_1^b + \pi_2 + \int V_k^b(x, d, k, p^b)dx + \int V^c(x, d, p^c)dx.$$

Social welfare under the different goods can be compared by using the prices calculated in steps one and two. Straightforward algebra demonstrates that when at least one consumer purchases compatibility, social welfare is greater when good b is offered.

Maximizing $W(p^a, p^c)$ and $W(p^b, p^c)$ with respect to each price implies $p^a = p^b = p^c = 0$, and good b is offered if at least one consumer purchases compatibility $(0.5 \leq d - k)$. Using the socially optimal prices and the prices calculated in steps one and two, it is also straightforward to demonstrate which consumers are making the same purchase decisions as under the socially optimal outcome.

Network externality and choice of product quality

The existence of a network externality and varying degrees of compatibility between products affect the quality decisions of firms under different degrees of competition.

For example, under given standard linear demand functions, each duopolist sells a smaller quantity of the product than if it were alone in the market when the two firms compete in quantity using Cournot type competition. If consumers care about the quality of their product and the cost of quality is independent of output, the previous result still holds, and the monopolist chooses a greater quality product than each duopolist. The result occurs because the average cost of quality is decreasing with respect to output, so the average cost of quality is less for the monopolist. However, when consumers care about the network size of their good, each duopolist may choose a greater quality product than the monopolist. This is because for a given network externality function, an increase in the degree of compatibility between products increases the output of each duopolist's product. The increase in compatibility increases the network size of each duopolist's product, so the demand for the product increases. Thus the average cost of quality to each duopolist decreases, and the quality of each duopolist's product eventually exceeds the quality of the monopolist's product. Whenever the quality is greater under a duopoly, social welfare also is greater under a duopoly when a duopoly is the equilibrium outcome. Although both the fixed cost of entry, and the cost of quality must be paid by each firm, the condition that a duopoly must be profitable implies that the fixed cost of entry is small enough such that social welfare is greater under a duopoly. However, when the network size is larger under a duopoly and both types of competition are profitable, social welfare may be greater under a monopoly. This is because the quality of the monopolist's product can be significantly greater than the quality of each duopolist's product when each has a larger network size. The social welfare may be greater under a monopoly if the fixed cost of entry is moderate.

The results of the model can be used to conclude, for example, that if the degree of compatibility between Intel based PCs and Apple computers is relatively small, Intel's chip is of higher quality (faster) with its large market share.

On the other hand, if the degree of compatibility between products is relatively large and the network externality is significantly strong, then Intel's chip would be of higher quality if Apple and Intel based PCs split the market. In addition, a comment about the welfare implication of Intel's large market share, and how it relates to the network externality and the degree of compatibility between products can be made using the results of the model.

There are a number of previous results concerning the choice of product quality in the presence of network externalities. However, none concerns the combined effect of the level of competition, the magnitude of the network externality, and the degree of compatibility on the quality decisions of firms. This chapter includes a game which determines the quality and network sizes of each firm, and when each type of competition exists in the presence of network externalities. The welfare implications of the equilibrium outcome are examined. Esser and Leruth (1988) were among the first in the vertical product differentiation literature to consider network externalities. They allowed two firms to first choose the quality of the product and then the network size. With heterogeneous consumers, firms are able to differentiate their products through the choice of quality and network size in order to avoid a high degree of competition. Bental and Spiegel (1995) and Economides and Flyer (1995) also model competition in quality using vertical differentiation, but they identify the quality of the product to be the size of the network.

Choi (1994a) models the choice of quality as a commitment mechanism for compatibility between generations of goods in the presence of network externalities. Because a monopolist sells a good to later consumers which is incompatible with the good sold to earlier consumers when quality is small, the earlier consumers rationally choose to delay their purchase. By choosing the quality of the earlier consumers' products to be larger than is socially efficient, the monopolist can credibly commit that the later consumers' products will be compatible with the earlier consumers' products. The model below incorporates a similar cost function to that used by Choi, and in both models, the cost of quality involves decreasing average costs. However, Choi only examines the quality level chosen by a monopolist, and not how the choice of quality is affected by the degree of competition.

Kristiansen (1996) asks the question: how does the existence of a network externality affect the degree of risk undertaken by firms participating in the R & D of quality? The entrant has a disadvantage relative to the incumbent in that it must offer a product with a greater quality to overcome the advantage the incumbent has with its established network. Thus the entrant chooses a riskier R & D of quality and the incumbent chooses a more certain R & D of quality than if no network externality existed. From a welfare perspective, the optimal solution would involve the entrant choosing an even riskier strategy and the incumbent choosing a more certain strategy. In the model below there is no uncertainty concerning the choice of quality. However, the choice of quality is compared under different levels of competition with a more general network externality function and varying degrees of compatibility.

Modelling product quality

A consumer's utility is a function of the size of the network, the quality of the product, and the price of the product purchased. More precisely, the utility of consumer s who purchases good j is

$$U_s(x_j, x_k, q_j, p_j, r_s) = r_s + v(x_j + cx_k) + q_j - p_j. \tag{1}$$

$v(x_j + cx_k)$ represents the network externality function which is identical for all consumers. v is concave and increasing in the network size, $x_j + cx_k$, it is twice continuously differentiable; its derivative is such that $\lim_{t \to \infty} v'(t) \leq 1$, and $v(0) = 0$. x_j and x_k are the quantities sold of good j and good k, respectively, and c represents the exogenous degree of compatibility between good j and good k with $0 \leq c \leq 1$. q_j is the quality of good j, and it represents a portion of the benefits derived independently of the network effect. r_s is consumer's s basic willingness to pay for a good, so it is independent of both the network externality and quality of the good. It is assumed that consumers are heterogeneous in their basic willingness to pay with r_s uniformly distributed between each integer and spread throughout the interval $(-\infty, A]$ $(A > 0)$. Finally, p_j represents the price of good j.

There are two identical firms. Each firm is a profit maximizer, with Cournot conjectures, both the quality (q_j) and quantity (x_j) of its product. Firm j's profit function is

$$\pi_j (x_j, q_j, p_j) = p_j x_j - c(q_j) - F.$$

$c(q_j)$ is the cost of producing q_j units of quality, and it is assumed to be strictly convex $c(0) = 0$. More precisely, $c(q_j) = q_j^2$ (somewhat relaxed later on). F is the fixed cost of entering the market for each firm.

The derivation of the demand function is conducted as follows. When either one or two products exist, a consumer purchases good j only if utility is greatest from purchasing good j. More precisely, a consumer purchases good j only if

$$r_s + v(x_j + cx_k) + q_j - p_j \geq \max\{r_s + v(x_k + cx_j) + q_k - p_k, 0\}. \tag{2}$$

A necessary condition for both firms to have positive sales under a duopoly is for equation (2) to hold with equality

$$\overline{p_j} = p_j - v(x_j + cx_k) - q_j = p_k - v(x_k + cx_j) - q_k = p_k \tag{3}$$

This equality simply says that the hedonic (quality adjusted) prices of the two goods must equal one another. Consumer s then purchases a good if $\overline{p} \leq r_s$ (a consumer must earn non-negative utility from purchasing a good). Therefore, $A - \overline{p} = x_j + x_k$, and the demand function for Firm j can be written as

$$p_j = A + v(x_j + cx_k) + q_j - x_j - x_k. \tag{4}$$

The price Firm j receives depends on the network size of its product, the quality of its product, and the total output of both firms. The firms are assumed to be Cournot competitors, and consumers are assumed to have fixed expectations about the network size of the product (the assumption about consumer expectations is relaxed later on).

Using equation (4), it is now possible to define the profit function for Firm j:

$$\pi_j(x_j, x_k, q_j) = x_j(A + v(x_j^e + cx_k^e) + q_j - x_j - x_k) - q_j^2 - F. \qquad (5)$$

By similar computations, the profit function for a monopolist must be

$$\pi_j(x_j, q_j) = x_j(A + v(x_j^e) + q_j - x_j) - q_j^2 - F. \qquad (6)$$

In an evolving competitive game, any two firms sequentially decide whether or not to enter the market. Then firms, which entered the market, simultaneously choose the quality of their good. The same firms then simultaneously choose quantity after seeing the quality decisions of the other firms. However, before making a purchase, consumers observe the quality but not the quantity of each firm's product. Consumer expectations about the quantity, and thus network size, for each good are known by both firms before entry occurs. The type of equilibrium examined is a Cournot equilibrium between firms with fulfilled expectations of consumers. This states that consumer expectations are fixed in advance of the Cournot game, and consumer expectations about each good's network size are correct in equilibrium.

The assumption that the firms must choose quality before quantity seems natural. A firm must decide what to produce before they decide how much to produce. If firms were to choose the quantity before quality, there would be no strategic interaction between firms in the choice of quality. Each firm would choose quality to equal one-half of their total output, so quality would be greater under a duopoly only if output is greater under a duopoly. When the choice of quality precedes quantity, firms strategically compete against one another in both quality and quantity. The additional competition allows quality to be greater under a duopoly when a duopolist chooses a smaller output than the monopolist.

The equilibrium analysis would be conducted as a subgame perfect equilibrium among firms (Tirole, 1988; Shapiro, 1989). Thus each firm's decision concerning entry, quality, and quantity can be determined through backwards induction. Because consumers are assumed to have fulfilled expectations, consumers are able to reason, but with myopic behaviour. More precisely, consumers expectations are fixed before firms choose their strategic behaviour. Consumers do not adjust their expectations if prices differ from those expected, so firms cannot manipulate their beliefs.

A fulfilled expectations equilibrium must satisfy $x_j = x_j^e$ for each active firm, so off the equilibrium path beliefs of consumers are wrong.

There are three types of equilibrium outcomes which can occur when both firms are active: (1), both firms have a positive symmetric network size; (2), only one firm has a positive network size; and (3), both firms produce a positive asymmetric network size. The second type of equilibrium is a monopoly outcome, and examples of the third type of equilibrium are hard to find.

The number of firms entering the market is easily determined. Whenever being a duopolist is profitable, Firm B enters the market if Firm A has entered the market. Thus when duopoly profits are positive ($\pi_d \geq 0$) both firms offer the good regardless of the level of monopoly profits. When monopoly profits are positive ($\pi_m \geq 0$) and duopoly profits are negative, only Firm A enters the market. When both monopoly and duopoly profits are negative, neither firm offers a good.

Some equilibrium results

Because the firms have Cournot conjectures about quantity, each firm has a reaction function for its quantity decision which depends on its competitor's quantity, its own quality choice decided in the previous stage, and consumer expectations. The notation $v_j \equiv v(x_j^e + cx_k^e)$ is used for brevity. Firm j's reaction function to the quantity choice of Firm k, given its quality choice is

$$r_j(x_k) = \frac{A + \bar{q}_j + v_j - x_k}{2} \tag{7}$$

Therefore, in equilibrium, quantities must satisfy

$$s_j(x_j^e, x_k^e, \bar{q}_j, \bar{q}_k) = \frac{A + 2\bar{q}_j - q_k + 2v_j - v_k}{3} \quad \text{for a duopoly,}$$

and $s_j(x_j^e, \bar{q}_j) = (A + \bar{q}_j + v_j)/2$ for a monopoly. Using this information, both firms are now able to predict the effect their choice of quality has on each firm's output and thus prices. Thus due to the Cournot conjectures about quality and backwards induction, each firm has a reaction function for its quality decision which only depends on the other firms quality decision and consumer expectations. Through backwards induction, the reaction function for the duopolist (Firm j) in quality is

$$a_j(q_k) = 2(A - q_k + 2v_j - v_k)/5. \tag{8}$$

Equilibrium quality choices under a duopoly must therefore satisfy

$$b_j(x_j^e, x_k^e) = 2(A + 4v_j - 3v_k)/7.$$

Given the choice of quality, the output of the duopolist must satisfy

$$s_j(x_j^e, x_k^e) = 3(A + 4v_j - 3v_k)/7.$$

$v_j = v_k$ due to symmetry. Thus $s_j(\cdot) = s_k(\cdot) = s_d$ under a duopoly outcome, and $s_j(\cdot) = s_m$ under a monopoly outcome. In addition, because consumer expectations are fulfilled in equilibrium, the fixed-point solutions for quality and quantity under the duopoly and monopoly outcomes are:

$$q_d = 2(A + v(x_d (1 + c)))/7, \quad x_d = 3(A + v(x_d (1 + c)))/7. \tag{9}$$

$$q_m = (A + v(x_m))/3, \quad \text{and} \quad x_m = 2(A + v(x_m))/3. \tag{10}$$

Substituting the variables from equations (9) and (10) into the profit functions for each type of outcome (equations (5) and (6)), the profits under the duopoly and monopoly outcomes are:

$$\pi_d = 5(A + v(x_d (1 + c)))^2/49 - F \tag{11}$$

and

$$\pi_m = (A + v(x_m))^2/3 - F. \tag{12}$$

Using the profits under each type of outcome, it is straightforward to determine the equilibrium outcome with respect to the fixed cost of entering the market.

Quality comparisons

Whenever the network externality function in a consumer's utility function is small, the monopolist produces a higher-quality product than a duopolist if the monopoly outcome is profitable. However, when the network externality becomes significant and there is a relatively large degree of compatibility, each duopolist produces a higher-quality product than the monopolist. Two examples are given.

Example 1 $v(z) = \alpha(z)^\beta$. (i) $\alpha = 0$: no network externality. Quality is greater under a monopoly. (ii) $\alpha = \beta = 1$: linear network externality. Quality is greater under a duopoly if $c > 0.66$. (iii) $\alpha = A = 1$, and $\beta = 0.5$: concave network externality. Quality is greater under a monopoly. (iv) $\alpha = 3$, $A = 1$, and $\beta = 0.5$: concave network externality. Quality is greater under a duopoly if $c > 0.89$.

Example 2 $v(z) = \alpha z + z^\beta$. The network externality function is strictly concave, and with parameters with the ranges $0.5 \leq \alpha \leq 1$ and $0.66 < \beta < 1$, there exists a critical degree of compatibility such that quality is greater under a duopoly if $c^* < c \leq 1$.

In Example 2 it is easy to construct network externality functions such that quality is greater under a duopoly. However, not many attractive functions would be able to obtain the result. For example, $v(z) = \alpha(z)^\beta$ does not satisfy the condition but for α relatively large and β not too small, there exists a critical degree of compatibility such that the quality is greater under a duopoly for any larger degree of compatibility (see Example 1). However, there is a test to check whether or not there exists a critical degree of compatibility such that quality is greater under a duopoly if the degree of compatibility exceeds the critical level.

Proposition 1   Quality is greater under a duopoly if and only if $x_d > 0.75x_m$. There exists a $c^* \in (0, 1)$ such that $c^* < c \le 1$, the quality of the product is greater under a duopoly if and only if $6\nu(1.5\ x_m) > A + 7\nu\ (x_m)$ (when both types of competition are profitable).

Proof   Using the equilibrium quality choices given in equations (9) and (10), it is found that

$$q_d > q_m \quad \text{if and only if } 6\nu\ (x_d\ (1 + c)) > A + 7\nu\ (x_m) \tag{13}$$

when both types of competition are profitable. Solving $\nu(x_d(1 + c))$ and $\nu(x_m)$ using the quantities given in equations (9) and (10), and substituting these solutions into equation (13), it is shown that $q_d > q_m$ if and only if $x_d > 0.75x_m$ for every $c > c^*$. From equation (13), the critical degree of compatibility such that $x_d = 0.75x_m$ must satisfy $6\nu\ (0.75\ x_m\ (1 + c^*)) = A + 7\nu\ (x_m)$. To demonstrate that $c^* \in (0,1)$, it must be the case that $6\nu\ (0.75\ x_m\ (1 + c^*)) < A + 7\nu\ (x_m) < 6\nu\ (0.75\ x_m\ (1 + c^*))$. The first inequality is necessarily true for all ν, but the second is true only if the slope of ν is relatively large at x_m.

These results to date show the effect the degree of competition has on quality depends on the concavity and magnitude of the network externality function at the monopolist's output level and on the degree of compatibility. A monopolist is more likely to produce a larger quantity of the good, so the average cost of quality is less for the monopolist due to decreasing average costs. However, due to the Cournot conjectures about the choice of quality, the duopolist chooses a larger quality than would maximize joint profits. Which effect is stronger depends on the strength of the network externality function and the degree of compatibility. When the network externality function is small (relatively concave at the monopolist's output level), the effect of increasing returns to scale is stronger than the effect from the higher degree of competition, so the monopolist has a greater quality product. If the degree of compatibility between products is relatively small, the gap between the quality of the monopolist's and duopolist's products actually widens as the network externality becomes stronger. This is because the network size is larger under a monopoly, so the demand for the monopolist shifts outward more so than the demand for the duopolist as the network externality function increases. However, for a significantly large degree of compatibility, the duopolist has a larger network size than the monopolist. The duopolist still sells a smaller quantity than the monopolist in most cases, but the competition effect on quality outweighs the decreasing average cost due to the larger network size.

Thus only $x_d > 0.75x_m$ is required for quality to be greater under a duopoly.

Cost of quality

Regardless of the network externality, the ratio of quality to quantity is always greater for a duopolist than the monopolist. This implies that the quality choice relative to the number of goods produced is greater under a duopoly, or in other words, the duopolist competes more heavily in quality than it does in quantity. This raises an interesting question, under which type of competition is more money spent on quality per good produced, and does it depend on the network externality function? When there is no network externality, it is easy to show that the cost of quality per good produced is greater for a duopolist than the monopolist. However, if the network externality function is significantly large, the monopolist spends more per good produced on quality if the degree of compatibility between the duopolists' products is relatively small. Two examples are now given. In addition, sufficient conditions on the network externality function such that the amount spent on quality per good produced is greater under a monopoly for a range of degrees of compatibility are presented.

Example 3 $v(z) = \alpha(z)^\beta$. (i) $\alpha = 0$: no network externality. The cost of quality of good produced is greater under a duopoly. (ii) $\alpha = \beta = 1$: linear network externality. The cost of quality per good produced is greater under a monopoly if $c < 0.44$. (iii) $\alpha = \beta = 0.5$ and $A = 1$: Concave network externality. The cost of quality per good produced is greater under a duopoly. (iv) $\alpha = 2$, $A = 1$, and $\beta = 0.5$: concave network externality. The cost of quality per good produced is greater under a monopoly if $c < 0.25$.

Example 4 $v(z) = \alpha z + z^\beta$. The network externality function is strictly concave, and within parameters of the range $0.42 \leq \alpha \leq 1$, and $-0.77 < \beta < 1$, there is a critical degree of compatibility such that the amount spent on quality per good produced is greater under a monopoly if $0 \leq c < c'$.

Comments

The quality to quantity ratio is always 0.66 (2/3) for a duopolist and 0.50 (1/2) for the monopolist regardless of the network effect. This implies that the duopolist spends $0.44x_d$ on quality per good produced, and the monopolist spends only $0.25x_m$ on quality per good produced. Thus if each duopolist's output is greater than 0.56 (9/16) of the monopolist's output, each duopolist spends more on quality per good produced. When there is no network externality, this is easily satisfied. However, when the degree of compatibility is relatively small but the network externality function is significantly large, the monopolist's output becomes much larger than 1.77 (16/9) of the duopolist's output. Thus a monopolist spends more on quality per good produced than the duopolist.

The duopolist competes more heavily in quality than quantity because it is chosen first and thus affects the output decisions of each firm. However, due to the convexity of the cost function for quality, the total quality and quantity levels are important as well. The monopolist spends less on quality per good produced with no network externality function, but when the degree of compatibility is significantly small and the network externality function is relatively large and not too concave, the quality of the monopolist's product becomes much greater than the quality of the duopolist's product relative to when no network externality exists. Thus due to the convexity of the cost function, the monopolist spends more on quality per good sold when the network effect is significantly large and the degree of compatibility is relatively small. However, as the degree of compatibility increases, the network size of the duopolist's product increases, but the amount spent on quality per good produced also increases.

Assessing social welfare

The social planner can choose the type of competition, but firms must still make positive profits in order to enter the market. Equations (14) and (15) give the precise welfare levels (given $p_d = x_d$ and $p_m = x_m$) under a duopoly and a monopoly, respectively.

$$\text{Welf}_d = 2(x_d^2 - q_d^2 - F) + (2x_d)^2/2 = 4(A + \nu(x_d(1 + c)))^2/7 - 2F \qquad (14)$$

$$\text{Welf}_m = x_m^2 - q_m^2 - F + x_m^2/2 = 5(A + \nu(x_m))^2/9 - F. \qquad (15)$$

When the quality of the duopolist's product is greater than the quality of the monopolist's product it must be the case that the network size under the duopoly $(x_d/(1 + c))$ is greater than the network size under a monopoly (see equation (13)). With both the quality and network size greater under a duopoly than under a monopoly, it is not difficult to show that welfare must be greater under a duopoly when fixed costs are ignored. Below, it is shown that even though both the fixed costs and the cost of quality must be paid by both firms under a duopoly, social welfare is greater under a duopoly whenever the quality under a duopoly is greater than the quality under a monopoly.

Example 5 $\nu(z) = z$. Letting $F = \pi_d + F$ (where π_d includes fixed costs), a sufficient condition for $\text{Welf}_d > \text{Welf}_m$ is found to be that $c > 0.62$. In Example 1, it was derived that $q_d > q_m$ if and only if $c > 0.66$. Thus whenever $q_d > q_m$ it must be the case that $\text{Welf}_d > \text{Welf}_m$.

Proposition 2 When $q_d > q_m$, it must be the case that social welfare is greater under a duopoly than under a monopoly.

Proof Equations (14) and (15) combine to show that welfare is greater under a duopoly if and only if

$$36(A + \nu(x_d(1 + c)))^2 - 63F > 35(A + \nu(x_m))^2 \qquad (16)$$

when both a monopoly and a duopoly are profitable. Letting the fixed cost, F, be such that $\pi_d = 0$, welfare is greater under a duopoly only if $\nu(x_d(1+c)) > 0.08A + 1.08\,\nu(x_m)$ when $\pi_m \geq 0$.

From equation (13) and the fact that equation (16) is most restrictive when $\pi_d = 0$, it is clear that when $q_d > q_m 0$, welfare is greater under a duopoly for all fixed costs such that min $\{\pi_d, \pi_m\} \geq 0$. If $\pi_d \geq 0 > \pi_m$, the monopolist does not offer the product and the result is trivial.

A duopoly is the equilibrium outcome for a relatively large fixed cost when the conditions such that quality is greater under a duopoly are satisfied. In addition, when the network size is greater under a duopoly, social welfare increases more under a duopoly than under a monopoly as the network externality function increases.

Thus as the network externality function increases (while the duopoly has a larger network size), the critical fixed entry cost such that welfare is greater under a monopoly becomes relatively large as well. Because welfare under a monopoly does not depend on the degree of compatibility, it is straightforward to show that as the degree of compatibility increases the critical fixed cost such that welfare is greater under a monopoly eventually exceeds the fixed cost such that a duopoly no longer is an equilibrium outcome. As it turns out, this degree of compatibility is less than the degree of compatibility such that quality is greater under a duopoly regardless of the concavity of the network externality function.

A further interesting question might be: Is it always the case that social welfare is greater under a duopoly outcome when the network size is greater under a duopoly than under a monopoly $(x_d(1+c) > x_m)$? As the arguments below show it is possible that the social welfare is greater under a monopoly despite the fact that the network size is greater under a duopoly outcome. Intuitively, when $x_d(1+c) = x_m + \varepsilon$ it must be the case that $q_m > q_d$, so the monopolist is offering a superior product. However, the monopolist also charges a greater price, so the benefits of the monopolist's superior product must be weighed against the benefits of intense competition under a duopoly. If fixed costs are ignored, social welfare is always greater under a duopoly when the duopolist has a larger network size. However, because both the fixed cost of entry and the cost of quality must be paid by each firm, there exists a range of fixed costs such that a duopoly is the equilibrium outcome, but social welfare is greater under a monopoly.

Under no network externality, it is possible to have social welfare greater under a monopoly regardless of the degree of compatibility. This is because under a duopoly the fixed costs must be paid by both firms, and from the first example, the quality of the monopolist's product is always much greater than the quality of the duopolist's product. However, if there exists a network externality, the consumers care about both the quality of the product and the network size. When the degree of compatibility is such that the network size under the two types of competitions is relatively close, the range in fixed costs such that a duopoly is profitable and social welfare is greater under a monopoly is increasing with the magnitude of the network externality function. Thus when network effects are

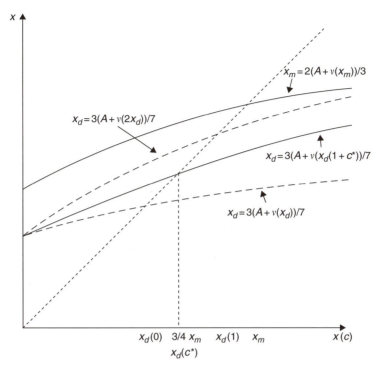

Figure 7.1 Quality comparison with respect to quantity.

relatively large, social welfare is greater under a duopolist when a duopolist has a network size only a little larger than the monopolist's network size, but as the network externality decreases, social welfare can be greater under a monopoly even when the duopolist has a network size significantly larger than the monopolists network size (see Figures 7.1 and 7.2).

Free entry and consumer expectations

So far only the scenario of a monopoly or duopoly has been considered. Now free entry is allowed. For notational purposes we take

$$X_{N-i}(c) \equiv x_{N-i}(1 + c(N-i-1)),$$

that is the network size under $N-i$ firms given each firm produces x_{N-i} units of output. Key questions would be raised how free entry would impact on social welfare. Does $q_N > q_i$ ($0 < i < N$) imply that social welfare is greater when N firms enter the market than if only i firms entered the market? When only two firms existed, we have shown that if a duopolist produces a greater quality product than

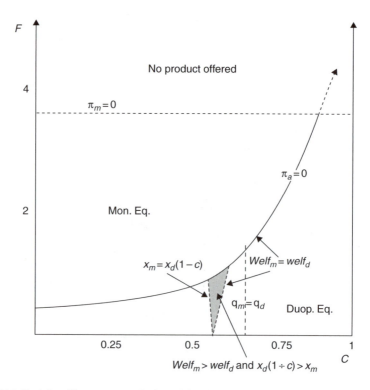

Figure 7.2 Social welfare vs network size with a linear network externality.

the monopolist, social welfare was greater under a duopoly whenever the fixed cost of entry was such that a duopoly was profitable. The following result, a variant of Proposition 2, is also true under free entry.

When $q_N > q_i$ ($0 < i < N$) it must be the case that social welfare is greater under N firms than under i firms regardless of the equilibrium outcome. This can be proved by induction on Proposition 2.

As when there existed only two potential entrants, the network size is larger under N firms than i firms whenever the quality is greater under N firms. Thus consumers get the best of both worlds, the larger network size and a higher-quality product. However, as before, each firm that enters the market must pay both the fixed cost of entry and the cost of quality. When the network externality function increases both the critical fixed cost such that welfare is greater under i firms and the fixed cost such that N firms is profitable increase. However, when the degree of compatibility is increased, the critical fixed cost such that welfare is greater under i firms is eventually greater than the fixed cost such that N firms are profitable. The critical degree of compatibility where this occurs is less than the critical degree of compatibility such that $q_N > q_r$.

To allow for free entry raises two more interesting questions. Is it possible that social welfare is greater under a monopoly, but the network size is larger under N firms?

To examine social welfare at equivalent network sizes across different degrees of competition, the degree of compatibility must increase as the number of profitable firms increases. The limit of the degree of compatibility such that the network size under N firms exceeds the network size under a monopoly approaches 2/3 from below as the number of entrants become large, and the limit of the degree of compatibility such that the network size under N firms exceeds the network size under $N-1$ firms approaches 1. Notice too that no lower boundary on fixed costs was required in both parts of the corollary regardless of the strength of the network effect. This is because social welfare is always greater with less firms when the network sizes are equal (when more than two firms have entered the market).

When only two firms existed, it was found that social welfare could be greater under a monopoly when the duopoly had a larger network only if fixed costs were positive. With more than two firms entering the market, the critical fixed cost such that welfare is greater with less firms entering eventually becomes greater than zero as the degree of compatibility increases if there exists a network effect. This follows from the earlier statement as a variant of Proposition 2.

In the model above, it was assumed that firms took consumer expectations as given. That is consumer expectations were fixed in advance of the Cournot game, and consumer expectations about each product's network size were correct in equilibrium. Thus firms could not expand the demand for their product by increasing the network for their product. The possibility that consumers can see the output produced for each product before a purchase is made is now explored. That is, the profit function for duopolist Firm j is

$$\pi_j (x_j, x_k, q_j) = x_j (A + \nu (x_j + cx_k) + q_j - x_j - x_k) - q_j^2 - F. \tag{17}$$

Similarly, the profit function for a monopolist must be

$$\pi_j (x_j, q_j) = x_j (A + \nu (x_j) + q_j - x_j - x_k) - q_j^2 - F. \tag{18}$$

When firms can affect a consumer's expectation of the network size, the network externality must be relatively small and the degree of compatibility relatively large for a duopolist to provide a positive quality. However, the quality of the duopolist's product increases as the network externality parameter increases, and the quality of the duopolist's product decreases as the degree of compatibility increases if the duopolist is providing a positive quality. This is because although the quality and quantity decision variables are both strategic substitutes, a change in the magnitude of the network effect and a change in the degree of compatibility have opposite effects on the reaction functions of each firm.

As the network externality becomes stronger, both quantity and quality become stronger strategic substitutes. However, the reaction functions of each firm (both quantity and quality) shift outward enough such that the quantity and quality of each firm's product increase. In addition, as the network externality function increases, the choice of quality has a smaller effect on demand, and if the network externality function becomes too strong the duopolist decides not to offer any quality (the choice in quality does not affect profits). Thus the network externality must be relatively small for the duopolist to produce a positive quality.

As the degree of compatibility increases, both quantity and quality become less strategic substitutes. However, the reaction functions of each firm (both quantity and quality) shift inward enough such that the quantity and quality of each firm's product decreases. This is because, with a greater degree of compatibility, the duopolist's competitor's output has a greater effect on the size of its own network. This effect increases the demand for both firm's products which lessens competition. This lessening of competition allows profits to increase. The result that quality decreases when the degree of compatibility increases sharply contrasts the case when the firms have no effect on consumer expectations. In previous results, derived from Proposition 1, it was shown that if the degree of compatibility exceeds some critical level then quality is greater under a duopoly only if the degree of compatibility is less than some critical level. In addition, the critical degree decreases in magnitude of the network externality when expectations are assumed given, but increases in the magnitude of the network externality when firms affect expectations.

Conclusions

This chapter focused on product development, compatibility, and market share as well as on competition and product quality in network economies.

On the first issue we designed a model which demonstrates that a firm making its product potentially compatible with a competitor's product does not necessarily increase its market share. The key to this result is that the firm offering the potentially compatible product may be initially targeted towards a market which is limited in size. If this is the case, potential compatibility makes the firm more attractive when competing against another product, but it does not significantly expand the number of sales in its uncontested market. Thus the number of additional consumers who purchase the new superior product is limited.

More precisely, the addition of a potentially compatible product forces the non-compatible firm to reduce its price to avoid losing too many consumers in the contested market. As a result, the number of products sold in the non-compatible firm's uncontested market increases, and the loss of sales in the contested market is limited. However, due to the added benefits of potential compatibility, the number of products sold by the potentially compatible firm in both its uncontested market and the contested market increases. When the size of the potentially compatible firm's uncontested market is unrestrictive, the firm offering potential compatibility always increases its market share in equilibrium. However, when the potentially compatible firm's product is built such that its uncontested market is limited in growth, the firm may actually lose market share if potential compatibility is offered.

The model demonstrates why it was feasible for Apple's market share to decrease when it offered its new computer that was based on the Intel compatible PowerPC chip. As is feasible with the model presented, Apple's profits increased but its market share decreased when it offered a product that was potentially compatible with its competitor's product. Regardless of the effect on market share, the model demonstrates that social welfare is greater under potential compatibility when at least one consumer purchases compatibility, and in addition, too few consumers purchase compatibility in equilibrium.

On the second issue we have shown that a duopolist produces a greater quality product than the monopolist if and only if both the network externality and degree of compatibility are significant. It also was shown that the monopolist spends more on quality per good produced than a duopolist if and only if the network externality is relatively large and the degree of compatibility is relatively small. In addition, the model demonstrated that whenever quality is greater under a duopoly, social welfare also is greater under a duopoly. However, the likelihood that social welfare is greater under a monopoly when the network size is greater under a duopoly increases with the strength of the network externality function but decreases with the degree of compatibility. Next, a general cost function was introduced, but the main results of the paper remained the same. The model was altered to include the possibility that firms could alter consumer expectations about its product's network size. It was shown that quality could still be greater under a duopoly than a monopoly, but this was for different reasons than noted before. When consumer expectations could be affected, quality was greater under a duopoly only if the degree of compatibility was significantly small such that the goods were strong strategic substitutes.

When quality was introduced it remained the case that when the network externality is large but compatibility between products is small, a monopoly may be the socially optimal level of competition. In fact it became more likely that a monopoly is the socially optimal level of competition due to its greater quality. However, when the degree of compatibility between products was significant and quality was introduced into the model, it became more likely that a duopoly is socially preferred.

References

Arthur, W. B. (1989) 'Competing Technologies, Increasing Returns, and Lock-In by Historical Events', *The Economic Journal* 99: 116–131

Bental, B. and M. Spiegel (1995) 'Network Competition, Product Quality, and Market Coverage in the Presence of Network Externalities', *The Journal of Industrial Economics* 43(2): 197–208

Bulow, J., J. Geanakoplos, and P. Klemperer (1985) 'Multimarket Oligopoly: Strategic Substitutes and Complements', *Journal of Political Economy* 93: 488–511

Choi, J. P. (1994a) 'Network Externality, Compatibility Choice and Planned Obsolescence', *The Journal of Industrial Economics* 42(2): 167–182

——(1994b) 'Irreversible Choice of Uncertain Technologies with Network Externalities', *Rand Journal of Economics* 25(3): 382–401

Choi, J. P. (1996) 'Do Converters Facilitate the Transition to a New Incompatible Technology?: A Dynamic Analysis of Converters', *International Journal of Industrial Economics* 14(6): 825–835

Chou, C. and O. Shy (1990) 'Network Effects without Network Externalities', *International Journal of Industrial Organization* 8: 259–270

—— (1993) 'Partial Compatibility and Supporting Services', *Economics Letters* 41: 193–197

Church, J. and N. Gandal (1992) 'Network Effects, Software Provision and Standardization', *The Journal of Industrial Economics* 40(1): 84–104

David, P. A. 'Clio and the Economics of QWERTY', *American Economic Review* 75(2): 323–373

Desruelle, D., G. Gaudet, and Y. Richelle (1996) 'Complementarity, Coordination and Compatibility: The Role of Fixed Costs in the Economics of Systems', *International Journal of Industrial Organization* 14(6): 747–768

Economides, N. (1989) 'Desirability of Compatibility in the Absence of Network Externalities', *American Economic Review* 79(5): 1165–1181

—— (1996) 'Network Externalities, Complementarities, and Invitations to Enter', *The European Journal of Political Economy* 12(2): 211–233

—— and F. Flyer (1995) 'Technical Standards Coalitions for Network Goods', Working Paper EC-95-12, New York University

—— and C. Himmelberg (1995) 'Critical Mass and Network Size with Applications to the US Fax Market', Working Paper EC-95-11, New York University

Esser, P. and L. Leruth (1988) 'Marketing Compatible, Yet Differentiated Products', *International Journal of Research in Marketing* 5: 251–270

Farrell, J. (1992) 'Converters, Compatibility and the Control of Interfaces', *The Journal of Industrial Economics* 40(1): 9–36

—— and G. Saloner (1985) 'Standardization, Compatibility and Innovation', *Rand Journal of Economics* 16(1): 70–83

Fudenberg, D. and J. Tirole (1989) 'Noncooperative Game Theory for Industrial Organization: An Introduction and Overview' in R. Schmalensee and R. D. Willig (eds), *Handbook of Industrial Organization*, Vol. 1, Amsterdam: North Holland

Katz, M. L. and C. Shapiro (1985) 'Network Externalities, Competition, and Compatibility', *The American Economic Review* 75(3): 424–440

—— (1986) 'Technology Adoption in the Presence of Network Externalities', *Journal of Political Economy* 94(4): 822–841

—— (1994) 'Systems Competition and Network Effects', *The Journal of Economic Perspectives* 8(2): 93–115

Kristiansen, E. G. (1996), 'R&D in Markets with Network Externalities', *International Journal of Industrial Organization* 14(6): 769–784

Matutes, C. and P. Regibeau (1988) 'Mix and Match: Product Compatibility with Network Externalities', *The Rand Journal of Economics* 19(2): 221–234

—— (1992) 'Compatibility and Bundling of Complementary Goods in a Duopoly', *The Journal of Industrial Economics* 40: 37–54

Salop, S. C. (1979) 'Monopolistic Competition with Outside Goods', *The Bell Journal of Economics* 10: 141–156

Shapiro, C. (1989) 'Theories of Oligopoly Behavior', Chapt. 6 in R. Schmalensee and R. D. Willig (eds), *Handbook of Industrial Organization*, Vol. 1, Amsterdam: North Holland

Shy, O. (1996) 'Technology Revolutions in the Presence of Network Externalities', *International Journal of Industrial Organization* 14(6): 785–800

Tirole, J. (1988) *The Theory of Industrial Organization*, MIT Press, Cambridge

8 Network economies for the Internet

Conceptual models

Introduction

With advances in computer and networking technology, thousands of heterogeneous computers can be interconnected to provide a large collection of computing and communication resources. These systems are used by a growing and increasingly heterogeneous set of users which are identified with the present Internet. A macroscopic view of distributed computer systems reveals the complexity of the organization and management of the resources and services they provide. The complexity arises from the system size (e.g. number of systems, number of users) and heterogeneity in applications (e.g. online transaction processing, e-commerce, multimedia, intelligent information search) and resources (CPU, memory, I/O bandwidth, network bandwidth and buffers, etc.).

The complexity of resource allocation is further increased by several factors. First, in many distributed systems, the resources are in fact owned by multiple organizations. Second, the satisfaction of users and the performance of applications are determined by the simultaneous application of multiple resources. For example, a multimedia server application requires I/O bandwidth to retrieve content, CPU time to execute server logic and protocols, and networking bandwidth to deliver the content to clients. The performance of applications may also be altered by trading resources. For example, a multimedia server application may perform better by releasing memory and acquiring higher CPU priority, resulting in smaller buffers for I/O and networking but improving the performance of the communication protocol execution.

Finally, in a large distributed system, the set of systems, users, and applications is continuously changing. We address some of the issues of Quality of Service (QoS) and pricing, and efficient allocation of resources (computational resources) in networks and systems.

Massive complexity makes traditional approaches to resource allocation impractical in modern distributed systems such as the Internet. Traditional approaches attempt to optimize some system-wide measure of performance (e.g. overall average response time, throughput, etc.). Optimization is performed either by a centralized algorithm with complete information, or by a decentralized consensus based algorithm (Low and Varaiya, 1993).

The current and future complexity of resource allocation problems described makes it impossible to define an acceptable system-wide performance metric. What single, system-wide performance metric adequately reflects the performance objectives of multimedia server and an online transaction processing system? Centralized or consensus-based algorithms are impractical in dynamic systems owned by multiple organizations. Resource allocation complexity due to decentralizations and heterogeneity is also present in economic systems. In general, modern economies allocate resources in systems whose complexity overwhelms any algorithm or technique developed for computer systems (Scarf, 1967). Here we discuss the similarities between complex distributed systems and economies. Competitive economic models could provide algorithms and tools for allocating resources in distributed computer systems. There is another motivation that has come about due to the commercialization of the Internet.

The debate has begun in the area of multiple QoS levels and pricing. How should pricing be introduced to provide many service levels in the Internet? Should pricing be based on access cost or should it be based on usage and QoS received by the end user? Will usage-based or flat-rate pricing help the Internet economy grow, and help in accounting and improving the efficiency of the Internet, and make users benefit much more? Similar issues are being investigated in the ATM networking community. We address some of the issues of QoS and pricing and efficient allocation of resources (computational resources) in networks and systems.

Design goals

In designing resource allocation and control mechanisms in complex distributed systems and networks several goals need to be considered:

- Partition large complex allocation problems into smaller, disjoint allocation problems.
- Decentralize resource access, allocation, and control mechanisms.
- Design reliable, fault-tolerant, and robust allocation mechanisms.
- Design scalable architectures for resource access in a complex system.
- Provide QoS guarantees to users of applications, on performance criteria, and develop pricing mechanisms for QoS based charging. Some of the QoS criteria in distributed systems include the following: (i) average response time, (ii) throughput, (iii) application failure probability, (iv) information loss, packet loss in communication networks, and (v) maximum response time (message delay).
- Define system performance criteria that reflect in aggregate the diverse individual criteria of users and applications.
- Design a unified framework in which users have transparent access to the services of a distributed system, and services are provided in an efficient manner.

The rationale of economic models in networking

There are intrinsic interfaces between human information processing and networking that show the usefulness of economic modelling.

Decentralization   In an economy, decentralization is provided by the fact that economic models consist of agents which selfishly attempt to achieve their goals. There are two types of economic agents: suppliers and consumers. A consumer attempts to optimize its individual performance criteria by obtaining the resources it requires, and is not concerned with system-wide performance. A supplier allocates its individual resources to consumers. A supplier's sole goal is to optimize its individual satisfaction (profit) derived from its choice of resource allocation to consumers.

Limiting complexity   Economic models provide several interesting contributions to resource-sharing algorithms. The first is a set of tools for limiting the complexity by decentralizing the control of resources. The second is a set of mathematical models that can yield several new insights into resource-sharing problems.

Pricing and performance   Most economic models introduce money and pricing as the technique for coordinating the selfish behaviour of agents. Each consumer is endowed with money that it uses to purchase required resources. Each supplier owns a set of resources, and charges consumers for the use of its resources. The supplier prices its resources based on the demand by the agents, and the available supply. Consumers buy resources or services such that the benefit they receive is maximized. Consumer-agents buy resources based on maximizing performance criteria. As a whole the system performance is determined by some combination of the individual performance criteria.

Usage accounting, billing, and dimensioning   By using economic models for service provisioning in distributed systems, accounting for QoS becomes an important task for suppliers, as they have to keep track of the resource usage in order to price the resources, and thereby charge or bill the users for QoS. In addition, pricing can be used to understand the user demands and thereby dimension systems appropriately.

Administrative domains   Often large distributed systems and computer networks spread over several domains, the control of resources is shared by multiple organizations that own distinct parts of the network. In such an environment each organization will have a set of services that it supports. Economic principles of pricing and competition provide several valuable insights into decentralized control mechanisms between the multiple organizations and efficient service provisioning.

Scalability   A key issue in designing architectures for services in large computer networks and distributed systems is scalability. With the ever-growing demand for new services, flexible service architectures that can scale to accommodate new services are needed. Economic models of competition provide, in a natural fashion, mechanisms for scaling services appropriately based on service demand and resource availability.

As has been pointed out by Roy Radner (1993), 'computer scientists … are more like engineers than economists … generally concerned with improving things, rather than proving that things are optimal under some unrealistic and restrictive assumptions … '.

The approach suggested is directed towards striking a balance between improving and making things optimal.

Internet resources

The evolution of Internet pricing poses interesting resource-allocation problems. Flat-rate pricing has been a key condition that allowed the Internet to expand very fast. It is interesting to note that flat-rate pricing has been more prevalent in the US than in Europe which partially explains higher user diffusion rates in the US than in Europe or Japan among private users.

But as the Net has grown in size and complexity, not discounting engineering advances in network (management) technologies, it is now becoming more obvious that other pricing schemes being able to cope with severe congestion and deadlock should come forward. New pricing schemes should not only be able to cope with a growing Internet traffic but also be able to foster application development and deployment vital to service providers. Usage-based pricing of this new kind should make the internet attractive to many new users. Casual users will find it more affordable, while business users will find a more stable environment.

Several routes with different capacities exist between a source and a destination (Figure 8.1). Classes of traffic compete for resources/services between the

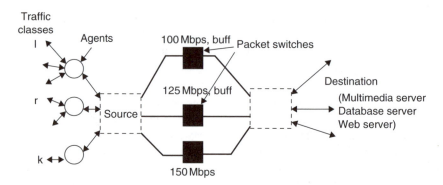

Figure 8.1 Traffic classes, agents to generate multiple routes between sources and destination.

source and the destination. The packet switches contain buffer and link resources which are shared.

Without an incentive to economize on usage, congestion can become quite serious (and so can expansion). The problem is more serious for data networks like the Internet than for other congestible transportation network resources because of the tremendously wide range of usage rates. A single user at a modern workstation can send a few bytes of e-mail or put a load of hundreds Mbps on the network, for example, by downloading videos demanding as much as 1 Mbps. Since the maximum throughput on most current backbones is only 40–60 Mbps, it is clear that even a few users with relatively inexpensive equipment could block the network. There is a witness of these problems a few years ago after America Online introduced a flat fee for its internet services and experienced a massive and persistent breakdown with disgruntled customers. A natural response by shifting resources to expand technology will be expensive and not a satisfactory solution in the long run because of the imminent potential of creating overcapacities (Odlyzko, 1998). Many proposals rely on voluntary efforts to control congestion. Many participants in congestion discussions suggest that peer pressure and user ethics will be sufficient to control congestion costs. But as MacKie-Mason and Varian (1995) suggest we essentially have to deal with the problem of overgrazing the commons, for example, by overusing a generally accessible communication network. A few proposals would require users to indicate the priority they want each of the sessions to receive, and for routers to be programmed to maintain multiple queues for each priority class. The success of such schemes would depend on the users' discipline to stick to the assigning of appropriate priorities to some of their traffic. However, there are no effective sanction and incentive schemes that would control such traffic, and therefore such a scheme is liable to be ineffective. This is why pricing schemes have gained increasing attention and various approaches and models have been discussed in the network community (Shenker *et al.*, 1996; Wang *et al.*, 1997).

Quality of Service (QoS)

With the Internet we observe a single QoS: 'best effort packet service'. Packets are transported first-come, first-served with no guarantee of success. Some packets may experience severe delays, while others may be dropped and never arrive. Different kinds of data place different demands on network services (Shenker, 1995). E-mail and file transfer requires 100 per cent accuracy, but can easily tolerate delay. Real-time voice broadcasts require much higher bandwidth than file transfers, and can tolerate minor delays but they can tolerate significant distortion. Real-time video broadcasts have very low tolerance for delay and distortion. Because of these different requirements network allocation algorithms should be designed to treat different types of traffic differently, but the user must truthfully indicate which type of traffic he/she is preferring, and this would only happen through incentive compatible pricing schemes. Network pricing could be looked at as a mechanism design problem (Cocchi *et al.*, 1991). The user can indicate the 'type' of transmission and the workstation in turn reports this type to the network. To ensure truthful revelation of preferences, the reporting and billing mechanism must be incentive compatible.

Pricing congestion

The social cost of congestion is a result of the existence of network externalities. Charging for incremental capacity requires usage information. We need a measure of the user's demand during the expected peak period of usage over some period, to determine the share of the incremental capacity requirement. In principle, it might seem that a reasonable approach would be to charge a premium price for usage during the predetermined peak periods (a positive price if the base usage price is zero), as is routinely done for electricity pricing (Wilson, 1993). However, in terms of Internet usage, peak demand periods are much less predictable than for other utility services. Since the use of computers would allow scheduling some activities during off-peak hours, in addition to different time zones around the globe, we face the problem of shifting peaks. By identifying social costs for network externalities the suggestion by MacKie-Mason and Varian (1995) is directed towards a scheme for internalizing this cost as to impose a congestion price that is determined by a real-time Vickrey auction. The scheme requires that packets should be prioritized based on the value that the user puts on getting the packet through quickly. To do this, each user assigns his/her packets a bid measuring his/her willingness-to-pay (indicating effective demand) for immediate servicing. At congested routers, packets are prioritized based on bids. In line with the design of a Vickrey auction, in order to make the scheme incentive compatible, users are not charged the price they bid, but rather are charged the bid of the lowest priority packet that is admitted to the network. It is well known that this mechanism provides the right incentives for truthful revelation. Such a scheme has a number of desirable characteristics. In particular, not only do those users with the highest cost of delay get served first, but the prices also send the right signals for capacity expansion in a competitive market for network services. If all of the congestion revenues are reinvested in new capacity, then capacity will be expanded to the point where its marginal value is equal to its marginal cost.

Internet communication technologies: ATM and B-ISDN

We take a particular platform of the Internet, ATM or B-ISDN, as an example to develop the economic principles of the network economy.

The Internet and Asynchronous Transfer Mode (ATM) have strongly positioned themselves for defining the future information infrastructure. The Internet is successfully operating one of the popular information systems, the World Wide Web (WWW), which suggests that the information highway is forming on the Internet. However, such a highway is limited in the provision of advanced multimedia services such as those with guaranteed QoS. Guaranteed services are easier to support the ATM technology. Its capability far exceeds that of the current

Internet, and it is expected to be used as the backbone technology for the future information infrastructure. ATM proposes a new communications paradigm. ATM allows integration of different types of services such as digital voice, video, and data in a single network consisting of high-speed links and switches. It supports a Broadband Integrated Services Digital Network (B-ISDN), so that ATM and B-ISDN are sometimes used interchangeably, where ATM is referred to as the technology and B-ISDN as the underlying technical standard. ATM allows efficient utilization of network resources, and simplifies the network switching facilities compared to other proposed techniques in that it will only require one type of switching fabric (packet switch). This simplifies the network management process (Minzer, 1989). The basic operation of ATM, and generally of packet-switched networks, is based on statistical multiplexing. In order to provide QoS the packets need to be served by certain scheduling (service) disciplines. Resource allocation algorithms depend heavily on the scheduling mechanism deployed. The scheduling is to be done at the entrance of the network as well as the switching points. The term 'cell' designates the fixed-size packet in ATM networks. ATM allows variable bit rate sources to be statistically multiplexed. Statistical multiplexing produces more efficient usage of the channel at the cost of possible congestion at the buffers of an ATM switch (Figure 8.2). When the congestion persists, buffer overflow occurs, and cells are discarded (or packets are dropped). Therefore, resources (i.e. bandwidth and buffer space) need to be carefully allocated to meet the cell loss and the delay requirements of the user. The delay and the cell loss probability that the user wishes the network to guarantee are referred to as the QoS parameters. Overall, QoS is usually defined in terms of cell loss probability, delay bounds, and other delay and drop-off parameters. How can one provide such QoS with guarantees? The general approach is to have an admission or performance algorithm that takes into account the traffic characteristics of the source and assigns suitable amounts of resources to the new connection during channel establishment. The admission algorithm is responsible for calculating the bandwidth and buffer space necessary to meet the QoS requirements specified by the user. The algorithm depends on how the traffic is characterized and the service disciplines supported by the switches.

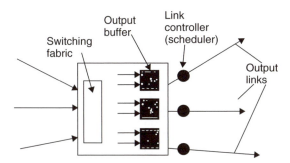

Figure 8.2 Packet switch (node) with output links and output buffers.

Although the Internet is capable of transporting all types of digital information, it is difficult to modify the existing Internet to support some features that are vital for real-time communications. One important feature to be supported is the provision of performance guarantees. The Internet uses the Internet Protocol (TCP/IP), in which each packet is forwarded independently of the others. The Internet is a connectionless network where any source can send packets any time at speeds that are neither monitored nor negotiated. Congestion is bound to happen in this type of network. If congestion is to be avoided and real-time services are to be supported, then a negotiation (through pricing or rationing) between the user and the network is necessary. ATM is a connection-oriented network that supports this feature. A virtual channel is established, and resources are reserved to provide QoS prior to data transfer. This is referred to as channel establishment.

Traffic in B-ISDN

In a B-ISDN environment high-bandwidth applications such as video, voice, and data are likely to take advantage of compression. Different applications have different performance requirements, and the mechanisms to control congestion should be different for each class of traffic. Classification of these traffic types is essential in providing efficient services. There are two fundamental classes of traffic in B-ISDN: real-time and non-real-time (best effort) traffic. The majority of applications on the Internet currently are non-real-time ones (Paxson, 1994) based on TCP/IP. TCP/IP is being preserved with an ATM technology (Chao, 1994). The Internet can support data traffic well but not real-time traffic due to the limitations in the functionality of the protocols. B-ISDN needs to support both non-real-time and real-time traffic with QoS guarantees. Most data traffic requires low cell loss, but is insensitive to delays and other QoS parameters. Applications such as Telnet require a real-time response and should therefore be considered real-time applications. Video is delay-sensitive and, unlike Telnet, requires high bandwidth. High throughput and low delay are required of the ATM switches for the network to support video services to the clients. This puts a constraint on the ATM switch design in that switching should be done in hardware and the buffer sizes should be kept reasonably small to prevent long delays. On the other hand, best-effort traffic tends to be bursty, and its traffic characteristics are hard to predict. This puts another, opposite constraint on an ATM switch, which requires large buffers at the switching point, further complicating its design (Figure 8.3).

Congestion control

Statistical multiplexing can offer the best use of resources. However, this is done at the price of possible congestion. Congestion in an ATM network can be handled basically in two ways: reactive control and preventive control (Gilbert, 1992). Reactive control mechanisms are commonly used in the Internet, where control is triggered to alleviate congestion after congestion has been detected. Typical examples of reactive control are (i) explicit congestion notification (ECN),

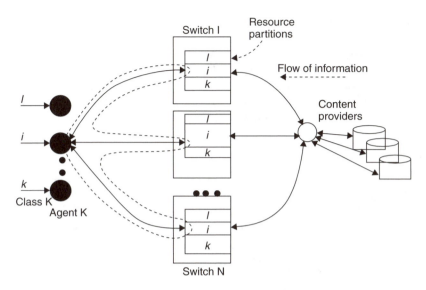

Figure 8.3 Resource partitions for K agents on N link suppliers.

(ii) node to node flow control, and (iii) selective cell discarding. In the more advanced preventive control approach, congestion is avoided by allocating the proper amount of resources and controlling the rate of data transfers by properly scheduling cell departures. Some examples of preventive control mechanisms are (i) admission and priority control, (ii) usage parameter control, and (iii) traffic shaping.

Reactive and preventive control can be used concurrently, but most reactive controls are unsuitable for high-bandwidth real-time applications in an ATM network since reactive control simply is not fast enough to handle congestion in time. Therefore, preventive control is more appropriate for high-speed networks.

Service discipline

Traffic control occurs at various places in the network. First, the traffic entering the network is controlled at the input. Second, the traffic is controlled at the switching nodes. In either case, traffic is controlled by scheduling the cell departures. There are various ways to schedule departure times, and these mechanisms are part of service disciplines. The service discipline must transfer traffic at a given bandwidth by scheduling the cells and making sure that it does not exceed the buffer space reserved (or the delay bound assigned) for each channel. These functions are usually built into the hardware of the ATM switch and into the switch controller. When implementing a service discipline in an ATM network, it is important to choose are simple enough that can be easily integrated into an ATM switch. However, the discipline must support the provision of QoS guarantees.

This also means that the service discipline is responsible for protecting 'well-behaved' traffic from the 'ill-behaved' traffic and must be able to provide certain levels of QoS guarantees (Ferguson and Huston, 1998). The service discipline also needs to be flexible enough to satisfy the diverse requirements of a variety of traffic types, and to be efficient, that is, to permit a high utilization of the network. Various service disciplines have been proposed, and many of them have been investigated thoroughly and compared (Zhang and Knightly, 1994). An important class is that of disciplines used in rate-allocating servers.

Bandwidth–buffer trade-off

A simple example on the representation of QoS parameters is the bandwidth–buffer trade-off. Bandwidth can be traded for buffer space and vice versa to provide the same QoS. If a bandwidth is scarce, then a resource pair that uses less bandwidth and more buffer space should be used. Resource pricing is targeted to exploit this trade-off to achieve efficient utilization of the available resources. The pricing concept for a scarce resource is well known in economics, but in the context of exploiting the bandwidth–buffer trade off, Low and Varaiya (1993) use non-linear optimization theory to determine centralized optimal shadow prices in large networks. With respect to large-scale application, however, the complex optimization process limits the frequency of pricing updates, which causes inaccurate information about available resources. In order to make pricing in the context of a buffer–bandwidth trade off more adjustable and flexible it should be based on decentralized pricing procedures according to competitive bidding in large markets where prices will be optimal prices if the markets are efficient. This would also allow flexible pricing which results in accurate representation of available resources in that prices are updated as the instance connect request arrives. The subsequent procedure is based on distributed pricing as a more feasible alternative to optimal pricing.

Modelling approach

Most studies of resource allocation mechanisms have used a performance model of the resource, where the very concept of the resource is defined in terms of measurable qualities of the service such as utilization, throughput, response time (delay), and so on. Optimization of resource allocation is defined in terms of these measurable qualities. One novelty introduced by the economic approach is to design a system which takes into account the diverse QoS requirements of users, and therefore use multi-objective (utilities) optimization techniques to characterize and compute optimum allocations. Economic modelling of computer and communication resource sharing uses a uniform paradigm described by two-level modelling: QoS requirements as inputs into a performance model that is subject to economic optimization.

In the first step, one transforms QoS requirements of users to a performance (example: queueing service model). This model establishes quantifiable parameterization of resource allocation. For example, average delay QoS requirement, when based on a FIFO queueing model, is a function of resources, bandwidth and buffer, and user traffic demands. These parameters are then used to establish an economic optimization model. The question of whether the resource is a piece of hardware, a network link, a software resource such as a database or a server, or a virtual network entity such as a TCP connection is not of primary importance. The first modelling transformation eliminates the details and captures the relevant behaviours and the optimization parameters.

Our approach evolves in the following sequence. Many users present QoS demands, which are translated into demands on resources based on a performance model. The suppliers compute the optimal allocations based on principles of economic optimization and market mechanisms. Once the optimization is done, the results provide inputs to mechanisms for QoS provisioning, such as scheduling of resources and admission of users in networks and load balancing in distributed systems. We present briefly an overview of the problems and contributions.

Optimal allocation and QoS

We motivate and solve a problem of allocating resources and providing services (QoS) to several classes of users at a single link. The resources at the link are buffer space and bandwidth. The link (network provider) prices per unit buffer and bandwidth resources. The consumers (user traffic classes), via economic agents, buy resources such that their QoS needs are satisfied. The network provider prices resources based on demand from the consumers. The ingredients are as follows:

- Economic models: we use competitive economic models to determine the resource partitions between user traffic classes, which compete to obtain buffer and bandwidth resources from the switch suppliers.
- Optimal allocations using economic principles: we look for Pareto optimal allocations that satisfy QoS needs of agents. Agents represent QoS via utility functions which capture the multiple performance objectives.
- Pricing based on QoS: we compute equilibrium prices based on the QoS demands of consumers. Prices are set such that the market demand and supply are met. Prices help in determining the cost of providing a service.
- Priorities: using the economic framework, we show a simple way to support priority service among the user-classes (or agents).
- Decentralization: we show a natural separation between the interactions of the user-classes (represented by agents) and the network switch suppliers. The interaction is purely competitive and market based. This decentralization promotes scalable network system design.

Scheduling and pricing mechanisms

We consider a dynamic system where sessions arrive and leave a traffic class, and demand fluctuates over time. In such a setting we investigate practical mechanisms, such as packet-level scheduling to provide bandwidth and buffer guarantees, admission-control mechanisms to provide class QoS guarantees, practical pricing to capture the changing demand, and charging mechanisms for user sessions within a class.

- Scheduling algorithms for class-based QoS provisioning: we provide novel scheduling mechanisms, which allocates bandwidth and buffer for meeting the demand from traffic classes. The scheduling mechanism allocates bandwidth, which is computed from the economic optimization.
- Admission Region and Control: we compute the admission-control region of the agents on the economic model. Due to the natural separation between who controls the admission of sessions into the traffic class, the admission region can be determined.
- We propose simple pricing models which capture the changing demand and are easy to implement. We also propose novel QoS-based charging mechanisms for sessions in a class with applications to charging in ATM Networks and Integrated Services Internet.

We first consider a network economy, of many parallel routes or links, where several agents (representing user classes) compete for resources from several suppliers, where each supplier represents a route (or a path) between a source and destination. Agents buy resources from suppliers based on the QoS requirements of the class they represent. Suppliers price resources, independently, based on demand from the agents. The suppliers connect consumers to information providers, who are at the destination; the flow of information is from information providers to the consumers. We formulate and solve problems of resource allocation and pricing in such an environment.

We then consider a server economy in a distributed system. Again, we use a similar model of interaction between agents and suppliers (servers). The servers sell computational resources such as processing rate and memory to the agents for a price. The prices of resources are set independently by each server based on QoS demand from the agents. Agents represent user classes such as transactions in database servers or sessions for Web servers that have QoS requirements such as response time. Using such economic models, our contributions are as follows:

- We propose a decentralized model of network and server economies, where we show efficient QoS provisioning and Pareto allocation of resources (network and server resources) among agents and suppliers, which are either network routes or servers (content providers).
- We show how prices for resources are set at the suppliers based on the QoS demands from the agents.
- We propose alternative dynamic routing algorithms and admission-control mechanisms based on QoS preferences by the user classes for the network economy, and we propose a simple way to perform transaction routing. We also show static optimal routing policies by the agents for the network and server economies.

Allocation and pricing models

In economic models, there are two main ways to allocate resources among the competing agents. One of them is the exchange-based economy and the other is the price-based economy. In the exchange-based economy, each agent is initially endowed with some amounts of the resources. They exchange resources until the marginal rate of substitution of the resources is the same for all the agents. The agents trade resources in the direction of increasing utility (for maximal preference). That is, two agents will agree on an exchange of resources (e.g. CPU for memory) which results in an improved utility for both agents. The Pareto optimal allocation is achieved when no further, mutually beneficial, resource exchanges can occur. Formally, an allocation of resources is Pareto Optimal when the utility derived by the competing economic-agents is maximum. Any deviation from this allocation could cause one or more economic agents to have a lower utility (which means the agents will be dissatisfied).

In a price-based system, the resources are priced based on the demand, supply, and the wealth in the economic system. The allocations are done based on the following mechanisms. Each agent is endowed with some wealth. Each agent computes the demand from the utility function and the budget constraint. The aggregate demand from all the agents is sent to the suppliers who then compute the new resource prices. If the demand for a resource is greater than its supply, the supplier raises the price of the resource. If there is surplus supply, the price is decreased. The agents again compute their demands given the current prices and present the demand to the suppliers. This process continues iteratively until the equilibrium price is achieved where demand equals the supply (Figure 8.4).

Bidding and auctioning resources is another form of resource allocation based on prices. There are several auctioning mechanisms such as the Sealed Bid Auction, Dutch Auction, and English Auction. The basic philosophy behind

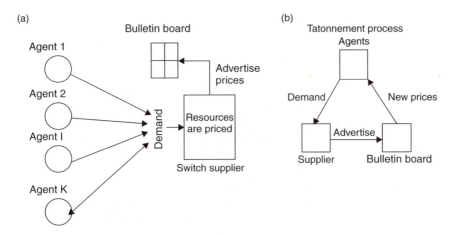

Figure 8.4 Economic players: K agents competing for resources from a supplier.

auctions and bidding is that the highest bidder always gets the resources, and the current price for a resource is determined by the bid prices.

What are the economic-based problems?

Some of the interesting problems encountered when designing an economic based computer system are discussed and stated.

- How do agents demand resources? This is a fundamental question regarding the agents preferences on the resources they consume. Are there smooth utility functions that can capture the agents preferences of the resources? Are there utility functions that can capture the diversity of the agents preferences?
- How are the prices adjusted to clear the economy or to clear the markets? In an economic model, efficient allocation of resources occurs when the demand equals the supply at a certain equilibrium price vector.
- What rational pricing mechanisms do the suppliers adopt? This question raises issues on pricing mechanisms that will attract agents (consumers).
- How do suppliers provide price guarantees to agents? This is a fundamental question in advertising and providing price guarantees to agents. Delays in information about prices, and surges in demand can cause prices to vary. Therefore agents can make bad decisions.
- What are the protocols by which the consumers and suppliers communicate to reserve resources?
- What are the general allocation principles? Can economic models give insight into the allocation mechanisms that can cause the computer system to reach equilibrium? Can these principles be used practically to evolve the computer system in a way that price equilibrium can be achieved?

Network economy

The economic model consists of the following players: Agents and Network Suppliers and Consumers or User Classes. Consumers (or user classes) request for QoS. Each user class has several sessions (or user sessions). Users within a class have common preferences. User classes have QoS preferences such as preferences over packet-loss probability, max/average delay and throughput. Users within a class share resources.

Agents and Network Suppliers: Each user class is represented by an agent. Each agent negotiates and buys services (resource units) from one or more suppliers. Agents demand for resources in order to meet the QoS needs of the user classes. Network providers have technology to partition and allocate resources (bandwidth and buffer) to the competing agents. In this competitive setting network providers (suppliers) compete for profit maximization.

Multiple Agent–Network Supplier Interaction: Agents present demands to the network suppliers. The demands are based on their wealth and QoS preferences of their class. The demand by each agent is computed via utility functions which represent QoS needs of the user classes. Agents negotiate with suppliers to determine the prices. The negotiation process is iterative, where prices are adjusted to clear the market; supply equals the demand. Price negotiation could be done periodically or depending on changes in demand.

Each agent in the network is allocated a certain amount of buffer space and link capacity. The buffer is used by the agent for queueing packets sent by the users of the class. A simple FIFO queueing model is used for each class. The users within a class share buffer and link resources.

Agent and supplier optimality: Agents compete for resources by presenting demand to the supplier. The agents, given the current market price, compute the affordable allocations of resources (assume agents have limited wealth or budget). The demand from each agent is presented to the supplier. The supplier adjusts the market prices to ensure demand equals supply.

The main issues which form the economic model are:

- Characterization of class QoS preferences and traffic parameters via utility functions, and computation of demand sets given the agent wealth and the utility function.
- Existence and computation of Pareto optimal allocations for QoS provisioning, given the agent utility functions.
- Computation of equilibrium price by the supplier based on agent demands, and conditions under which price equilibrium exists. Price negotiation mechanisms between the agents and suppliers.

Problem formulation

Network model: The network is composed of nodes (packet switches) and links. Each node has several output links. Each output link is associated with an output buffer. The link controller, at the output link, schedules packets from the buffers and transmits them to other nodes in the network. The switch has a buffer controller that can partition the buffer among the traffic classes at each output link. We assume that a processor on the switch aids in control of resources.

We have confined ourselves to problems for a single link (output link) at a node, but they can be applied to the network as well. Let B denote the output buffer of a link and C be the corresponding link capacity. Let $\{c_k, b_k\}$ be the link capacity and buffer allocation to class k on a link, where $k \in [1,K]$. Let $p = \{p_c, p_b\}$ be the price per unit link capacity and unit buffer at a link, and w_k be the wealth (budget) of traffic class k. The utility function for TC_k is $U_k = f(c_k, b_k, Tr_k)$. The traffic of a class is represented by a vector of traffic parameters (Tr_k) and a vector of QoS requirements (such as packet-loss probabilities, average packet delay and so on).

Agent (TC: traffic class) buys resources from the network at the given prices using its wealth. The wealth constraint of agent TC_k is: $p_b *b_k + p_c *c_k \leq w_k$. A budget set is the set of allocations that are feasible under the wealth constraint (budget constraint). The budget set is defined as follows:

$$B(p) = (x : x \in X, px \leq w_k). \tag{1}$$

Computation of demands sets: The demand set for each agent is given by the following:

$$\Phi(p) = (x : x \in B(p), U(x), \forall\, x \in B(p)\}. \tag{2}$$

The goal of TC_k is to compute the allocations that provide maximal preference under w_k and p. Each TC_k performs the following to obtain the demand set (defined above):

Find: $\{c_k, b_k\}$

such that: $\max U_k = f(c_k, b_k, Tr_k)$

Constraints: $p_b b_k + p_c c_k \le w_k$ $\tag{3}$

$c_k \in [0, C], b_k \in [0, B]$

Utility parameters

In the previous section, we show a general utility function which is a function of the switch resources; buffer (b) and bandwidth (c). The utility function could be a function of the following:

- Packet loss probability $U_l = g(c, b, Tr)$
- Average packet delay $U_d = h(c, b, Tr)$
- Packet tail utility $U_t = v(c, b, Tr)$
- Max packet delay $U_b = f(b, b_T)$
- Throughput $U_c = g(c, c_t)$.

The variables b and c in the utility functions refer to buffer-space allocation and link bandwidth allocation. In the utility functions U_b and U_c; the parameters b_T and c_T are constants. For example, the utility function $U_b = f(b, b_T)$ for max packet delay is simply a constant as b increases, but drops to 0 when $b = b_T$ and remains zero for any further increase in b (Figure 8.5a,b).

We look at utility functions which capture packet-loss probability of QoS requirements by traffic classes, and we consider loss, max-delay, and throughput requirements. After this we proceed to utility functions that capture average delay requirements, followed by utility functions that capture packet tail utility requirements. We also could give examples of utility functions for agents with many objectives; agents have preferences over several QoS parameters as shown below.

$$U = f(U_l, U_d, U_t, U_b, U_c) \tag{4}$$

Packet loss

The phenomenon of packet loss is due to two reasons: the first, packets arrive at a switch and find that the buffer is full (no space left) and, therefore, are dropped.

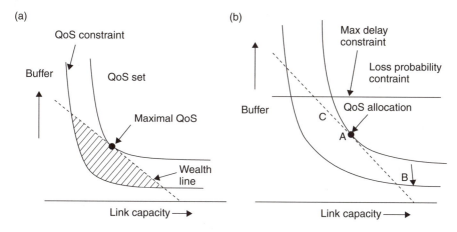

Figure 8.5 Agent QoS set, given constraint (*a*) Loss probability and max delay constraints (*b*).

The second is that packets arrive at a switch and are buffered, but they do not get transmitted (or scheduled) in time, then they are dropped. A formal way of saying this: for real-time applications, packets, if delayed considerably in the network, do not have value once they reach the destination.

We consider K agents, representing traffic classes of M/M/1/B type, a single server queueing system (B equals in packets), competing for resources from the network provider. The utility function is packet loss utility (U_1) for the user classes. We choose the M/M/1/B model or traffic and queueing for the following reasons:

- The model is tractable, where steady state packet-loss utility is in closed-form, and differentiable. This helps in demonstrating the economic models and the concepts.
- There is a specific interest in M/M/1/B or M/D/1/B models for multiplexed traffic (such as video), where simple histogram-based traffic models capture the performance of queueing in networks (Kleinrock, 1976; Wolff, 1989).

For more complex traffic and queueing models (example of video traffic) we can use tail utility functions to represent QoS of the user class instead of loss utility.

In the competitive economic model, each agent prefers less packet loss, as the more packet loss, the worse the quality of the video at the receiving end. Let each agent TC_k have wealth w_k, which it uses to purchase resources from network provider.

Let each TC transmit packets at a rate λ (Poisson arrivals), and let the processing time of the packets be exponentially distributed with unit mean.

Let c, b be allocations to a TC. The utility function U for each TC is given as follows:

$$U = f(c,b,\lambda) = \begin{cases} \dfrac{(1 - \lambda/c)(\lambda/c)^b}{1 - (\lambda/c)^{+1+b}} & \text{for } \lambda < c \qquad (5) \\[2em] \dfrac{1}{b+1} & \text{for } \lambda = c \\[2em] \dfrac{(-1+)(\lambda/c)(\lambda/c)^b}{-1 + (\lambda/c)^{1+b}} & \text{for } \lambda > c \end{cases}$$

The above function is continuous and differentiable for all $c \in [0,C]$, and for all $b \in [0,B]$. We assume that $b \in R$ for continuity purposes of the utility function.

Equilibrium price and convergence

Pareto efficient allocations are such that no traffic class can improve upon these allocations without reducing the utility of one or more traffic classes. The more formal definition of Pareto efficiency is given in Varian (1993). The set of Pareto allocations that satisfy the equilibrium conditions forms the Pareto surface.

Each agent computes the demand set, which is a set of allocations, that maximizes the preference under the wealth constraint. The demand set is obtained by minimizing the utility function under the budget constraint. The Lagrangian is given below with L as the Lagrange multiplier.

$$\min[f(c,b,\lambda) - L^*(p_c^* c + p_b - w)] \quad c \geq 0, b \geq 0. \qquad (6)$$

The function $f(c,b,\lambda)$ is smooth, strictly convex, and compact, thus the demand set is just one element [1,2]. Using the Kuhn-Tucker optimality conditions, the optimal resource allocation vector is obtained, where L is the Lagrange multiplier

$$\frac{\partial U}{\partial c} = L^* p_c, \qquad \frac{\partial U}{\partial b} = L^* p_b. \qquad (7)$$

From this the equilibrium condition is obtained. This condition states the marginal rate of substitution is equal among the competing traffic classes. The economic problems are to establish competitive equilibrium, compute the equilibrium prices p_c^*, p_b^* and Pareto optimal allocations. The equilibrium condition is shown as follows:

$$\frac{\partial U/\partial c}{\partial U/\partial b} = \frac{p_c^*}{p_b^*}. \tag{8}$$

Using the utility function given by equation (5), the price ratio is given below. From the equation, it is evident that the price ratio is a function of the resource allocations and the traffic parameter λ.

$$\frac{p_c}{p_b} = g(\lambda,c,b) = \frac{-\lambda + \lambda(\lambda^b/c) - \lambda b + cb}{(\lambda - c)c \, \log(\lambda/c)} \tag{9}$$

This equation can be rewritten in the following way, where function N has a nice interpretation. It is the ratio of the effective queue utilization ($\rho(1 - U)$) to the effective queue emptiness ($1 - \rho*(1 - U)$), where $\rho = \lambda/c$.

$$\frac{p_c}{p_b} = \frac{N - b}{c \log \rho} \quad \text{where } N = \frac{\rho*(1 - U)}{1 - \rho*(1 - U)} \tag{10}$$

This can also be interpreted as the effective number in an equivalent M/M/1 queueing system, where the system utilization is $\rho = \rho(1 - U)$. For an M/M/1 system, the average number in the system is $\rho/1 - \rho$.

The following gives the equilibrium condition for K agents competing for resources from a single network provider. From this condition, and the resource constraints, the Pareto allocations and the corresponding equilibrium price ratios can be computed.

$$\frac{p_c}{p_b} = \frac{b_1 - N_1}{c_1 \log(\rho_1)} = \frac{b_2 - N_2}{c_2 \log(\rho_2)} = \cdots = \frac{b_k - N_K}{c_K \log(\rho_K)}. \tag{11}$$

Using the buffer constraint $b_1 + b_2 + b_3 + \cdots + b_k = B$, the equilibrium price ratio and optimal buffer allocation for each agent i can be represented by the following equations:

$$\frac{p_c^*}{p_b^*} = \frac{\sum_i N_i - B}{\sum_i (c_i \log(\rho_i))} \tag{12}$$

$$b_i = N_i - \frac{\left(\sum_i N_i - B\right)(c_i \log(\rho_i))}{\sum_i (c_i \log(\rho_i))} \tag{13}$$

The issue of determining the equilibrium prices, so that supply equal demand is an open question (Figure 8.6).

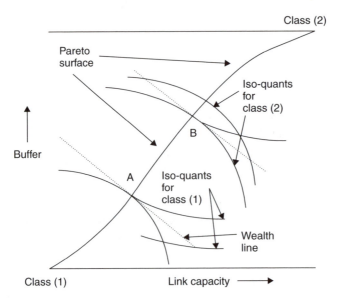

Figure 8.6 Edgworth Box diagram. Link capacity along the x-axis and buffer space along the y-axis. TC_1 and TC_2 compete for resources at both ends of the resource box. Any point (c, b) in the box represents an allocation $\{c, b\}$ to class (1) and an allocation $\{C - c, B - b\}$ to class (2). The wealth line is the wealth constraint of both the TCs. Isoquants are contours of a function $f(c, b, \lambda) = \beta$ (constant).

Competitive pricing algorithm

1   Set initial prices: $P_c = p_c^0, p_b = p_b^0$.
2   Compute demand set, that is, find minimum of min $[U_i = f_i(c_i, b_i \lambda_i)]$ $\forall i \in [1, K]$ given $p_c c_i + p_b b_i \leq w_i$ (wealth constraint).
3   Demand: $D_c = \sum_{i=1}^{i=K} c_i, D_b = \sum_{i=1}^{i=K} b_i$.
4   If $(D_c - C) < (>)0$, then $p_c = p_c - (+)\Delta_c$.
     If $(D_b - B) < (>)0$, then $p_b = p_b - (+)\Delta_b$.
     Go back to step (2).
5   Else if $D_c = C$ at p_c, and $D_b = B$ at p_b, then the equilibrium is attained and prices are at equilibrium.

The algorithm computes iteratively the equilibrium prices in a competitive economy using the utility functions. Given the wealth in the economy, the prices converge to a point on the Pareto surface which can be computed using the first-order conditions. Once the prices are computed the network service provider releases the resources to the agents.

Example of two agents and one supplier

We consider two agents, representing traffic classes of the M/M/1/B model. The utility function is shown in equation 5. The agents have wealth w_1 and w_2 respectively. The agents compete for resources, which then are used to provide services to users.

Two classes We consider two competing traffic classes. Using the equilibrium conditions, the equilibrium price ratio is given by,

$$\frac{P_c^*}{P_b^*} = \frac{N_1 - b_1}{c_1 \log \rho_1} = \frac{N_2 - b_2}{c_2 \log \rho_2}. \tag{14}$$

The above equation states that at equilibrium, the log of the ratio of utilizations of the two traffic classes is equal to the ratio of the time to evacuate the residual buffer space of the traffic classes. Rewriting the above equation:

$$\frac{\log \rho_1}{\log \rho_2} = \frac{N_1 - b_1}{c_1} \cdot \frac{c_2}{N_2 - b_2}. \tag{15}$$

By using the resource constraints $c_1 + c_2 = C$ and $b_1 + b_2 = B$, the equilibrium conditions become a function of just two variables. The Pareto surface is the set of allocations that satisfy equation (14). The function N_i and U_i (for all $i \in \{1,2\}$) have several interesting properties for different values of ρ_i. We study the properties of these functions for various regions of ρ_1 and ρ_2, where ρ_1 and ρ_2 are utilizations of TC_1 and TC_2 respectively.

- $\rho_1 < 1$, $\rho_2 < 1$: As the buffer is varied to infinity, the utility function (loss utility) becomes 0, and the effective average number (N_1, N_2) becomes the average number in an M/M/1 queue. The $\lim_{b1 \to \infty} N_1 = \rho_1/1 - \rho_1$, $\lim_{b1 \to \infty} U_1 = 0$. The quantity $b_1 - N_1 \geq 0$ for $b_1 \in [0, \infty)$.
- $\rho_1 > 1$, $\rho_2 > 1$: The allocated capacity is less than the mean rates of TC_1 and TC_2. We consider the case where the buffer tends to infinity. $\lim_{b1 \to \infty} N_1 = \infty$, $\lim_{b1 \to \infty} U_1 = 0$. The quantity $b_1 - N_1 < 0$ for $b_1 \in ([0, \infty)$.
- $\rho_1 \to 1$, $\rho_2 \to 1$: The quantity is $N_1 = b_1$, $N_2 = b_2$. The equilibrium condition for offered loads equal to 1 is $b_1^*(b_1 + 1)/2^* \lambda_1 = b_2^*(b_2 + 1)/2^* \lambda_2$.

Several other cases such as $\rho_1 > 1$, $\rho_2 > 1$ are omitted, but are essential in determining the Pareto surface.

For the two competing traffic classes, the following relation between the utility functions of the traffic classes with respect to the Pareto optimal allocations is obtained:

$$\frac{\log U_1}{\log U_2} = \frac{(b_1 - N_1)}{c_1} \cdot \frac{c_2}{(b_2 - N_2)}, \tag{16}$$

$$\frac{\log U_1}{\log U_2} = \frac{(b_1 - N_1)}{(b_2 - N_2)} \cdot \frac{c_2}{c_1}. \tag{17}$$

This relation has an interesting physical meaning: the loss of the ratio of the utilities of the traffic classes is equal to the ratio of the time to evacuate the residual buffer in the queues. The residual buffer is simply: $b_i - N_i$, where N_i is given by equation (10).

Conclusions

We demonstrate the application of economic tools to resource management in distributed systems and computer networks. The concepts of analytical economics were used to develop effective market-based control mechanisms, and to show the allocation of resources are Pareto optimal.

Methodologies of decentralized control of resources, and pricing of resources are based on QoS demand of users. We bring together economic models and performance models of computer systems into one framework to solve problems of resource allocation and efficient QoS provisioning. Such a scheme can be applied to pricing services in ATM networks and Integrated Services Internet of the future.

There are drawbacks to this form of modelling where several agents have to use market mechanisms to decide where to obtain service (which supplier?). If the demand for a resource varies substantially over short periods of time, then the actual prices of the resources will also vary causing several side effects such as indefinite migration of consumers between suppliers. This might potentially result in degradation of system performance where the resources are being under-utilized due to the bad decisions (caused by poor market mechanisms) made by the users in choosing the suppliers.

Unlike economies, the resources in a computer system are not easily substitutable. The future work is to design robust market mechanisms and rationalized pricing schemes which can handle surges in demand and variability, and can give price guarantees to consumers over longer periods of time. Another drawback is that resources in a computer system are indivisible resulting in non-smooth utility functions which may yield sub-optimal allocations, and potential computational overhead.

In summary, economic models are useful for designing and understanding Internet-type systems. The Internet currently connects hundreds of millions of users and thousands of sites. Several services exist on many of these sites, notably the WWW which provides access to various information sources distributed across the Internet. Many more services (multimedia applications, commercial transactions) are to be supported in the Internet. To access this large number of services, agents have to share limited network bandwidth and server capacities (processing speeds). Such large-scale networks require decentralized mechanisms to control access to services. Economic concepts such as pricing and competition can provide some solutions to reduce the complexity of service provisioning and decentralize the access mechanisms to the resources.

References

Chao, J. and D. Ghosal (1994) 'IP or ATM on Local Area Networks', *IEEE Communications Magazine*, April

Clearwater, S. (1995) *Market based Control: A Paradigm for Distributed Resource Allocation*, Singapore: World Scientific Publishing

Cocchi, Ron, D. Estrin, S. Shenker, and L. Zhang (1991), 'A Study of Priority Pricing in Multiple Service Class Networks', *Proc. of SIGCOMM* 91: 123–130

Ferguson, F. and G. Huston (1998) *Delivering Quality of Service on the Internet and Corporate Networks*, New York: Wiley

Gilbert, W. E. (1992) 'The Five Challenges to manage Global Networks', *IEEE Communcations Magazine,* July

Gupta, A. and D. O. Stahl (1995) *An Economic Approach to Networked Computing with Priority Classes*, Cambridge, MA: MIT Press

Kahin, B. and J. Keller (eds) (1995) *Public Access to the Internet*, Cambridge, MA: MIT Press

Kleinrock, L. (1976) *Queueing Systems*, Vol. 2, New York: Wiley

Kurose, J. F. and R. Simha (1989) 'A Microeconomic Approach to Optimal Resource Allocation in Distributed Computer Systems', *IEEE Trans. on Computers* 38(5): 705–707

Lazar, A. A. (1991) 'Control of Resources in Broadband Network with Quality of Service Guarantees', *IEEE Communications Magazine*, October, 66–73

Low, S. and Varaiya (1993) 'A New Approach to Service Provisioning in ATM Networks', *IEEE Trans. on Networking*, November

MacKie-Mason, J. K. and H. R. Varian (1995) 'Pricing the Internet', in B. Kahin and J. Keller (eds), *Public Access to the Internet*, Cambridge, MA: MIT Press, 269–314

Minzer, S. (1989) 'Broadband ISDN and Asynchronous Transfer Mode(ATM)', *IEEE Communications Magazine*, September

Odlyzko, A. (1998) 'The Economics of the Internet: Utility, Utilization, Pricing and Quality of Service', ATT Research Memorandum (www.research.att.com/(amo/doc/internet.economics.pdf.)

Paxson, V. (1994) 'Growth Trends in TCP/IP', *IEEE Communications Magazine*, April

Radner, R. (1993) 'The Organization of Decentralized Information Processing', *Econometrica* 62: 1109–1146

Scarf, H. (1967) *Computation of Economic Equilibria*, Cowles Foundation, New Haven: Yale University Press

Shenker, S. (1995) 'Service Models and Pricing Policies for an Integrated Services Internet', in *Public Access to the Internet*, Cambridge, MA: MIT Press, 315–337

Shenker, S., D. Clark and D. Estrin and S. Herzog (1996) 'Pricing in Computer Networks: Reshaping the Research Agenda', *ACM Computer Communications Review* 26: 19–43

Varian, H. R. (1993), *Mircoeconomic Analysis*, New York: Norton Press.

Wang, Q., J. M. Peha and M. A. Sirbu (1997) 'Optimal Pricing for Integrated Services Network', in L. M. Mcknight and J. P. Bailey (eds), *Internet Economics*, Cambridge, MA: MIT Press, 353–376

Wilson, R. (1993) *Nonlinear Pricing*, Oxford: Oxford University Press

Wolff, R. W. (1989) *Stochastic Modeling and the Theory of Queues*, Englewood Cliffs, NJ: Prentice Hall

Zhang, E. and E. Knightly (1994) 'Providing End-to-end Statistical Performance Guarantees with Interval Dependent Stochastic Models', *Proc. of ACM Sigmetrics* 2: 25–32

9 Network economies for the Internet

Application models

Introduction

On the basis of the conceptual framework of Network Economies, Chapter 8, we will motivate and solve two problems of allocating resources and providing services (QoS) to several classes of users in view of network links and the collection of servers. In the first case we address the informational links in its supply/demand infrastructure, in the second case we focus on the transaction based aspect of the Internet, most recently identified with e-commerce on the business-to-consumer as well as business-to-business dimension. For both we start with some stylized examples that reflect the present internet structure.

We first consider a network economy of many parallel routes or links, where several agents (representing user classes) compete for resources from several suppliers, where each supplier represents a route (or a path) between source and destination. Agents buy resources from suppliers based on the QoS of the class they represent. Suppliers price resources, independently, based on demand from the agents. The suppliers connect consumers to information providers who are at the destination, the flow of information is from information providers to consumers. We formulate and solve problems of resource allocation and pricing in such an environment. We then consider a server economy in a distributed system. Again we use a similar model of interaction between agents and suppliers (servers). The servers sell computational resources such as processing rate and memory to the agents for a price. The prices of resources are set independently by each server based on QoS demands from the agents. Agents represent user classes such as transactions in database servers or sessions for Web servers that have QoS requirements such as response time. Resource allocation in networks relate to computational models of networks, as developed in the works of Radner (1993), Mount and Reiter (1994), van Zandt (1998), see also Gottinger (1998). Here they emanate from certain types of queueing systems (Kleinrock, 1976; Wolff, 1989) on generalized networks (see Figure 9.1).

This chapter is organized as follows. In the next section we present two examples, one of simple network routing, the other on network transactions that provide similar platforms of network allocation decisions. Based on a simple decentralized model for the network economy we apply the principles of

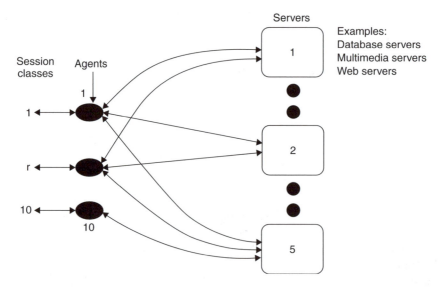

Figure 9.1 Several sessions (session classes) request for transaction or multimedia services from servers. The servers offer response-time services for information
retrieval. Agents represent user classes where a single agent represents a single
user class.

economic optimization between agents and suppliers, Pareto Optimality and price
equilibrium for agents competing for resources from suppliers in the section on
'Price equilibrium'. In the section on 'Agent routing and admission' we present a
routing algorithm which considers the dynamic nature of session arrival and
departure. Some numerical results for optimal allocation and for the routing
mechanism are presented. In the section on 'The server economy' we present the
server economy, and show the Pareto optimal allocations and price equilibrium
when agents are competing for resources from servers (suppliers). Correspondingly,
in the section on 'Transaction routing' we apply transaction routing policies to
handle the dynamics of user behaviour. Conclusions follow in the final section.

Two examples

Example 1   Network Routing. The first example shows a network representing
many user classes or types of users wishing to access specific content providers.
The users have a choice of routes to connect to the servers. Several routes exist
between the source and the destination. At the destination there are various kinds
of content providers, such as databases, digital libraries, and Web servers. Each
route is independent (parallel) and they have different amounts of resources. The
resources are buffer and bandwidth. For simplicity we assume that each route is
a single link between a source and a destination, and we assume that each route
has one packet switch that buffers packets and transmits them. User classes have

several QoS requirements such as packet-loss utility, maximum end-to-end delay, and average packet delay. The QoS requirements are due to applications such as digital video libraries, access to multimedia databases, and Web servers. Sessions are set up between the source and the destination along one of the routes to access the content providers. The applications, for smooth operation, demand a certain QoS from the network routes and the end-nodes (content providers), for an end-to-end QoS. For example, video applications generate bursty traffic, and this can lead to packet loss in the network depending on the allocation of network resources for the video sessions. Video applications can tolerate a certain amount of packet loss, but beyond a threshold, the QoS of the video at the user workstation will deteriorate. In addition, maximum delay requirement is necessary to design buffer play-out strategies for smooth operation of the video application at the user workstation.

From the demand side, the demand at the network changes due to random arrivals and departures of user sessions of the traffic classes. The new session arrival may require the user class to acquire more resources to ensure a certain QoS level. In addition, when a new session arrives, a decision has to be made as to which route to choose from. In the example, resources are finite, and therefore have to be used efficiently in order to provide QoS. The traffic classes are allocated resources only for a certain period of time. The main reason being that session arrival and departure rates could change, causing fluctuations in demand, and therefore resources have to be reallocated to meet the change in demand. The traffic classes can renegotiate for resources once their ownership of resources expires.

From the supply side, consider that each route is a supplier, and let each traffic class be represented by an agent. The agent on behalf of the class negotiates for resources from the suppliers based on QoS requirements of the class.

Each supplier has to guarantee buffer and bandwidth resources, depending on the demand from the agents. The supplier has ensured efficient utilization of the network resources, so that the resource limits are fully exploited given the QoS requirements of classes. The task of the agents is to represent the QoS needs of the traffic class, given a certain performance framework from the supplier. Every time a session of a certain traffic class arrives, a decision must be made on which route to take between the source and destination. This depends on the agent, who can choose a route based on preferences of the traffic class, and the available resources in the routes. Therefore, dynamic mechanisms are necessary to ensure the right decision making in routing a newly arrived session. In a dynamic network the available resources at each route could be different, and in addition there is competition from other agents who have similar tasks to perform. With many routes between source and destination, the routing or placing of sessions along a route or a link must be done in a decentralized fashion. This is necessary to handle many routes and many traffic classes, each of which could have diverse QoS requirements. A framework to decentralize the various functions or tasks in admitting and routing sessions, and scheduling to switch bandwidth and buffer among the traffic classes is a challenging problem. In addition, the framework must ensure flexible QoS provisioning and promote efficient utilization of resources.

Example 2   Transaction Processing. In this example, users request services from the content providers, and users are grouped into classes. The user classes are transaction classes for databases or just sessions for computation or information retrieval, which request access services from one or more of the servers (content providers).

Consider a transaction processing system, where transactions that arrive are routed to one of many systems in order to satisfy performance objectives such as average response time or per-transaction deadlines. In commercial online transaction processing systems, it is very common for transactions to be processed on heterogeneous servers which have different operating systems, database management systems, hardware and software platforms, and a host of various communication protocols. Transactions are grouped into transaction classes, transactions in the same class have common workload characteristics and performance objectives. Transactions arrive at random times to their respective classes and therefore need to be routed dynamically to one of the servers. Each transaction class could have different preferences over the performance objectives and they have different processing requirements from the servers.

In a transaction processing system it is quite difficult to match the quantities of resources for an efficient usage with the diverse QoS requirements of user classes. For example, a queue could be assigned to each class at each server in order to provide various service levels, or a queue at each server could be shared among the classes. For a queue that is shared by many classes the complexity of service provisioning increases as transactions from each class have to be distinguished in order to provide service levels. The allocation mechanism determines the throughput of each queue and the buffer allocation at the server. In addition, efficiency could mean a server-wide performance measure of session level throughput, given the QoS requirements of the transaction classes.

In order to handle many transaction classes and provide access to various services, the control of resources must be decentralized for reasons of efficiency and transparency. Each server (supplier) has to offer resources such as processing, memory and input/output, and services such as average response time and throughput. This cannot be done in a centralized fashion, if we consider all the servers, instead decentralized mechanisms are needed to distribute user sessions (transaction sessions) among the servers and provide the QoS needs of classes. In addition, each server has to implement practical mechanisms, such as processor scheduling, to partition resources among the various transaction classes or provide priority services among the classes.

In this example, when a user session arrives, the problem of choosing a server in order to provide a service is needed. Consider each class is represented by an agent. If a new session arrives the agent has to know if there are enough available resources to provide the required QoS. Consider that agents represent transaction classes, and they compete for resources from the various databases, and remove this burden from the servers. The problem for the agents is to choose the right server and to make sure QoS is guaranteed to the class it represents, and use the allocated resources judiciously. This implies mechanisms for optimal routing need to be designed.

With random arrival and departure of user sessions, the agent must handle routing and admission of sessions in a dynamic way. The problem of efficient resource management by the agents and optimal allocation of resources by the servers, due to changing demand is challenging. The allocation of resources cannot be static and time-periods of renegotiation of resources and services will affect the way routing and admission of sessions is done. In addition, servers will have to adapt to changing demand in order to reflect the new allocations. For example, consider that depending on the time of day, demand at the servers fluctuates, and demands could be independent from server to server. The challenge is in determining the time-intervals based on demand.

Results from the network economy

The network consists of V nodes (packet switches) and N links. Each node has several output links with an output buffer. The resources at output link are transmission capacity (or link capacity) and buffer space. The link controller at the output link schedules packets from the buffer. This is based on how the buffer is partitioned among the traffic classes and the scheduling rule between the traffic classes (see Figure 8.3).

Sessions are grouped into traffic classes based on similar traffic characteristics and common QoS requirements. Sessions that belong to a class share buffer and link resources, and traffic classes compete for resources at a packet switch. Each session arrives to the network with a vector of traffic parameters Tr, vector of QoS requirements and wealth. A session is grouped or mapped to a corresponding traffic class. A traffic class has common QoS requirements, and we consider QoS requirements per traffic class rather than per session. Once a session is admitted along a path (a route), it will continue along that path until it completes.

Each agent k performs the following to obtain the demand set on each link. The allocations are buffer (b) and bandwidth (c) on each link for each agent. The wealth is distributed across the links by each agent to buy resources.

That is, the problem is to find pairs c_k^*, b_k^* such that max $U_k = f(c_k, b_k, Tr_k)$, constraints $p_b b_k + p_c c_k \le w_k$.

In the above formulation, each agent k buys resources from each link. The allocation for agent k is $c_k^* = \{c_k^{*1}, c_k^{*2}, \ldots, c_k^{*N}\}$ and $b_k^* = \{b_k^{*1}, b_k^{*2}, \ldots, b_k^{*N}\}$. An agent can invest wealth in either some or all the links. We assume that at each link there is competition among at least some of the agents for buying resources. As previously, Chapter 8, we show a general utility function which is a function of the switch resources: buffer (b) and bandwidth (c). A utility function of the agent could be a function of:

- Packet-loss probability $U_t = g(c, b, Tr)$
- Average packet delay $U_d = h(c, b, Tr)$
- Packet-tail probability $U_l = v(c, b, Tr)$
- Max packet delay $U_b = f(b)$
- Throughput $U_c = g(c)$.

We consider that an agent will place demands for resources based on a general utility function, which is a combination of the various QoS requirements:

$$U = f(c, b, Tr) = x_1 U_1 + x_d U_d + x_b U_b + x_c U_c + x_t U_t$$

where U_1 is the packet-loss probability utility function, U_d is the average delay utility function, U_t is the packet-tail probability, U_b is the utility function for max-delay requirements, and U_c is for bandwidth (throughput) requirements. x_1, x_d, x_b, x_c, x_t are constants. Agents could use such a utility function. As long as the convexity property with respect to buffer b and bandwidth c holds, Pareto optimal allocations and price equilibria exist. However, if they are not convex, then depending on the properties of the functions, local optimality and price equilibrium could exist. To show the main ideas for routing and admission control, we use packet-loss probability as the main utility function (U_1), which means we assume that x_1 from the above equation are the only constant and the rest are zeros. For doing this, we need first some further specifications of the loss probability. Further on we show results for Pareto optimality and price equilibrium. In general, one can assume that agents, on behalf of user classes, demand for resources from the link suppliers based on the utility function shown above. The agent uses the utility function to present the demand for resources over the whole network of parallel links.

Loss probability specifications   At each output link j the resources are buffer space B^j and link capacity C^j.

Let $\{c_k^j, b_k^j\}$ be the link capacity and buffer allocation to class k on link j where $k \in [1, K]$. Let p_c^j and p_b^j be the price per unit link capacity and unit buffer respectively at link j, and w_k be the wealth (budget) of a traffic class k. For a link j from the source to the destination, the packet loss probability (utility) for traffic class k is given by the following

$$U_k = P_{\text{loss}} = 1 - \prod_{j=1}^{N} (1 - P_k^j), \tag{1}$$

where P_k^j is the packet-loss probability at link j of agent k.

The goal of the agent is to minimize the packet-loss probability under its wealth or budget constraints. If the traffic classes have smooth convex preferences with respect to link capacity and buffer allocation variables at each link, then the utility function U_k is convex with respect to the variables (Hara and Zipkin, 1987).

Price equilibrium

Let each TC (represented by an agent) transmit packets at a rate λ (Poisson arrivals), and let the processing time of the packets be exponentially distributed with unit mean. Let c, b be allocations to a TC. The utility function (packet-loss probability for M/M/1/B queues as in Wolff, 1989) U for each TC at each link is given by

$$
U = f(c,b,\lambda) = \begin{cases} \dfrac{(1 - \lambda/c)(\lambda/c)b}{1 - (\lambda/c)^{1+b}} & \text{for } \lambda < c \\[4mm] \dfrac{1}{b+1} & \text{for } \lambda < c \\[4mm] \dfrac{(-1+)(\lambda/c)(\lambda/c)^{b}}{-1+(\lambda/c)^{1+b}} & \text{for } \lambda > c \end{cases} \tag{2}
$$

The allocation variables at each node for each traffic class are c (link capacity) and b (buffer space). The utility function is continuous and differentiable for all $c \in [0,C]$, and for all $b \in [0,B]$. We assume that $b \in \Re$ for continuity purposes of the utility function.

With agents competing for resources in a network of parallel links, the overall utility function U can be obtained by using the utility function above. We have the following theorem.

Proposition 9.1   The packet-loss probability function for agent k shown in (2), assuming an M/M/1/B model for each link, is decreasing convex in c_k^j for $c_k^j \in [0,C_j]$, and decreasing convex in b_k^j, $\forall\, b_k^j \in [0,B_j]$.

Proof   See Appendix.

The goal of each agent is to maximize the preference (which is minimizing packet-loss probability) under the budget constraint. Each traffic class computes a demand set using the wealth constraints and the current prices.

The demand set can be computed using Langrange multiplier techniques. Using the utility function given by equation (2) and the first-order equilibrium conditions, the price ratio at each link j is given by the following:

$$
\frac{\partial U_k/\partial c_k^j}{\partial U_k/\partial b_k^j} = \frac{p_c^j}{p_b^j} = \frac{N_k^j - b_k^j}{c_k^j \log \rho_k^j}, \quad N_k^j = \frac{\rho_k^{j*}(1 - P_k^j)}{1 - \rho_k^{j*}(1 - P_k^j)} \tag{3}
$$

where function N_k^j is the ratio of the effective queue utilization $(\rho_k^{j*}(1 - P_k^j))$ to the effective queue emptiness $1 - \rho_k^{j*}(1 - P_k^j)$ and $\rho_k^j = \lambda_k^j/c_k^j$.

Consider K traffic classes of M/M/1/B type competing for resources (link and buffer) in a network of parallel links. Then the following theorem is stated:

Proposition 9.2   Let each traffic class k have smooth convex preferences represented by the utility function shown in equation (2) Given that $\Sigma_1^k c_i = C$ and $\Sigma_1^k b_i = B$ for all $i, k \in [1, K]$, then the Pareto surface exists. Given the wealth constraint w_k of the traffic classes, the Pareto optimal allocation and the price equilibrium exist.

The proof is based on the fact that the utility functions are decreasing convex and smooth in the resource space (preferences are convex and smooth). The proof is essentially the same as in Chapter 8 for Pareto optimality, except that the preferences are shown here to be convex in link capacity and buffer space at each link (given the traffic parameters of each traffic class at each link) in the network of parallel links using the M/M/1/B model.

Agent routing and admission

For a session that arrives to a traffic class in the network, the agent has several routes to choose from between the source and the destination. The agent can choose a route that benefits the traffic class it joins. This means that an agent is searching for the right set of service providers (or links) to reach the destination. Several interesting questions arise in a market economy with many users and suppliers: will the network economy be efficient in service provisioning? What are the negotiation protocols between the users and the suppliers so that services are guaranteed? What is the session-blocking probability per class, given session arrival and average session holding time per class?

The static description of the problem is simply to find the best allocation of sessions among the suppliers. The allocation can satisfy efficiency criteria such as throughput of the number of sessions per class admitted to the overall network. For example, consider the static case that A_i is the session arrival rate (Poisson with distribution) for class i, and Ω_i is the average session holding time of sessions of class i. Let Agent i be allocated c_{ij} link capacity on link j. Let the maximum number of sessions that can be admitted per link j for class i, such that certain QoS level is satisfied. Let the space be $\{n_{i1}, n_{i2}, ..., n_{iN}\}$. Then the problem for the agent is simply to determine the flow of sessions among the network of links, given the above parameters. Formally, the agent has to find the following: find $\{\rho_{i1}, \rho_{i2}, ..., \rho_{iN}\}$, minimize $1 - \Pi_1^N(1 - P_{\text{block}})$ given that $\{c_{ij}, b_{ij}\}$ and constraints $\Sigma_1^N \rho_{ij} = \rho_i$ where $\rho_{ij} = A_i/\Omega_i$ for all $j \in [1, N]$ is the session level utilization, and $\Sigma_1^N A_{ij} = Ai$ and $\rho_i = A_i/\Omega_i$. For the main goal of agent i is to maximize the throughput of the sessions through the network. This is one of the many efficiency requirements of agent i.

We now discuss dynamic routing algorithms for each agent i that routes a session over the network along one of the routes (or links). The dynamic routing algorithms depend on the state of the network portion owned by agent i. For example, the routing decisions will be made based on the number of sessions currently active on each of the links for class i.

Consider a parallel link network as explained in the section on 'Two examples' where each link is a supplier. The routing algorithm is as follows: the agent representing the traffic class will choose the supplier which can give a better QoS for the overall class. This means that the suppliers in the network are ordered in the decreasing order of preference by the agent based on the utility derived by joining them. This routing algorithm is described as follows for a network consisting of several parallel links between a source and a destination. If a session of type TC_k arrives, then it is routed to a link j which gives the maximum preference (maximum QoS) to the class from among the set of suppliers. The routing mechanism yields the guideline: route to j such that max $U_k(\Phi(p))$ for all j where $\Phi(p)$ is the demand at supplier j. $U_k(\Phi(p))$ is the overall utility derived by traffic class k if the session joins supplier j. This mechanism essentially states that the agent will choose the service provider which gives the maximum utility (or in this case minimal packet-loss probability) to the traffic class. The routing algorithm (by the agent) first computes $P_k^j(\Phi(p))$ for all the suppliers, where $P_k^j(\Phi(p))$ is the packet loss probability of traffic class k at link j in the parallel link network. The agent then ranks the class utility derived by joining a supplier, and then ranks them in decreasing order of preference.

Admission control   The agent will admit the session on one of the many routes (links) provided the QoS of the traffic class it joins is honoured. If the agent has the same preference over a subset of the suppliers (a tie for suppliers), then one of them will be chosen at random. If all the sessions of a traffic class are identical (same traffic load and parameters), then the agent can compute the admission space, and the number of sessions that can be admitted without violating the QoS constraints of the class over all the links. Formally, find $\{n_1^*, n_2^*, \ldots, n_N^*\}$ given that $\{c_{ij}^*, b_{ij}^*\}$ with constraints $q_i^c = \{q_{i1}^c, q_{i2}^c, \ldots\}$.

The agent has to find the maximum (n_j^*) of admissible sessions at each link, given the Pareto allocation for agent i on each link j, and given the QoS constraints of the class $i(q_i^c)$ which, for example, could be packet-loss probability, max-delay, and average delay requirement per class.

Several interesting questions arise under the class-welfare based routing: what is the session-level-blocking probability per class, given the session-arrival rate and average holding time per class? How does it depend on the session arrival rate and holding time? Does this routing algorithm balance the loads in such a fashion that a traffic class benefits in the long run by the routing algorithm?

We study some of the questions numerically. We use simulations where two traffic classes (two agents) compete for resources in a two-node (link) parallel network, that is, just two suppliers. The sessions of traffic class k arrive to the network at a Poisson rate of γ_k. The session holding time is exponentially distributed with mean ν_k ($k \in [1, 2]$). Each session of class k arriving has average packet arrival rate λ_k (traffic parameters are Poisson arrivals) and the mean service time is exponentially distributed with mean one. The state space is basically a Markov chain with four parameters $\{n_1^1, n_2^1, n_1^2, n_2^2\}$ representing the number of sessions of traffic class k at each of the links. However, for each agent the state space is two dimensional. Numerical studies indicate that the routing algorithms are stable. The results can be obtained using simulations and Markov chain models of two user classes and two suppliers (links). The session-blocking probability is in the order of $1/10^7$ for an offered load (at the session or call level) $\gamma_k/\nu_k = 2.0$. It is evident that the dynamic algorithm is better than the static one as we increase $\rho = A/\Omega$. The agent that routes a session can choose one of the links dynamically based on the state of the link. Let class 1 be allocated bandwidth and buffers in such a way that ten sessions can be admitted to supplier 1 and fifteen to supplier 2 for agent 1. This admission region assumes that a packet loss probability of $1/10^8$ is the QoS requirement by class 1.

The server economy

We now discuss the server economy where servers offer processing resources and memory to agents representing user classes. The agents compete for these resources and buy as much as possible from suppliers. The agents perform 'load balancing' based on the QoS preferences of the class it represents.

The economic model consists of the following players: Agents and Server Suppliers, Consumers or user classes and Business. User sessions within a class have common preferences. User classes have QoS preferences over average delay and throughput, and in some cases completion times of sessions (deadlines). Users within a class share resources at the servers.

Agents and network suppliers   Agents represent user classes. An agent represents a single user class. Agents negotiate with the supplier and buy resources from service providers. Agents on behalf of user classes demand resources to meet the QoS needs. Suppliers compete to maximize revenue. Suppliers partition and allocate resources (processing rate and memory) to the competing agents.

Multiple agent network supplier interaction   Agents present demands to the suppliers. The demands by agents are based upon their wealth and user-class preferences. The demand by each agent is computed via utility functions which represent the QoS needs of the class. Agents negotiate with suppliers to determine the prices. The negotiation process is iterative where prices are adjusted to clear the market. Price negotiation could be done periodically or depending on changes in demand.

The agent and network supplier become service providers in the market. The role of the supplier is to provide technologies to sell resources (buffer and bandwidth units) and to partitioning them flexibly based on the demand by the agents. The agents transform the goods (buffer and bandwidth) and provide QoS levels to the user classes. The agents strive to maximize profits (minimize buying costs) by using the right utility functions and the right performance models in order to provide QoS to the user class. More users within a user class implies more revenue for the agent. The agent is decoupled from the traffic class and the supplier.

In this economy, user classes are transaction classes that send transactions to database servers for processing. The transaction processing time at each of the server is based on the type of transaction. Consider K classes of transactions and each class is represented by an agent (economic agent). In the economy, the agents negotiate with the servers for server capacity. We assume that transactions of any class can run on any of the database servers. Therefore, agents negotiate with all the servers for server throughput (or processing speed). A model where K agents compete for services in a transaction processing system, and where transaction classes do not share the service queues is shown in Figure 9.2.

Each class could do the following based on its preferences on average delay and throughput: (i) each agent i can minimize its average response time under throughput constraints, (ii) each agent i can maximize throughput of its transactions under an average delay constraint, (iii) each agent i can look at a combination of QoS requirements and have preferences over them.

Therefore, each class can choose either one of these preferences and let the agent control the flow of transactions through the system. The problem now becomes a multi-objective optimization problem as every agent is trying to maximize its benefit in the system based on the class of QoS preferences. Consider that the classes wish to choose various objectives, the utility function assumes $U = x_d U_d + x_l U_l$ where U_d is the utility function for average delay and U_l is the utility function for throughput, and x_d and x_l are constants. Consider that there are requirements for transaction completion time. Instead of scheduling transactions to meet deadlines, we try to minimize the number of transactions that have missed the deadlines (in a stochastic sense). Consider that each transaction class is assigned a service queue at each server, then we try to minimize the probability of the number of transactions of a class exceeding a certain threshold in the buffer. This is the tail probability $P(X > b)$ where X is the number of transactions of a class in a queue at a server, and b is the threshold for the number in the queue, beyond which transactions miss deadlines. If we include this QoS requirement then the above utility function will be $U = x_d U_d + x_l U_l + x_t U_t$ where U_t is the tail probability utility function and x_t is a constant.

Pareto Optimality   We now have a simple formulation for classes competing for server capacity (processing rate) in order to minimize average delay (or average response time). The utility function is simply $U = x_d U_d$ as the rest of the constants are zero. Let p_j be the price per unit processing rate at server j. The maximum processing rate at server j is C_j. The problem therefore for each agent is the following: find $\{c_{ij}^*\}$ such that min $U_d = \{\Sigma_{j=1}^{N} W_{ij}\}$ with constraints $\Sigma_{j=1}^{N} \lambda_{ij} = \gamma_i \ \forall i$, $\Sigma_i^{N} c_{ij}^* p_j w_i \ \forall i$.

In the above problem definition, each agent will try and minimize the utility function under the wealth constraint and under the throughput constraint. This constraint is necessary to make sure that positive values of throughput are obtained as a result of the optimization. The transaction agents compete for

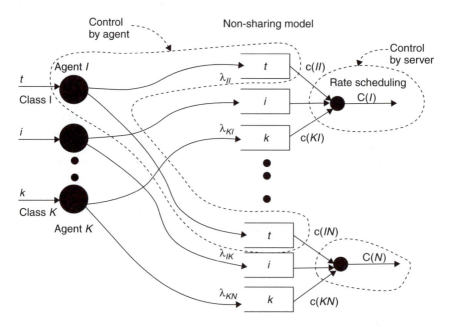

Figure 9.2 Non-sharing model: K agents compete for services in a transaction processing
system with N servers.

processing rate at each server, and transaction servers compete for profit. The
objectives of the transaction classes are conflicting as they all want to minimize
their average response time. In the above formulation $W_{ij} = \lambda_{ij}/(c_{ij} - \lambda_{ij})$ this is the
average number of class i transactions in queue at system j. The average delay in
the system for each class i is simply the average number in the system divided by
the overall throughput $\sum_{j=1}^{N} \lambda_{ij}$.

The main goal of the agent representing the transaction class is to minimize a
utility function which is simply the average number in the overall system. This will
also minimize the average delay or average response time of the transaction class.

Proposition 9.3   The utility function U_d is convex with respect to the resource
allocation variable c_{ij} where $\lambda_{ij} \in [0, c_{ij})$, and $c_{ij} \in (0, C_j]$

The proof follows from Chapter 8.

The utility function U_d is discontinuous when $\lambda_{ij} = c_{ij}$.

Demand set   The demand set for an agent i, given the prices (p_j of server j)
of the processing rates (or capacities) at the servers is $\{c_{i1}, c_{i2}, \ldots, c_{iN}\}$ over
all the servers. We use the standard techniques of optimization to find the
demand set, which is given as follows for all $j \in [1, N]$

$$c_{ij} = \lambda_{ij} + \left(\left(w_i - \sum_{j=1}^{N} \lambda_{ij} p_j \right) / \sum_{j=1}^{N} \sqrt{\lambda_{ij}} p_j \right) \sqrt{\lambda_{ij}} / p_j.$$

Price equilibrium Once the demand set is obtained, then using the wealth constraints, we can solve for the equilibrium price. This is not easily tractable. However, numerical results can be computed using the tatonnement process whereby agents compute the demand set, given the processing-rate prices by each server. An iteration process between the agents and the servers takes place. This will converge to an equilibrium price, when demand equals the supply which is $\sum_{j=1}^{K} c_{ij} = C_j$.

We now state formally the result for K agents competing for processing resources from N servers.

Proposition 9.4 Consider K agents competing for processing resources from N servers. If the utility function of these agents is U_d and the performance model at the servers is an M/M/1 model, then price equilibrium and Pareto optimality exist.

The proof of this proposition is the same as described in Chapter 8. The utility function U_d is continuous and decreasing convex with respect to the allocation variables c_{ij}. The function is discontinuous when $\lambda_{ij} = c_{ij}$. Due to this, Pareto allocations or price equilibrium may not exist. However, we solve this problem by stating that the agents, when they present their demands, have to make sure that the transaction throughput rate λ_{ij} at a server has to be lower than the capacity allocation c_{ij}. If this is not met then the price iteration process or the tatonnement process will not converge. We assume that the servers know the transaction throughput or arrival rate from each agent during the iteration process.

Transaction routing

The static routing problem for the agent i, once the allocation of processing rates at the N servers is done for agent i, can be formulated as:

Find $\{\lambda_{ij}\}$ such that min $\{\sum_{j=1}^{N} W_{ij}\}$ with constraints $\sum_{j=1}^{N} \lambda_{ij} = \gamma_i \, \forall i$. Here, W_{ij} is the average response time for agent i traffic when sent to server (supplier) j. We use a simple M/M/1 model of the queueing system, where $W_{ij} = \lambda_{ij}/(c_{ij} - \lambda_{ij})$ (average number of agent i transactions in server j). This or the average delay can be minimized (the same result will be obtained for either one of them). The optimal arrival rate vector to the servers or the optimal flow of transactions, assuming a Poisson distribution for arrivals with rate λ_{ij} is given by

$$\lambda_{ij} = c_{ij} - \frac{\sqrt{c_{ij}}}{\sum_{j=1}^{N} \sqrt{c_{ij}}} \cdot \left(\sum_{j=1}^{N} c_{ij} - \lambda_{ij} \right).$$

This result gives the optimal flow of transactions of class i to the servers, given the capacity allocation to the agent i. Using this, a simple random routing policy which can split transaction traffic optimally can be designed. This policy does not assume the current state of the servers, the number of transactions of agent i queued for service at server j. A simple, but well-known routing algorithm is illustrated here.

Dynamic routing algorithm　The Join Shortest Queue (JSQ) algorithm routes transactions of class i to a system j is found by obtaining the minimum of the following

$$\min\left\{\frac{Q_{i1} + 1}{c_{i1}}, \frac{Q_{i2} + 1}{c_{i2}}, \cdots, \frac{Q_{iN} + 1}{c_{iN}}\right\},$$

where Q_{ij} is the queue length of server j or the number of transactions of class i queuing up for service at server j. If there are ties, then one of the queues is picked at random (or with equal probability).

Conclusions

We have developed a decentralized framework for QoS provisioning based on economic models. A new definition of QoS provisioning based on Pareto efficient allocations is given. These allocations are not only efficient (from a Pareto sense) but also satisfy the QoS constraints of competing traffic classes (or users). We have shown that Pareto optimal allocations exist in a (transaction based) network economy (parallel link network), also represented as a server economy. A methodology is provided for the network service providers to price services based on the demands placed by the users. Prices are computed based on the load of the traffic classes and the corresponding demand.

Prices are excellent indicators of available QoS at each node and link in the network. A dynamic session routing algorithm is coupled with admission control mechanisms to provide QoS to the traffic classes, for a network as well as a server economy.

We have not investigated several issues related to the dynamics of the overall system. For example, if we assume time is divided into intervals, and during each time interval prices of resources are stable. The price negotiation is done between the agents and the suppliers at the beginning of the time interval. However, each supplier (server) could have time intervals which are different from the rest. This can cause the agents to negotiate with each supplier independently.

Economic models can provide several new insights into resource sharing and QoS provisioning in future networks and distributed systems which will connect millions of users and provide a large number of servers.

Pricing and competition can provide solutions to reduce the complexity of service provisioning and efficiently utilize the resources.

Appendix: proofs of Pareto optimal allocations

We start by giving the first derivative of P with respect to the buffer variable b:

$$P' = \frac{\rho^b(1 - \rho)\log[\rho]}{(1 - \rho^b)^2}$$

$$\log_{c\to\lambda} P' = -\frac{1}{(1 + b)^2}, \tag{A.1}$$

where $\rho = \lambda/c$. This function is negative for all $b \in [0,B]$ and for all $\rho > 0$.
The second derivative with respect to b yields

$$P'' = \frac{(1 - \rho^b)\rho^b(\log[\rho])^2(1 - \rho)}{(1 - \rho^b)^3}$$

$$\lim_{c\to\lambda} P'' = \frac{2}{(1 + b)^2}. \tag{A.2}$$

This function is positive for all $b \in [0, B]$ and all $\rho > 0$. Similarly, the function P can be shown to be continuous (smooth) and decreasing convex in c for all $c \in [0,C]$, by rewriting function P to the following:

$$P' = \frac{1}{1 + c/\lambda + (c/\lambda)^2 + \cdots + (c/\lambda)^b}. \tag{A.3}$$

From this the first derivative can be shown to be negative and the second derivative to be positive for all $c \in [0,C]$, hence the proof.

In the system of parallel links the overall packet-loss probability (QoS parameter) for a traffic class k is given as follows:

$$U_k = P_{\text{loss},k} = 1 - \prod_{j=1}^{N}(1 - P_k^j), \tag{A.4}$$

where P_k^j is the packet-loss probability of TC_k on link j (or supplier).

This utility function is the same as equation (1), however, this is the packet-loss probability in a network consisting of parallel links rather than a route between a source and destination as considered in equation (1).

References

Gottinger, H. W. (1998) 'Introduction to Complexity' in *Informatics: The Future of Information Society*, Memoirs 1008, Graduate School of Informatics, Kansai University Japan, 53–74, 201–228

Harel, A. and P. H. Zipkin (1987) 'Strong Convexity Results for Queueing Systems', *Operations Research* 35(3): 405–418

Kleinrock, L. (1976) *Queueing Systems, Applications*, Vol. 2, New York: Wiley Interscience

Mount, K. R. and St. Reiter (1994) 'On Modeling Computing with Human Agents', in M. Majumdar (ed.), *Organizations with Incomplete Information*, Cambridge: Cambridge University Press

Radner, R. (1993) 'The Organization of Decentralized Information Processing', *Econometrica* 62: 1109–1146

Van Zandt, T. (1998) 'The Scheduling and Organization of Periodic Associative Computation: Efficient Networks', *Review of Economic Design* 3: 93–127

Wolff, R. W. (1989) *Stochastic Modeling and the Theory of Queues*, Prentice Hall: Englewood Cliffs, NJ

10 Macroeconomics of network industries

Introduction

While network effects in micro structures, that is, on industry levels, have been our primary concern in previous chapters, we now address network effects on a macro scale involving productivity, growth, and the business cycle. The network effect is here strongly facilitated through computerization and information technologies (ITs). The emerging computerization pervades through many sectors of the economy, and communication by network technologies such as the Internet (the network is the computer) is a strong catalyst. Eventually, through this synergy most sectors of the economy will be impacted by network effects. Thus, networking and computerization may have far-reaching impacts on the pace and path of the economy but they could also make the economy more vulnerable to economic shocks.

We will address three important issues: IT, networks and productivity, endogeneous growth and increasing returns.

Brynjolfsson and Hitt (2000) provide some examples on some productivity-enhancing activities on the enterprise level: (i) computerization of ordering along the supply chain, (ii) Internet-based procurement system (EDI), and (iii) computer-based supply chain integration.

The relationship between technology and productivity used, on the economy or sector level, found little evidence of relationship in the 1980s. The investment between 1977 and 1989 rose several hundred per cent but was barely reflected in a rise in output per worker. There was this famous saying by Nobel prize-winning economist Robert Solow (1987): 'You can see the computer age everywhere except in productivity statistics'.

More recently, in the 1990s, such a positive relationship on the firm level was established empirically. On a short-term basis: a one-year difference in IT investments vs a one-year difference in firm productivity should be benchmarked by benefits equal to costs.

However, benefits are supposed to rise by a factor of 2–8 in forecasting future benefits (in productivity growth).

Economic techniques focus on the relatively observable aspects of investment, such as price and quantity of computer hardware in the economy, but neglect intangible investments in developing complementary new products, services, markets, and business processes.

Current statistics typically treat the accumulation of intangible capital assets, new production systems, and new skills as expenses rather than as investments. This leads to lower levels of measured outputs in periods of net capital accumulation. Output statistics miss many of the gains of IT brought to consumers such as variety, speed, and convenience. For instance, US productivity figures do not take account of quality changes, in particular, in services industries: (a) financial services sector (ATMs), (b) health care (CAM/diagnosis), and (c) legal services (online information).

Economic transformation

The story of the revolution in IT is a story of technology and a story of innovations in business organization and practice. The network economy is as much a story about changes in business organization, market structures, government regulations, and human experience as it is about new technology. Information technology builds the capabilities to process and distribute digital data to multiply the scale and speed with which thought and information can be applied. And thought and information can be applied to almost everything across the board. Computer chips, lasers, broadband Internet, and software are the key components of the technology that drives the network economy.

Productivity growth and technological change in the core sectors of the information-processing revolution has been immense. Sceptics can see this productivity explosion as just another example of a 'leading sector' – an explosion of invention and innovation that revolutionizes productivity in a narrow slice of the economy. There have been many such leading sectors in the past – air transport in the 1960s, television in the 1950s, automobiles in the 1920s, organic chemicals in the 1890s, railroads in the 1870s. Yet they did not change the standard dynamics of economic growth, they defined it.

But what we are experiencing is not just a decade-long boom as technology opens up new possibilities in a leading sector of economic growth, we are experiencing something deeper and broader. Semiconductors, computers, and communications do constitute a large leading sector, but this is not the whole story. Some technological changes do not just amplify productivity in one sector but enhance productivity in all economic sectors. They open new possibilities for economic organization across the board. They change what can be done and how it can be done across a wide range of industries. And they require changes in ideas about property and control, in the way that the government regulates the economy, in order for these new possibilities to be realized.

Innovative users began to discover how they could employ the computer in new ways. For example, American Airlines used computers to create its SABRE automated reservations system. The insurance industry first automated its traditional process, its back office applications of sorting and classifying. But insurance companies then began to create customized insurance products. The user cycle became one of first learning about the capabilities of computers in the course of automating established processes, and then applying that learning to generate innovative applications. As computing power has grown, computer-aided product design from airplanes built without wind-tunnels to pharmaceuticals designed at the molecular level for particular applications has become possible. A major function of a computer is that of a 'what-if' machine. The computer creates models of 'what-if': that is, what would happen if the airplane, the molecule, the business, or the document were to be built up in a particular way. It thus enables an amount and a degree of experimentation in the virtual world that would be prohibitively expensive in resources and time in the real world.

What does it mean to say that computing is becoming pervasive? The new production and distribution processes that pervasive computing makes possible are visible at the checkout counter, the petrol station, and in transportation services. The most important part of pervasive computing is the computers that we do not see. They become embedded in traditional products and alter the way such products operate. In automobiles, anti-lock brakes, air bags, and engine self-diagnosis and adjustment are performed by embedded microprocessors that sense, compute, and adjust. The level of automotive performance in systems from brakes to emission control is vastly greater today than it was a generation ago because of embedded microprocessors, and it extends to the choice of transportation modes through the emergence of 'intelligent transportation systems' (ITS).

Now much more than before we see the computer as a network (the 'network is the computer'). As the cost of communication bandwidth dropped, it became possible to link individual sensing, computing, and storage units. Today it is well taken that an automated teller machine (ATM) verifies the bank balance we hold in a bank in a distant city. The key point is not that rapid transmission has become technically feasible, but that the costs of data communication are dropping so far and fast as to make the wide use of the network for data transmission economically feasible for nearly every use imaginable. With the early data use of data networks it was once again leading-edge users who created new applications in their pursuit of competitive advantage. The experimental nature of the Internet in the beginning, its evolution to a full-scale global data and communication network is a case in point. Networking began either as private corporate networks, or, as in the case of the French Minitel, as a public network with defined and limited services. And data communications networks began their exponential expansion as experimenting users found new useful applications and configurations.

But few foresaw the true long-run potential of high-speed data networking until the TCP/IP protocol and the World-Wide Web (WWW) revealed the potential benefit of linking networks to networks. Every computer became a window into the world's data store. And as the network grew it became more and more clear that the value of the network to everyone grew as well – a principle that is now termed Metcalf's Law (see Appendix B).

The build-up of the Internet has been so rapid in large part because the Internet could be initially run over the existing voice telecommunications system. Even before the new technologies designed from the ground up to manage data communications emerged, the global Internet had already established its reach. The first generation Internet has grown exponentially world-wide during the last decade.

Some of the elements of the next generation of data networks are already evident. First, for consumers and small businesses one dramatic advance will be broadband to the home to create high-bandwidth (Ferguson, 2002). The acceleration in speed will change the kinds of tasks that can be accomplished over the Internet.

Second, wireless voice networks will soon be as extensively deployed as the wired phone network. Widely diffused wireless data networks will set off another round of experimentation and learning.

Third, the capacity and cost of the very backbone of the network will evolve dramatically over the next years, bringing new architectures, lower costs, ongoing experimentation and new applications.

Technological advance and diffusion clouds the view of how the growth of the network will transform business organization and business competition. How will the entire economy be linked into information processing and data communications? The prospects are still grossly uncertain because the growth of the network promises to transform the whole society. Traditional businesses that act as intermediaries – like stockbrokers and travel agents – will be irrevocably altered. Traditional products like automobiles are already being marketed in new ways. Stores will not disappear, but the mix of stores and what stores do will change. New ways of reaching customers will in turn drive new ways of organizing production and delivering goods to consumers. Today we continue to see strategic experiments in the form of new companies trying to exploit the Web and established companies trying to defend their positions. But we do not know which of these experiments in corporate information and network strategy will be successful. We can, however, see which strategies have been successful in the recent past. Consider the retail sector, and take the consumer-goods distributor Wal-Mart. Wal-Mart starting as a conventional retail distributor, has evolved into a very efficient network retailer by successfully solving problems of control and distribution, by adopting consistently and on a large-scale basis modern information technology. So Wal-Mart is among the top firms that excel in the use of information and network technology related to output and revenue.

Some of those benefits may not come forward as rapidly as expected. Economic historian Paul David (1990) points out that it took nearly half a century for business users to figure out the possibilities for increased efficiency through factory reorganization opened up by the electric motor. Finding the most valued uses for the next wave of computer-and-communications technology will probably not take as long, but it will take time.

Assessing the transformation

Why, sceptics ask, are boosters of information processing and communications so sure that this current transformation is more important than the leading sectors we have seen in the past? Is the claim justified that the impact on our material welfare through the Internet is so much greater than the impact of the automobile, or of penicillin and other antibiotics, or of network television?

R. J. Gordon (2000) is one of the leading sceptics, and it is appropriate to discuss the line of his main arguments.

Even Gordon admits the pervasive impact of IT: 'A revival in productivity growth ... is impressive in comparison with the American historical record ...'

He argues, based on econometric estimation, that 'spillover effects on multi-factor productivity in the non-computer economy are absent or slightly negative'. However, Gordon looks at the computer primarily as a 'stand alone' IT, he only considers 12 per cent of US GDP as generated by the computer/semiconductor industry, but neglects the network effects of the economy, in particular, the computerized network industry and the Internet that comprises about 30 per cent of the US economy (most of the professional services, media, telecoms).

There also appear to be problems with measurements as suggested by Gordon:

* the comparative statistical basis is too small (only 5 years in the 1990s), which ignores that the innovation effect is cumulative depending on critical mass and spillover into several sectors
* neglect of synergy of IT and network economy (the 'network is the computer')
* neglect of intangible effects (quality, speed, new products)
* neglect of laggardness of IT effects, not considered in econometric estimation.

According to Gordon 'The second industrial revolution took place from 1860 to 1900 and was triggered through invention of electricity, internal combustion engine, the telephone, and led to increased productivity growth from 1913 to 1972'.

What is not mentioned is that productivity growth did not increase by the emergence of those technologies themselves but by the fact that they were embedded in products or even created a network industry.

A question mark is placed at: 'Does Information Technology and the Internet sustain a Third Industrial Revolution?' And the 'New Economy is certainly more about computers than pharmaceuticals'. Why this artificial distinction?

We can venture the thesis: Progress in Science is heavily carried through computers (Wolfram, 2002). In most cases of recent progress in science we could put forward the thesis that all science (now) is (in a way) computer science. Examples: Human Genome projects to disclose DNA classification, new drug designs, system products such as the heart pacemaker, as there are many new discoveries in astronomy, physics, biology, medicine, with new technology platforms which could snowball into new network industries. This is not yet reflected in the measurements, because it takes time to have this synergy come out in hard numbers.

Thus computers/communications is a cross-sectional technology impacting almost every sector of the economy, horizontally (industry and firm specific) as well as vertically (downstream and upstream, i.e. computers in basic research, basic IT research in non-computer industries, etc.).

The roadmap of this industrial revolution is new computing technology + networking leading to emerging industries which runs further than the cycle: maturing technology + networking leading to existing industries.

Compared to one of the five big innovations in the Second Industrial Revolution, how do they compare with the Internet today? How far goes the information revolution?

In terms of welfare impacts for the population concerned, Gordon asks, 'is for the population of Houston air conditioning more important than the Internet', or for the population of Minneapolis, 'is indoor plumbing more important than the Internet?'.

Gordon: 'The cost of computing has dropped exponentially, the cost of thinking is what it always was. I cannot type or think any faster than I did with my first 1983 personal computer that contained 1/100th of memory and operated 1/60th of the speed of my present model'.

This looks like a scientist who has everything in his head, and gets his ideas out where it does not make a difference what vintage the computer is and whether networked or not. Look at how one produces a 'paper', or launches a new product. Thinking is not an island, in fact, many ideas originate through a network. Criticality, size of network and speed matters, even if one finds out by speedy ways that somebody else had the idea before (because then he can realize his opportunity costs faster and pursue a more productive idea). Suppose a paper is incremental knowledge, as a new product, then its faster production and diffusion is higher productivity! Increasing network size and speed (say through broadband fibre optic lines etc.) could even make more than an order-of-magnitude difference.

Gordon: '…the main productivity gains of computers have already been achieved'.

Here one of the biggest weaknesses of the Gordon study is the presumption of projecting the past and existing functionality of present IT (computers) into the future.

Gordon: 'Much of computer usage is through competition, and thus "burned up" on an more aggregate level (Barnes & Nobles, Amazon) which does not show up in aggregate productivity (zero sum game) while (paradoxically?) on a micro level the rate of return on investment in computers substantially exceed other investments'.

This is an interesting argument, but does it stick? Yes, but it is only a one-shot effect, therefore, only a blip in the time series on productivity rates.

Gordon: 'The Internet creates no new products, they are already available'.

Again these are strong words. If we describe goods and services through commodity characteristics, then speed and higher quality (less 'externality bound') could be important characteristics defining a new product. If the Internet allows me to do things electronically which otherwise would need physical transportation, then it would be a partial or complete substitute (with zero mileage costs and almost zero pollution) for a fossil-fuel-type transportation device (Park and Roone, 2002).

The productivity paradox

But if this wave of technological innovation is so important, why has it not yet had a more powerful impact on our picture of the overall economy? Back in 1987 Robert Solow wrote in the *New York Review of Books*: 'How come we see the computer revolution everywhere but in the [aggregate] productivity statistics'. Solow shared the general view that computers-and-communications held a potential for economic revolution. Yet when he looked at the aggregate overall measurements of the state of the economy, he saw slow productivity growth.

After having made a detailed accounting of the computer's contribution to productivity statistics, J. Triplett (1998) of the Brookings Institution responded: 'You don't see computers in the productivity statistics yet, but wait a bit and you will.'

The fourteen years from the date generally accepted as the beginning of the productivity 'slowdown', the oil crisis years 1973–87, with Solow's observations, had seen measured output per hour worked in the non-farm business sector of the US economy grow at a pace of only 1.1 per cent per year. By contrast, the fourteen years before 1973 had seen measured output per hour worked grow at a pace of 2.8 per cent per year.

Even after Solow had asked his question the productivity performance worsened: between 1987 and 1995 measured output per hour worked for the US non-farm business sector grew at only 0.8 per cent per year (Council of Economic Advisers, 1999).

This 'productivity paradox' was sharpened because at the microeconomic level economists and business analysts had no problem finding that investments in high technology had enormous productivity benefits. Typical rates of return on investments in computers and networks amount to more than 50 per cent per year. Firms that invested heavily in IT and transformed their internal structures so that they could use their new technological capabilities flourished in the 1980s and 1990s – and their lagging competitors did not (Brynjolfsson and Hitt, 2000).

Attempts have been put forward to resolve the paradox. One comes from the economic historian Paul David (1990) arguing that it takes considerable time for an economy to restructure itself to take full advantage of the potential opened up by revolutionary technology. For example, David observed that it took forty years for the American economy to realize the productivity potential of the dynamo. Electric power became a reality in the 1880s. But it was not until the 1920s that there had been enough experimentation and use of electricity-based technologies for businesses to learn how to use electric power effectively, and for the inventions of Edison and Westinghouse to pay off in big leaps in industrial sector productivity.

Another resolution of the productivity paradox stems from the fact that while technologists look at the leading edge of technologies national income accountants see changes reflected in their aggregate data only when a critical mass has been building up. With a considerable lag in invention and innovation dates and its economic impacts there have been observations with innovations having taken place in 1760 that only led to a marked acceleration of economic growth in the 1840s and 1850s when industrial technology diffused widely.

One interesting explanation is provided by Sichel (1997), as to the lag of productivity growth, for example, the lack of critical mass. In the 1970s and 1980s computers were simply too small a share of total investment in total GDP to expect to see a strong contribution to aggregate economic growth – even if for each investing company the rate of return on IT investments was very high. This observation is superimposed by findings that manufacturing sectors that use computers most intensively showed a gain in relative productivity growth in the 1990s, although the most computer-intensive service sectors do not (McGuckin and Stiroh, 2001). This weak measured productivity growth of the services needs to be reconciled with the massive IT investments and high expectations of the new economy. However, as Sichel points out, what was true in the 1980s was no longer true in the 1990s: then investments in IT were more than half of total investment. From 1995 productivity growth has been accelerating, and computers and communications are the prime source for this recent acceleration in American economic growth. For OECD countries there have been comprehensive recent investigations supporting this view (OECD, 2000).

Still, there are conflicting arguments as to the extent of IT's contribution to productivity and economic growth.

The most comprehensive explorations are Onliner and Sichel (1994) and Jorgenson and Stiroh (1995, 1999). For both the growth accounting equation is calculated as:

$$d_tY = s_c d_t K_c + s_{nc} d_t K_{nc} + s_L d_t L + d_t \pi, \tag{1}$$

where $d_t Y = dY/dt$, the rate of growth of output, $d_t K_c$, $d_t K_{nc}$, and $d_t L$ are rates of growth of the inputs – K_c computer capital (or computer capital services), K_{nc} non-computer capital (services) and L, labour, s_i is the share of input i, and $d_t \pi$ the growth of multifactor productivity. This equation says that the rate of growth of output ($d_t Y$) equals the share-weighted growth in inputs (for example, $s_c d_t K_c$ is the rate of growth of computer capital, weighted by the share of computer capital in total cost), plus the rate of growth of multifactor productivity.

Jorgenson and Stiroh (1995) estimate the share of capital services provided by computer equipment capital, using the capital accounting framework developed by Jorgenson (1990); Onliner and Sichel (1994) use computer equipment's income share. The results of both papers are highly consistent. Computer equipment made a relatively small contribution to economic growth, even during the period of the 1980s when computer technology became so widely diffused throughout the economy. In the growth accounting framework of equation (1), even very rapid rates of input growth, and the growth of computing equipment has been rapid indeed, make only relatively small contributions to growth when the share of this equipment is small. In these calculations, computer equipment still accounts for only around 2 per cent or less of the physical capital stock, and under 2 per cent of capital services.

Onliner and Sichel (1994) enlarge the definition of computers to encompass all of information-processing equipment and also computing software and computer-using labour. The result remains unchanged. On any of these definitions the shares remain small and so does the growth contribution of IT.

To check the reasonableness of their results, Oliner and Sichel (1994) simulate results for the assumption that computers earn supernormal returns, as equation (1) implies that computers earn the same return as earned on other capital equipment. Romer (1986), Brynjolfsson and Yang (1996) all argued or implied that computers yield higher returns than investment in other capital. The alternative simulations raise the contribution of computing equipment to growth (from 0.2 to 0.3 or 0.4), but all of them confront the same problem: the share of computing equipment is simply too small for any reasonable return to computer investment to result in large contribution to economic growth.

Growth-accounting exercises calculate the computer's contribution to growth, not its contribution to multifactor productivity. As equation (1) shows, multifactor productivity's contribution to economic growth is separate from the contribution of any input, including the input of computers. If one interprets the productivity paradox as applying to multifactor productivity, growth-accounting exercises do not shed very much light on it.

In summary, computers make a small contribution to growth because they account for only a small share of capital input. Does the same small share suggest that they likewise cannot have an impact on productivity? Not so. The paradox remains a subject for discussion for other reasons to follow.

One reason is that computer impact is less observable in sectors of the economy whose output is poorly measured. Griliches (1994) noted that more than 70 per cent of private sector US computer investment was concentrated in wholesale and retail trade, financial insurance, and real estate and services. These are exactly the sectors of the economy where output is least well measured, and where in some cases even the concept of output is not well defined (finance, insurance, consulting services). That there are serious measurement problems in all these areas is well established. It is also the case that services account for a large part of output in advanced economies. Services that directly affect the calculation of GDP are those in personal consumption expenditures (PCE) and in net exports (and of course the output of the entire government sector is notoriously mismeasured).

Thus, services make up a large proportion of the aggregate productivity ratio and they are poorly measured. Of course, services include many that have probably not benefited appreciably from output-enhancing productivity improvements caused by computers.

The other position that the real computer impact is delayed and needs a critical mass is argued by David (1990). He has drawn an analogy between the diffusion of electricity and computers linking electricity and computers because both 'form the nodal elements' of networks and 'occupy key positions in a web of strongly complementary technical relationships'. Because of their network parallels, David predicts that computer diffusion and the effects of computers on productivity will follow the same protracted course as electricity. More than four decades have passed since the introduction of the commercial computer. In about forty five years the price of computing power has declined more than two thousand fold. No remotely comparable price decreases accompanied the dawning of the electrical age. David reports that electricity prices only began to fall in the fourth decade of electric power; and although Nordhaus (1997) estimates that the per lumen price of lighting dropped by more than 85 per cent between 1883 and 1920, two-thirds of that is attributable to improved efficiency of the light bulb, rather than to electric-power generation.

Because their price histories are so different, the diffusions of electric power and computing power have fundamentally different – not similar – patterns. In the computer diffusion process, the initial applications supplanted older technologies for computing. Water and steam power long survived the introduction of electricity; but old, pre-computer age devices for doing calculations disappeared long ago.

The global network economy

A strong companion of the network economy is deregulation, liberalization, and privatization.

We take the case of telecommunication as a prototype of a network industry. Once telecommunications deregulation began, deregulation in air travel and finance (banking, brokering, insurance) freed major companies in those industries to experiment with new applications of computing and telecommunications. The newly competitive environment in their own industries gave them every possible incentive to try to gain advantage on their competitors. Subsequently, other companies had to imitate the innovators, or leapfrog them by developing still newer applications – usually in conjunction with IT producers. Deregulation thus created eager experimenters willing to try new applications developed by IT firms.

In the US deregulated companies in key industries eagerly sought new competitive tools and experimented with new organizational forms and new products and services. In Japan, at least in the early stage, telecommunications remained a regulated monopoly, and so established companies and entrepreneurial groups could not experiment in how they used telecommunications; they could only do what NTT (the monopoly telephone company) had planned for them to do. Japanese banks and brokerages remained regulated, so there was little competitive pressure to seek out new IT applications to transform their businesses. Both the possibilities of experimenting with new uses for telecommunications and the supply of lead users eager to do that experimenting were absent.

Policies assuring competitive markets, deregulation, and competition policy, were essential. In the very beginning it was antitrust that moved the infant transistor technology into the competitive realm. The then-monopoly AT&T was forced to make the new technology – invented at Bell Labs – available to all. Had the transistor remained under monopoly control as the AT&T's development review process tried to think of uses for it, recent industrial history would be fundamentally (but unknowably different). It is highly likely that innovation and diffusion would have proceeded more slowly and narrowly, resulting in both fewer innovative products and fewer innovative competitive technology firms. New companies such as Fairchild, Intel, AMD, National Semiconductor took the new technology and led the process of innovation and risk taking that has brought prices down further and faster, and performance up further and faster, than with any other major new technology in history.

Most of the large integrated companies that dominated vacuum-tube consumer electronics – RCA, Philco, Sylvania – were soon bypassed by the new companies that were born and grew with new technology. New (and some reborn) technology producers working closely with innovative users created new applications, many of which were not initially obvious: from automobile door locks, anti-skidding brakes, through medical imaging and surgical equipment, to ATMs, personal computers, and gene sequencers.

The creation of competitive markets in telecommunications was not an easy policy to establish or to implement.

Deregulation and competition drove the rapid build-up of private networks in America and the rapid private take-up of Internet access. Now, as we move to next generation Internet, wireless networks, and high-speed Internet access in homes and small businesses, the question reposes itself: how to sustain competition and in which parts of the market?

The network economy is an 'idea economy'. Certainly economic growth has always been motored by ideas. Given the increasing pace of innovation that rests on ever new ideas and the importance of information-based products that are easily diffused in perfect form over digital networks, the question of intellectual property becomes central.

Ideas and 'information goods' have particular characteristics that distinguish them from ordinary goods. These include (1) marginal costs of reproduction and distribution that approach zero, (2) problems of transparency, and (3) non-rival possession. The emergence of a digitized network economy opens a broad range of issues. The network economy creates new products and transforms established industries with new ways. It transforms storage, search, diffusion, and indeed generation of ideas and information. It reopens issues such as rights to copy because previously copies generally involved degraded quality or substantial cost.

Summarizing, the Internet-based economy creates new opportunities and paradigms.

As laid out in Chapter 9 the transaction-based Internet is e-commerce. It has a very large regional and often global reach, it creates an enhanced form of competitiveness in competitive markets, eases market entry (but accelerates market exit), it provides a very fast mechanism which is highly cost efficient for incremental costs, it is highly able to induce significant increases in productivity through the entire business process such as: (i) just-in-time (JIT) delivery by data exchange, integration of production and sales processes of different companies, (ii) in many cases no inventory is necessary because of manufacturing on demand (disintermediation) – Dell Computer, (iii) lowering costs by planned product obsolescence, thus no price dumping (Compaq vs Dell), (iv) lower sunk capital, higher profitability, and greater reach.

These advantages exist in a stable or cyclical growth environment of the industry (as part of the network economy) but, for instance, JIT production based on effective demand only constitutes partial (incomplete) information, and can turn to a big disadvantage in a network economy along the supply chain because a cyclical downturn can reinforce itself in a cumulative, steep decline.

Summing up the Productivity Advantage of IT Industries

- IT is pervasive in all business activities (disaggregation of Value Chain) Orders-Marketing-Billing-Logistics. Allows to concentrate on certain activities and outsource others ⇒ Higher Specialization with Lower Capital Costs.
- Significant Increase of Market Transparency, Reduction of Transaction Costs and Barriers to Entry ⇒ Intensification of Competition.
- IT is truly global. More product information available all the time, sales around the clock and around the globe.
- Speeding up information and innovation, reducing product launch time. Database management: Saving of Individual Customer Profiles. Customer Relations Management (CRM).
- Business-to-Business (B2B) online ordering cuts procurement costs, by finding cheaper suppliers and reducing errors in orders.
- Much lower distribution costs in electronic delivery (financial services, software, music).

Intangible assets

Current statistics typically treat the accumulation of intangible capital assets, new production systems, and new skills as expenses rather than as investments. This leads to lower levels of measured outputs in periods of net capital accumulation. Output statistics miss many of the gains of IT brought to consumers such as variety, speed, and convenience.

Even though the most visible developments in digital markets recently has been in business-to-consumer (B2C) markets, the biggest economic changes are likely to be in the business-to-business (B2B) part of the value chain. B2B electronic commerce has been around longer than B2C commerce with the introduction of technologies such as electronic data interchange (EDI). However, now that the B2C part of the value chain is becoming digital, it is increasingly easy to integrate the whole value chain so that consumers become an important player in all steps of value creation. The most immediate impact of this change will be in logistics and supply chain management.

Logistics and supply chain management practices are changing to include customers in the value chain. Traditional logistics issues address the moving of physical items along the value chain so that a product is available at a retailer when a consumer wants to purchase it.

Information markets

The ability of the Internet to deliver a good, and not just create a transaction that requires fulfilment via some other channel, may be one of the key factors to enhance productivity increases across major sectors.

Information goods have unique properties including marginal reproduction costs that are close to, if not exactly, zero. Therefore, the pricing strategies must change as well to reflect the new economics. For instance, some of the financial information freely made available on the Web today by online brokerage companies was sold through proprietary networks for hundreds of dollars per month just a few years ago. Software, another information good, is also enjoying a new economic model of 'open source' where the source code that comprises the good is made freely available to use and improve on the design.

Information goods may be most affected by integrating consumers in the value chain. Instead of an information product being created *ex ante* for consumers to purchase, information products can be dynamically rendered based upon the wishes of the consumer. Not only will this enable (Internet) retailers to price discriminate, it can also help change the number of product offerings to an almost infinite set of products. While there may be mass customization of physical products once the consumer is included in the value chain, information products can be customized to individual consumers at almost no additional costs.

Digital information goods also raise interesting pricing opportunities. Traditional rules of thumb such as 'price equals marginal cost' or using a standard mark-up over cost are not very useful in this environment. Instead value-oriented strategies are likely to be more effective (Shapiro and Varian, 1999). At the same time, the special characteristics of digital goods combined with the Internet open up new opportunities including disaggregation of previously aggregated content such as newspaper or journal articles and/or massive aggregation items, such those sold by America Online (Bakos and Brynjolfsson, 1999).

Conclusions

Conventional economics views economic growth as a result of input accumulation and technical progress in a world of roughly constant returns to scale. While there is some debate about how to measure inputs and how to define technical progress, there is a consensus that much of economic growth involves trade-offs, for example, increasing capital means investment, savings, and foregone consumption, while increasing labour input requires education expenditure and foregone leisure. Any unexplained growth is labelled the contribution of total factor productivity (TFP), also known as the Solow residual, which reflects technical progress, spillovers, improved efficiency, scale economies, etc. The network or new economy view takes the idea of TFP very seriously and argues that important sectors benefit from increasing returns, externalities, standards, and network economies. In a network economy, more creates more. For example, the value of new IT products like an internet connection, a fax machine, or a software program increases when others invest and obtain compatible equipment. Thus investment of firm A improves the productivity and value of firm B's investment. This type of production spillover allows for an on-going growth that can quickly outpace traditional explanations. Related ideas include non-linear dynamics growth after a critical mass is reached, virtuous circles of positive feedback in fast-developing industrial sectors, and falling prices and increased quality via technology and scale economies. These ideas are not entirely new to conventional economics but in network economies they gain greater importance as the driving force of economy-wide growth.

Proponents point to commonplace observations about hardware and software use as evidence of increasing return and network effects. Since modern networks are typically high-tech, for example, communications systems like the Internet show many characteristics of increasing returns, the IT sector is seen as the vital force in the new economy. Globalization also plays a role by expanding the scope of markets and allowing critical sectors to grow and achieve the necessary size of scale effects. Finally, the very nature of the new digitized economy is seen as inherently different from the old industrial economy due to obvious physical production and pricing differences between information and physical products or commodities.

References

Bakos, Y. and E. Brynjolfsson (1999) 'Bundling Information Goods, Pricing, Profits and Efficiency', *Management Science* 45(12): 1613–1630

Brynjolfsson, E. and L. Hitt (2000) 'Beyond Computation: Information Technology, Organizational Transformation and Business Performance', *Journal of Economic Perspectives* 14(94): 23–48.

——and S. Yang (1996) 'Information Technology and Productivity; A Review of the Literature', *Advances in Computers* 43: 179–214

Council of Economic Advisers (1999) *Economic Report of the President*, Washington, DC: GPO

David, P. A. (1990) 'The Dynamo and the Computer: An Historical Perspective on the Productivity Paradox', *American Economic Review* (PP) 80: 315–348

Ferguson, Ch. (2002) 'The United States Broadband Problem: Analysis and Policy Recommendations', Working Paper, Washington, DC: Brookings Institution, 31 May

Gordon, R. (2000), 'Does the "New Economy" Measure up to the Great Inventions in the Past?', *Journal of Economic Literature* 14: 49–74

Griliches, Z. (1994) 'Productivity, R&D and the Data Constraint', *American Economic Review* 84(1): 1–23

Jorgensen, D. W. (1990) 'Productivity and Economic Growth', in E. Berndt and J. Triplett (eds), *Fifty Years of Economic Measurement*, Chicago: University of Chicago Press

——and K. J. Stiroh (1995) 'Computers and Growth', *Economics of Innovation and New Technology* 3: 295–316

——(1999) 'Computers and Growth', *American Economic Review* (PP) 89(2): 109–115

McGuckin, R. H. and K. Stiroh (2001) 'Do Computers Make Output Harder to Measure?', *Journal of Technology Transfer* 2: 295–321

Nordhaus, W. D. (1997) 'Do Real-Output and Real-Wage Measures Capture Reality? The History of Light Suggests Not', in T. F. Bresnahan and R. J. Gordon, *The Economics of New Goods*, National Bureau of Economic Research, Studies in Income and Wealth 58, Chicago: University of Chicago Press

OECD (2000) *A New Economy?: The Changing Role of Innovation and Information Economy in Growth*, OECD: Paris

Onliner, St. D. and D. E. Sichel (1994) 'Computers and Output Growth Revisited; How Big is the Puzzle?', *Brookings Papers on Economic Activity* 2: 273–334

—— (2000) 'The Resurgence of Growth in the Late 1990s: Is Information Technology the Story?', *Journal of Economic Perspectives* 14: 3–22

Park, J. and N. Roome (2002) *The Ecology of the Economy*, London: Greenleaf Publishers.

Romer, P. (1986) 'Increasing Returns and Long-Run Growth', *Journal of Political Economy* 94(5): 1002–1037

Sichel, D. E. (1997) *The Computer Revolution; An Economic Perspective*, Washington, DC: The Brookings Institution

Solow, R. E. (1987) 'We'd better watch out', *New York Times Book Review*, July

Triplett, J. E. (1999) 'Economic Statistics, the New Economy, and the Productivity Slowdown', *Business Economics* 34(2): 13–17

Wolfram, St. (2002) *A New Kind of Science*, Champaign: Wolfram Media

Appendix A*   The Japanese telecommunications industry

Introduction

In December of 1984 both Houses of Japan's Diet passed a set of three bills–the Telecommunications Business Act, the Nippon Telegraph and Telephone (NTT) Privatization Act, and the Omnibus Act – aimed at remodelling the nation's telecommunications industry. This transformation consists of the privatization of NTT, the entry of new facility-based carriers, and large-scale value-added service providers. Governmental reform councils made various recommendations on telecommunications, the Diet felt that NTT should no longer operate in a protected vacuum. Some partially attributed this change of heart to international pressures mainly from American companies and governmental officials.

Telecommunication deregulation has been the priority item on the world political and economic agenda of the 1980s and 1990s. Telecommunication is truly international in scope. The break-up of the world's largest telecommunication company, AT&T in the United States, and the privatization of the telecommunication system of Great Britain, and all over continental Europe have sent powerful signals for others to follow suit. It was also a triumph on the policy effects of 'Anglo-American' economics of predicting welfare-enhancing effects for consumers and industries alike, through deregulation, privatization, and liberalization of regulated industries dominated by public monopolies.

As regards the mechanics of deregulation, parallels can be drawn between the United States, Great Britain, and Japan, the three countries experiencing the most dramatic changes (Nogami and Prestowitz, 1992; Noll *et al.*, 1995). The liberalization measures taken in each country accommodated a shift from traditional telephone services to enhanced or value-added services, mainly to serve corporate data-communications users. The degree of competition and the extent to which the reform has been implemented, however, set Japan apart from the other countries. It reflects the peculiar institutional environment in which the different actors operate and interact.

* Appendix A is co-authored with Professor Makoto Takashima from Nagasaki University.

As to the factors that brought about the Japanese telecommunication reform, the recommendations submitted to the Prime Minister by the 'Rincho' committee for administrative reforms in 1982 seem to have represented a turning point in changing the government's policy (Ito, 1986). The recommendations made by Rincho reflected then Prime Minister Nakasone's commitment for change in telecommunications. Privatization of NTT was one of Nakasone's major legislative proposals.

The Telecommunication Business Law

This law is the backbone of NTT's privatization. For the first time since telegraphy was introduced in Japan, a law would allow new entrants to own telecommunication facilities. The Telecommunication Business Law categorizes telecommunication carriers into Type I carriers – those who operate their own telecommunication facilities – and Type II carriers – the value-added services providers, those who lease facilities.

The distinction between Type I and Type II categories is similar to the US approach of the basic/enhanced dichotomy. But in order to avoid the problematic (basic/enhanced) boundary between the two categories, the Japanese adopted a vertical division-facility-owned/rented instead of the horizontal division-basic/enhanced services. Though basic services virtually means the same thing, 'value-added services' used in connection with the Telecommunication Business Law is more encompassing than what is considered to be 'enhanced services' in the US. They include packet switching, circuit switching, protocol conversion, transmission speed conversion, format or product code conversion, voice mail, electronic mail, videotex, facsimile, information processing, provision of data base services, traffic flow monitoring, remote computing services, video transmission, point-of-sale (POS) systems among many others.

Definition of special and general type II carriers   After four years since privatization, the Ministry of Posts and Telecommunications (MPT), now the Ministry of Public Management, Home Affairs, Posts and Telecommunications (MPHPT), has clarified certain aspects of this law, the most ambiguous point of which being the definition of Special and General Type II classification. Article 21 states that Special Type II carriers offer services to 'many and unspecific persons' and have facilities exceeding the standards stipulated by MPT. General Type II carriers are companies other than Special Type II businesses that lease facilities from others. This provision, however, does not define 'many and unspecific persons', leaving the MPT to provide more details.

In an attempt to clarify this clause, the MPT noted that any Type II companies with more than 500 exchange access lines would be classified Special Type II. This restriction was initially applied to carriers serving more than 500 end-users. However, the MPT had counted only leased trunk lines in determining the size of a Type II carrier and had not taken subscriber lines into account. This makes the '500 access-line restriction' virtually useless, because each carrier trunk line can reach many users. Owing to the confusion created by the MPT, several large firms have classified themselves both as General and as Special Type II carriers. Next to NTT and KDD which respectively enjoyed a monopoly of the domestic and international telecoms markets, by March of 2001 (MPHPT, 2001) there were more than 343 Type I carriers, operating their own networks and 9,006 Type II carriers.

Entry limitation   Under the supply-demand-balance rationale, as stipulated in Article 10 of the Telecommunication Business Law, the MPT has authority to determine how many carriers should be allowed to operate in a particular service market and can deny entry if it is deemed to create excessive supply in any part of the country. But this restriction has been lifted by the partial revision of the law in 1997 due largely to the intervention by the Fair Trade Commission (FTC).

Rate-making power   Article 31 of this law stipulates that rate-making is subject to MPT's discretion rather than the Diet's where authority was held prior to privatization. This transition reduces the possibility of tariffs being used for political purposes and provides a new challenge to the MPT. Under its public-corporation status, NTT was also acting as policy maker. This can be observed clearly in the way in which NTT Public Corporation was organized. The structure of its Tokyo headquarters was almost identical to various government agencies and did not resemble that of private companies – the legacy from the days when it was called the Ministry of Telecommunication. Often, the telecommunication ministry merely submitted NTT's proposals to the Diet or passed ordinances based on them. For a long time there was no mechanism to independently assess the appropriateness of rates proposals at the MPT. The same article in the Telecommunication Business Law prescribes that all tariffs of Type 1 carriers should be determined 'in consideration of proper costs'. Subsequently, the MPT has defined 'proper costs'.

Equal access   Although Article 39 of this law provides the MPT with the author-ity to mandate interconnection between Type I carriers, 'equal access' was in the beginning not required by law as in the US. That is, MPT had requested NTT to modify its networks so that new facility-based carriers can offer services on an equal basis with the ex-monopolist. Originally, NTT was demanding three new interexchange carriers (Daini Denden, Japan Telecom, and Teleway Japan) to cover the whole cost of modifying its central exchange offices, but backed down after having been opposed by MPT, and it agreed to absorb approximately half of the cost of accommodating the new Type I carriers. Article 39 provides MPT with the authority to mandate interconnection between Type I carriers. The revision of the law in 1997 has added the provision of mandating Type I carriers to agree to the interconnection when it is requested by other carriers (Article 38).

   The Ministry of International Trade and Industry (MITI), however, has made some recommendations regarding the review of the Telecommunication Business

Law that run counter to MPT's decision (Kawakita, 1985; Johnson, 1989). The main thrust of MITI's recommendations was to call upon the MPT to loosen its regulatory grip on the telecommunication industry. The trade ministry observed that the basic philosophy underlying the way MPT had implemented the Telecommunication Business Law over the first three years had been to protect new facility-based carriers from bankruptcy. The ministry claimed that this priority does not necessarily serve the users' interests. This concern was addressed by MITI because it wanted to improve the welfare of corporations, the large ones in particular, that come under its jurisdiction. In that MITI can hardly be seen as protecting the general consumers' interests.

Next to MPT, MITI also had some policy-making power in the field of telecommunications. MITI claims jurisdiction over a large number of industries including computers and data communication. MITI's early decision to include data communication under its umbrella led to a continuous turf battle between MITI and MPT. Another government agency that monitors the telecommunications industry is the FTC. The FTC will play a constructive role in overseeing the telecommunications industry now that competition has been introduced in this arena. Its main objective is to discourage anticompetitive practices.

Ban on simple resale of private lines for voice transmission   Services offered by Type II carriers are almost identical to the value-added network services as known in the US. In the legal framework of the Telecommunication Business Law, however, Type II carriers can offer any services they wish, including simple resale of leased circuits for voice communications. In view of NTT's current rate structure, the Diet concluded that this situation will endanger NTT's management (Kira, 1987). Thus, Type II carriers are prohibited to resell private lines for voice transmission purposes.

Nippon Telegraph and Telephone Corporation Law

On 1 April 1985 NTT's legal status was altered from a public corporation to a special joint-stock company partially owned by the government through the Ministry of Finance (MoF). As guaranteed in the NTT Corporation Law, the net worth of the public corporation – amounting to 5,213.7 billion yen ($34,7 billion) – was disposed of as new capital and reserves for NTT (*NTT Annual Report*, 1985). The NTT Public Corporation Law and the Public Telecommunications Law, both of which embraced NTT's monopoly in principle were abolished at the same time as NTT Corporation Law and the Telecommunications Business Law were enacted on 1 April 1985. Also, some provisions of the Commercial Code will be applied to the privatized NTT in dealing with the company's stocks. NTT's corporate status was changed from a public corporation to a joint-stock company. More specifically, at least one-third of the latter's shares should be owned by the government and the rest will have been sold to the public.

Prior to its privatization, NTT had been the monopolist in most domestic communications-service markets. There are some exceptions, however. The direct use of microwave frequencies has been permitted to some institutions, but only for their internal use.

Entry barriers

What determines the degree of market competition? Government regulation immediately comes to mind as a significant factor if one deals with industries such as public utilities. Either manifestly or latently, various governments have espoused monopoly. This posture has created an artificial barrier to entry. Even with the recent worldwide trend towards liberalizing telecommunications regulation, some entry barriers often remain albeit in different forms (Beesley, 1997; Vickers and Yarrow, 1997). One means of examining Japan's telecommunications market structure is to analyse the various barriers to entry. Where a sufficient number of firms have already entered the market, barriers of effective competition are examined. The list below sums up the possible barriers to entry or to effective competition:

- Regulation
- Network externalities
- Technical expertise/R & D capability (learning curve)
- Economies of scale
- Conglomeration
- Dominant carrier's anti-competitive behaviour.

Regulation

The MPT has been a strong advocate of telecommunications competition. Paradoxically, however, sometimes it has been a fierce enemy from the standpoint of potential entrants. Firms interested in entering markets such as automobile telephone, pocket pager, toll, and international services have felt that their initiatives were curtailed by the ministry.

For example, when two firms proposed to offer automobile telephone services, the ministry claimed that there were not enough frequencies available for both firms. MPT, then, instructed those Type I carriers to form a joint venture. The veracity of the claim is to be questioned since details of frequency allocation have not been made public. This action is an illustration of the ministry's lack of transparency in decision-making. MPT seemed to take the view that more vigorous competition could be expected if there were only one company, rather than two, to counter NTT in this market. The negotiation to merge two applicants' operations, however, went into a deadlock before MPT finally decided to allow both firms to enter the specialized market in the limited geographical areas – the Nagoya Osaka areas to be served by a subsidiary of Daini Denden (DDI) and the Tokyo area to be served by a subsidiary of Teleway Japan (a subsidiary of KDD in 1998). Then in 2000, KDD became KDDI by merger with DDI, a long-distance and mobile-services affiliate of Kyocera Corp. and IDO, a Toyota subsidiary selling mobile-telephone services.

Another issue that can be identified as an artificial barrier created by the Japanese government has to do with the supply-and-demand balance. As discussed earlier, an article in the Telecommunications Business Law provides the MPT with the authority to deny entry into a market if such a move would create excessive supply in any part of the country. Criticism mounted when an application by Satellite Japan – the third satellite company to register for Type I category – was rejected by the ministry.

The focus of the debate regarding this matter was MPT's criteria for screening applicants. With the backing of Sony – a major shareholder – Satellite Japan's proposal was very similar to, if not stronger than, in terms of its financial background, service offerings, and technical expertise, of the other two satellite firms previously granted certification. This led many in the industry to believe that the earlier an application is filed, the better the chances to obtain authorization.

MPT's role in maintaining the supply – demand balance is quite important. Excessive capacity in heavy-capital industry can produce negative consequences for competition. In the short term, the supply – demand imbalance in utilities may bring higher prices, shifts in market share, and falling earnings. In the long term the imbalance leads to more serious consequences. Firms in the market can be forced to write off part of their assets, go bankrupt, or merge with others until supply is reduced sufficiently to be in line with demand.

Nevertheless, the negative effects of excessive capacity do not automatically justify MPT's past actions to have deterred entry in markets such as automobile telephone, pocket pager, toll, and international services. MPT's actions – that is, deterring entries in those markets – resulted in indirectly strengthening the incumbents' (NTT or its international competitor Kokusai Denshin Denwa (KDD's)) positions. It is easy to suggest for MPT to improve their methods of forecasting the future demand for various services. In reality, however, it is almost impossible to obtain accurate demand forecasts for any services. More pragmatic suggestions for MPT would be to arrange some schemes (e.g. auctioning) so that new entrants can use the incumbent's facilities to offer the services whose supply would be excessive if new entrants build their own facilities in addition to those of the incumbent's that are already available.

Network externalities

A network externality is said to exist for a service when users for this service get higher benefit the more people are going to use it (Armstrong, 1997). As in other telecommunications markets the Japanese market is dominated by a major network provider, for example, NTT, and network externalities clearly favour a dominant player. This feature of the telecommunications market, together with the fact that it is costly for a user to be connected to more than one network clearly demonstrates why network interconnection is so important with regard to competition policy. For example, if there were two networks which were not interconnected then a firm supplying any telecoms service over the smaller network would be placed at a severe competitive disadvantage. It is therefore evident that a dominant carrier such as NTT clearly has a strategic advantage to facilitate network externalities within its own network and to defend their benefits by hindering interconnection to new entrants, by setting interconnection charges at a high level to deter competition and to bundle services within its own network and price them at a significant discount. High interconnection charges and high leased-line rates have often been identified as the cause for the slow growth of the Internet in some European countries and Japan.

Technical expertise and R & D capability (learning curve)

Firms go through different phases of their life cycle, and a learning curve can be drawn. In industries where rapid technological changes take place, such as telecommunications, it is rather difficult for new entrants to catch up with market leaders. The superiority of incumbents can manifest itself not only in the quality of products they offer, but also in lower cost of production. Advantages to early comers are multifold, thus they can function as a barrier to effective later competition.

Prior to privatization, NTT established a subsidiary, General Communications Engineering, to provide new facility-based carriers (i.e. Daini Denden, Japan Telecom, Teleway Japan) with much-needed technical assistance to get their businesses started. It generated some additional revenues for NTT while fulfilling the expectation of the FTC, which has been active in ensuring viable competition in telecommunications. This indicates a clear technical lag between NTT and the other three Type I carriers. Ever since three new toll carriers started to offer private-line services, there has been no perceptible difference in quality between non-NTT carriers and NTT. But concerns have been expressed about non-NTT Type I carriers not having much experience dealing with functional breakdown of networks. In order to respond to an emergency, such as power failure or technical difficulties, NTT and Daini Denden submitted to MPT an application to allow them to interconnect with each other's network as a back-up. A similar application had been filed with the telecommunications ministry by Teleway Japan and Japan Telecom. Being supportive of the efforts, the MPT has authorized these arrangements.

Four Type I carriers (Tokyo Telecom Network, Chubu Telecom, Osaka Media Port, and Kyushu Telecom Network), partially owned by regional electric power companies, are the exceptions. It is apparently easier to transfer knowledge from one network industry to another. In Japan much of the truly significant high-technology research (including computers and semi-conductors) has been done by a dozen NTT Telecommunications Laboratories. The corporation currently has 6,000 researchers of whom more than 400 have PhDs in engineering. The number of patents held by NTT is one indication of the depth and width of its research activities. Every year, since 1988, NTT registered or applied between 1,000 and 4,000 advanced technology patents, a level that no other telecommunications company in Japan can match.

The ratio of R & D expense of NTT's total operating expenditures was 4.2 per cent in fiscal year 1997. The corporation's projected R & D budget for the last five fiscal years has been ranging between 250 and 300 billion yen, much less than that invested by some of ex-'Denden family' companies (i.e. NEC, Fujitsu, and Hitachi) in Japan. Those corporations, it is to be noted, intensely research a variety of products, whereas NTT's laboratory research focuses on computer software and telecommunications.

Considering the capital investment and the number of employees required, the new facility-based carriers will not be able to afford large-scale R & D for some time to come. Lack of in-house R & D capabilities is likely to force some non-NTT carriers, Daini Denden, Japan Telecom, and Teleway Japan in particular, to limit their services to what NTT offers. As Noll (1985) has pointed out, the R & D of the dominant carriers can negatively affect competition. The problem for regulators is that the benefits of R & D are not product-specific; therefore, it is almost impossible to assign the costs to any particular service. NTT, maintaining R & D activities that dwarf its competitors, has been expected by both public sectors to set ambitious research agendas in order to position Japan prominently in the worldwide competition on computers and communications. It is a challenging task for MPT to sort out these conflicting objectives.

In any case, NTT's R & D superiority has not prevented entries into various telecommunications markets. It can be, however, a barrier to effective competition in the future. In this respect, four regional Type 1 carriers (Tokyo Telecom Network, Chubu Telecom Consulting, Osaka Media Port, and Kyushu Telecom Network) have a potentially important role to play since they (Tokyo Telecom Network in particular) have more advanced R & D resources.

Economies of scale

Rapid technological advances in telecommunications have encouraged new entrants into the long-monopolized field (InfoCom, 1996). Being latecomers, non-NTT carriers have been able to take advantage of efficient transmission and switching systems more quickly than NTT. It naturally takes longer for NTT to update its large-scale network, especially for the local loops.

Economies of scale have been given as a reason for maintaining monopoly in industries that require heavy sunk costs. If more than one firm provides the same service, subadditivity is said to occur. This concept implies that costs of supplying a certain level of output would be higher when two or more firms operate in the market as opposed to one (Baumol *et al.*, 1982). More recently, some economists have concluded that new technology has reduced the Minimum Efficient Scale (MES) and, in turn, it has had an influence on scale economies to be less of a barrier to entry. Kahn (1995) adds that rapid growth of various service demands has shifted market demand to the right (in the usual supply – demand chart whose vertical axis represents the price of products and the horizontal axis the quantity of production). Thus, the spread between MES and total market demand would create more opportunities for entry.

In Japan, can we state that (a) new technology has reduced the Minimum Efficient Scale, thus scale economies are less of a barrier to entry than before, and (b) rapid growth of various service demands has shifted market demand and created more opportunities for entry? The answers are definitely positive. Economies of scale in Japanese telecommunication networks do not seem to exist to the extent that they become too high a barrier for newcomers. However, the barrier might not be low enough for entrants to compete effectively with NTT in the long term. No statistics have been made available on this matter in Japan.

MPT's White Paper on Telecommunications (1999) indicates that NTT's number of circuits have grown from 58,780,000 (1993) to 60,380,000 (1997), but relatively have declined from more than double of the three Type-I toll NCC carriers (DDI, Japan Telecom, and Teleway Japan, now KDD) to only 60 per cent more, an indication that the NCCs have made some inroads though not to the extent that they clearly challenge NTT's dominant position.

Conglomeration (deep pockets)

Nippon Telegraph and Telephone offers the most diverse range of telecommunications services in Japan. Tokyo Electric Power Company comes closest to NTT in terms of diversity of service offerings (through subsidiaries) and of the level of invested capital in various telecommunications services. This electric utility could emerge as a substantial competitive force vis-à-vis NTT. Besides Tokyo Telecom Network, there are other communications subsidiaries of Tokyo Electric Power.

What is most significant about Tokyo Electric Power is that not only does it invest in these companies but also it provides them with its resources (technical know-hows, experienced engineers, land, and buildings). Gradually, the other regional electric utilities will follow the same path. This is the critical difference with the three long-haul toll carriers (DDI, JT, and TJ). It does not necessarily mean, however, that the latter cannot compete effectively with NTT in each sub-market just because they do not have as deep pockets as the latter, or as Tokyo Electric Power for that matter.

MPT's regulatory posture vis-à-vis the group of local and short-haul toll service carriers that includes Tokyo Telecom Network (TTNet) Chubu Telcom Consulting (CBC), Osaka Media Port (OMP), and Kyushu Telecom network could have serious implications for NTT. TTNet, for example, undertook digitization of its network earlier than NTT did. With their fibre-optics networks, these firms appeared in 1998 well positioned to enter the long-haul toll service markets.

These firms have requested MPT's authorization to interconnect their respective networks so as to become a single full-fledged long-haul toll carrier. Even though economies of scale enjoyed by NTT do not seem to be so great as to prevent new entrants, one cannot deny the fact that they exist. From this point of view, the proposed toll carrier can represent a very effective competition to NTT especially with its collective financial and technical strength. The ministry, however, has been reluctant to allow the formation of still another giant company to offer nationwide services in an effort to secure the viability of other common carriers providing long-haul toll services. When one considers the possibility of establishing a very powerful duopoly (NTT being one of the components), it seems to be appropriate for the MPT not to allow the electric utilities to form a nationwide telecommunications network.

It was not until April 1997 that MPT authorized the nine communications subsidiaries of the electric power companies to interconnect their respective network.

In October 2001 these regional carriers established a single full-fledged long-haul full services company, PoweredCom, and launched business all over Japan except the Okinawa region. The change in attitude by the authorities was brought about by the fact that NTT's monopolistic positions in telecommunications markets have not yet been dissolved when fifteen years have passed after the liberalization of the industry. The revenue share of NTT in the regional market was 92.3 per cent in 1998 and that in long-haul and international market was 41.7 per cent in 1999 (MPT Council).

Anti-competitive behaviour of dominant carriers

Even though anti-competitive behaviour can be categorized under market conduct, it is also a barrier to effective competition and thus affects market structure.

Since privatization, NTT has established some 170 subsidiaries. Two of them, Nippon Information and Communication Inc. (NI&C) with IBM, and Internet, a joint venture with computer manufacturers such as NEC and Fujitsu, provide Value Added Network (VAN) services. These companies' facilities are co-located in NTT's local-exchange plants, which give them advantages over other VANS providers in terms of access to local loops and facilities whose maintenance is ensured by NTT.

In the US the issue of equal interconnection has been addressed by the Federal Communications Commission (FCC). The commission coined terms such as comparatively efficient interconnection (CEI) to 'ensure that the basic service available to a carrier's enhanced services is available to other enhanced service providers in an equally efficient manner' and open network architecture (ONA) to 'provide service on the basis of relatively equal cost of interconnection to the bottleneck' (FCC, 1986: paras 154 and 203). Being aware of these developments, Internet and NI&C competitors will likely demand equally efficient interconnection. The point was underlined in 1995 when new carriers complained to MPT that NTT was hindering their efforts to introduce new services by refusing to agree terms for interconnection with NTT's local network. For example, Japan Telecom charged in 1995 that for more than two years NTT had prevented it from offering frame relay services by refusing to agree to conditions for interconnection (*FT*, 1995). More recently, 1998, the EU complained about high interconnection charges and rules governing the right to lay underground cables thereby obstructing competition in Japan's telecoms market. Apparently the fee charged by NTT is about 60–100 per cent higher than the mid-point of the EUs recommended range. Also the EU Commission noted that it was thirty times more expensive to lay cable in Tokyo than in London affecting twenty-eight different laws regulating rights of way, involving eleven different ministries (*FT*, 1999).

The FTC had previously warned NTT Equipment Sales Division not to engage in certain anti-competitive practices. For example, complaints have been filed to the FTC that some NTT sales representatives promised customers particular phone numbers provided that they purchase the company's telephones. Needless to say, this can be only done by companies such as NTT, which engage in both telephone sales and provision of telephone services. (These blatant anti-competitive practices have recently decreased in numbers, however.) Therefore, both the MPT and the FTC have instructed NTT to divest its Equipment Sales Division.

Research and development

Prior to privatization, NTT's priority was to conduct prestigious basic research in which specialists took great pride. Laboratories at NTT engaged in long-term research where profit maximization was not necessarily a priority. To keep an edge in the new competitive environment, NTT is adjusting its R & D agenda towards a better response to users' needs and more marketable products and services.

In the area of very large-scale integration (VLSI), NTT had succeeded in developing the 16-megabit Dynamic Random Access Memory (DRAM) in 1986, universally considered a technological breakthrough at the time. NTT strengthened its research in various applied research areas since privatization.

From these accomplishments it can be seen that NTT does not fit a characteristic that is often associated with monopolies or oligopolies – namely, reluctance to pursue innovations. In fact, NTT Public Corporation had been part of the modus operandi of Japan's concerted industrial policy on computers and telecommunications. The MITI has been credited worldwide for being the engine of rapid growth in the computer industry. NTT, nonetheless, has played a prominent role in supplying resources for technological advancement. So far, the new entrants into telecommunications service markets have not been able to initiate technological breakthroughs. In view of the large capital investment and the high number of employees required, most of the new facility-based carriers will not be able to afford large-scale R & D for some time to come. In this area NTT stands out, with some 5,000 R & D staff members in eleven different laboratories and an annual budget of over 500 billion yen (1997). But Type 1 carriers associated with electric utilities, such as Tokyo Telecom network, may represent a potential threat to NTT's technical superiority in the future.

Diversification

Nippon Telegraph and Telephone has not been selective enough to ensure the managerial integrity and profitability of its subsidiaries. On the one hand, the corporation seems to feel the need to expand its operation to the fullest extent at this point, but might withdraw from some of its unprofitable businesses at a later date. On the other hand, some of NTT's subsidiaries are targeting segments of the industry that NTT considers crucial to its future strategies. Those firms will not be dismantled unless they turn out to be financial disasters. It is probable that NTT's offsprings such as NI&C, Internetwork Inc., NTT Software Corporation, and NTT Tokyo Software Supply Co. would be in this group. The main business activities of those subsidiaries will be concentrated on the development of software to facilitate protocol conversion which is a big threat to other VAN service providers.

Productive efficiency and profitability

Has NTT's productive efficiency improved since privatization? If we take as base year 1986 with operating revenues (¥) 5,091,409 and employees 303,951 and benchmark it against 1997 with operating revenues (¥) 6,322,343 and employees 145,373 we have seen almost a doubling of productive efficiency. Indeed, this rise in labour productivity is attributed, to a substantial degree, to a separation of maintenance services for telecommunications facilities and equipment from NTT. It appeared that the twelve affiliated regional companies in charge of these services for NTT have been established since 1986 and NTT has transferred employees to these companies. For NTT group including these subsidiaries, the consolidated figure for operating revenues was (¥) 9,450,013 and the number of employees proved to be 226,000 in fiscal year 1997. Despite this, however, it can be said that NTT's performance has improved as a whole over recent years.

This finding most likely means that overall performance of the Japanese telecommunications industry has improved as well during the past four years since NTT commands dominant market shares in almost all submarkets.

Has diversity of services (provided either by the incumbent or by new entrants) increased since privatization? Since competition has been introduced in April 1985, telecommunications users definitely have been offered a broader range of services. NTT started to offer new services such as toll-free dialling and non-subscription voice mail. There are other services that have been offered by new carriers and out of which market NTT has stayed – multi-channel access services, teleterminal services, computer communications services (with an NTT subsidiary in the market). Even among services that have been offered before privatization, various new features have been added to cater for the more specialized needs of customers. All these are the positive by-product of competition. Many users, however, have expected more new services – for example, the Japanese version of optional calling plans such as AT&T Software Defined Network (SDN).

Another question is what is the extent of market power that the Japanese situation fits: a competitive market with a dominant supplier.

Overall, NTT is still by far the most dominant player, commanding at least 70–80 per cent in almost all the markets, even though a significant degree of competition is emerging in mobile communications (PHS, in particular) and personal computer communication services. NTT's market dominance and its superiority in R & D over other carriers will put the corporation in an advantageous position for a long time to come. It should be noted, nevertheless, that damages done to NTT in the private-line and toll-service markets by competition is more extensive than originally thought. Overall, three new toll carriers have siphoned away

5–6 per cent shares in these markets. Since NTT obtains more than 80 per cent of its total revenues from telephone services, this small erosion of market shares has a rather significant impact on the corporation.

International competition

In terms of 1996 annual revenues, NTT is the world's largest telecommunication service provider, almost three times as large as British Telecom (BT) and less than double that of Deutsche Telecom (DT). NTT is operating in an environment characterized by low regulation in domestic markets, but also low globalization due to continued government restrictions on international activities (Japan's MPT, 1996). With the enactment of the Telecommunications Business Law in 1985, barriers to foreign entry into Japan's terminal equipment market were lowered and new carriers were allowed to enter the market. Type I carriers provide telecommunication networks requiring significant investments in infrastructure and continue to be regulated by MPT. Type I carriers must get the permission of MPT to offer their services and must obtain authorization for its tariffs, their content, user rights, and user restrictions. Type II telecommunication carriers are not involved in transmission and only require approval when providing intermediate communication services (Takano, 1992).

Three new carriers (DDI, Japan Telecom, and Teleway Japan) have entered the Type I long-distance business with backing from companies such as Sony, Kyocera, Japanese National Railways, and Japan Highway Public Corporation. New fibre-optic lines were laid along the power company's, national railway's, and national highway's right-of-way. Initially, foreign telecommunication firms were limited to 30 per cent participation in Type I carriers. For example, Hughes Communications Inc. invested 30 per cent in Japan Communication Satellite Co. as a Type I business. In spite of this limitation the new competitors have obtained over 50 per cent share of the communications-intensive Tokyo–Nagoya–Osaka belt and one-third of international communications by 1993. MPT initiated this shift by setting new carrier rates 30 per cent below NTT's rates. In seven years rates have dropped four times, from 400 to 200 yen for a three-minute call using NTT, and from 300 to 180 yen for the same service using new carriers. As a result, NTT's revenues remained flat between 1987 and 1993 as ordinary profits fell by over 70 per cent, from early 497 billion yen to 109 billion yen.

By mid-1991, sixty-seven new entrants were providing Type I long-distance, rural, mobile, and international telecommunication services. In October of 1993 MPT allowed the new common carriers to lower prices below all of NTT's rates. NTT had attempted to raise local telephone rates to offset the declining profits from long distance, but finally cut its rates to stay competitive. MPT rejected local-rate hikes (until recently), arguing that better utilization of NTT's current infrastructure would generate additional profits (Maeno, 1993).

Type II telecommunications carriers are those that are not involved in transmission and therefore do not require registration. They can offer communications services such as telephone, facsimile, telex, and VAN services, but do not provide network facilities. By 1992 there were nearly 1,000 new competitors. Japan Motorola Ltd., joined Tokyo Telemessage to offer pocket-pager services. Daini-Denden Ind. (DDI), Kansai Cellular Telephone Co., Ltd, and Nippon Ido Tsushin Inc. all introduced the Motorola cellular telephone system. IBM Japan, AT&T, and McDonnell Douglas have all entered Type II businesses (InfoCom, 1996).

In search of new markets and to respond to competitive pressures, NTT developed a plan to meet the future needs of its markets.

NTT were to add new VI & P (visual, intelligent, personal) telecommunication services in response to competition's more convenient and easier-to-use-services. Advanced VI & P services included: visual telecommunication services utilizing advanced image-processing technologies like high-definition video communications that provide clear text and 3-D graphics on life-size screens; intelligent services utilizing advanced information-processing functions for automatic translation and coded communications for secure secretarial services; and personal services like selective call forwarding for improved call blocking and communications.

MPT prohibited NTT from participating directly in international markets until 1992. Previously, Japan's telecommunication business had been divided between domestic and international services since the Second World War. KDD (Kokusai Denshin Denwa Kaisha) had been Japan's international telecommunications carrier. Internationally, NTT had been limited to consulting-type services through subsidiaries. Japan's MITI had argued that such regulations needed to be revised to allow telecommunication carriers to offer both domestic and international services. With the globalization of today's corporations, MITI argued that international information networks were needed and that MPT's regulations were limiting new carriers from responding to such market forces (Callon, 1995; Friedman, 1988).

Now with NTT bound to follow the fate of AT&T in the eighties, within the construction of a holding company, to be split into two regional NTTs with a third subsidiary free to expand internationally we are now, seeing a full-scale expansion of NTT in the international arena (Takashima *et al.*, 1997).

In the area of consulting type services NTT was already able to by-pass these regulatory restrictions. It established in 1985 NTT International Corporation (NTTI) to promote international business through telecommunication consulting activities. NTT Data Communications System Corporation, and NTT PC Communications Incorporated also are operating overseas. NTT had established an internal 'Department of International Business' to more aggressively pursue orders to establish overseas telecommunications networks.

NTT plans for its future core business to include telephone, textmail, value-added internet services, and visual-telephone services. Telephones using voice communication will emphasize 'pocket-phones' and 'pagers'. NTT has already introduced digital cellular networks, lightweight pocket phones (PHS), and 'wristwatch' pagers, with double-digit growth rates and more since 1993, though profit growth was less satisfactory. Textmail includes communications of characters and still image with on-line storage and retrieval capabilities. With the growing communications capabilities of ISDN, textmail will increase in importance.

The visual telephone provides image-based face-to-face communications and is expected to grow with the installation of broadband ISDN.

NTT has been held back by stifling regulations through MPT which has put it far behind other national carriers such as BT and the 'Baby Bells' in the US. Though it has taken some minor investments in small Asian telecoms, it really could not pursue an international strategy as becoming part of joint ventures.

In 1991 NTT began restructuring its organization to respond to the rapid changes in the industry. Lines of responsibility for each business segments were clarified and staff activities rationalized. The new staff structure unified the strategic planning activities for the company. Operations began being pushed out to the regional branch offices in hopes that more decentralized operations would allow NTT to respond more rapidly to growing local competition. But the organization is still technology and service-based rather than focusing on the type of customer. NTT's fast-growing mobile communications business (DoCoMo) was decentralized into regional companies. In July 1992, DoCoMo was separated from NTT as an independent company and was listed in the first division of the Tokyo Stock Exchange. After divestiture in 1998 the NTT holding company owned 67 per cent of the shares. It still keeps 64.06 per cent as of September 2001.

Revisions to the NTT Act, the KDD Act, and the Telecommunications Carriers Act, enacted in 1997, established a legal framework aimed at stimulating competition in the telecommunications sector. The revised NTT Act allowed KDD to enter the domestic communications market, and the revised KDD Act allowed NTT to compete in the international market. As a result, KDD commenced its domestic telephone service in mid-1998. The revision to the Telecommunications Carriers Act abolished restrictions on foreign capital investment in Type I carriers in the industry. These restrictions had served to protect the domestic telecommunications industry by forbidding foreign companies from becoming Type I designated carriers. The restrictions were abolished as part of Japan's response to the current environment of international deregulation.

Summarizing, NTT has responded to technological changes and market demands by attempting to develop new services. However, there are growing questions as to whether NTT can build Japan's next-generation digital communication network to support those services. Japan's MoF is unwilling to use public funds for the project, and NTT may be too weak to finance it alone. MITI is pushing for it, but MPT feels it cannot trust NTT to build it. During the bureaucratic squabbling, NTT announced that 'as long as there is capital, we can do it with our own hands just as we have always done' (InfoCom, 1996). It remains to be seen if such promises can still be kept. With growing domestic competition in all segments of the market, NTT's financial performance is at risk. As a result, efforts to pursue operations abroad will likely continue.

Conclusions

Despite the specific features of Japanese deregulation of the telecommunications sector that play to NTT's advantage we can clearly show that NTT is learning fast to play along the (new) information rules of network economies (Shapiro and Varian, 1999) which they can use to enhance or hold on to their strategic edge but also could make them vulnerable to fast pace change in technology and markets.

Various factors that might create entry barriers have been examined. These features are quite important in shaping the market environment that influence the rivalry among buyers and sellers.

As has been shown, government regulation can be a possible entry barrier. An article in the Telecommunications Business Law provides the MPT with the authority to deny entry into a market if such a move would create excessive supply in any part of the country. To maintain a balance between supply and demand of telecommunications services is an important undertaking. Imbalance can lead to serious consequences. Firms in the market can be forced to write off part of their assets, go bankrupt, or merge with others until supply is reduced sufficiently to be in line with demand.

On the other hand, deterring new companies to enter markets usually results in strengthening incumbents' positions, which has actually occurred in some Japanese telecommunication markets. A better alternative that MPT can adopt would be to arrange some schemes (e.g. auctioning) so that new entrants can use the incumbent's facilities to offer the services whose supply would be excessive if new entrants were to build their own facilities in addition to those of the incumbent's that are already in use.

Examining sales figures over the past years, brand loyalty to NTT seems much less prominent in recent years compared to the period immediately following NTT's privatization. The service quality and lower-price offerings by new Type I carriers seem to have swayed many large users. Also, other factors that encourage users to stay with NTT are gradually disappearing, for example, the limited geographical coverage by new entrants.

In industries associated with rapid technological advances, such as telecommunications, it is rather difficult for new entrants to catch up with market leaders. The superiority of incumbents can manifest itself not only in the quality of the products they offer (as a result of advanced R & D), but also in lower cost of production. Advantages to early comers are multifold, and can thus function as a barrier to effective competition for an extended period of time.

Technical specifications and business plans of NTT's network operations have been proprietary. Yet, the dominant carrier knows details of its Type 1 competitors' business plans (e.g. number of subscribers, their location, where and when they expand their services, etc.) because the latter has to depend on NTT for local connection. To be on an equal footing, those new carriers should be allowed to have access to the same information from NTT. The Ministry of Posts and Telecommunications is currently negotiating with NTT in order to make public more detailed business-related information. Proprietary information is another barrier to effective competition.

In the past, economies of scale have often been considered a barrier to entry specially regarding telecommunication markets. More recently in Japan as elsewhere in the West, new technologies have reduced the Minimum Efficient Scale, thus scale economies are less of a barrier to entry than before; and rapid growth of various service demands has shifted market demand and created more opportunities for entry. To precisely measure the degree of scale economies that NTT enjoys, detailed engineering studies have to be conducted. In the absence of elaborate cost studies, the tentative conclusion seems to be that economies of scale exists in Japanese telecommunication networks. They do not seem to be too high an entry barrier to deter new entrants. However, they might not be low enough for entrants to compete effectively with NTT on a long term.

Nippon Telegraph and Telephone offers the most diverse range of telecommunications services in Japan. This high degree of conglomeration might function as a barrier to effective competition. Tokyo Electric Power Company comes closest to NTT in terms of diversity of service offerings (through subsidiaries) and of the level of invested capital in various telecommunications services. As a major subsidiary of Tokyo Electric Power Company, Tokyo Telecom Network (TT Net) will have access to the parent company's resources. TT Net has been requesting the MPT to allow the formation of a single nationwide toll carrier through interconnection with its sister companies in other regions – Chubu Telecom Consulting (CBC), Osaka Media Port (OMP), and Kyushu Telecom Network.

The MPT's regulatory posture vis-à-vis this group of local and short-haul toll-service carriers could have serious implications for NTT and other new Type I carriers TT Net. With their fibre optics networks, these firms are well positioned to enter the long-haul toll-service markets.

Even though economies of scale enjoyed by NTT do not seem to be so great as to prevent new entrants, one cannot deny the fact that they exist. From this point of view the proposed toll carrier can represent a very effective competition to NTT especially with its collective financial and technical strength. The ministry, however, has been reluctant to allow the formation of still another giant company to offer nationwide services in an effort to secure the viability of other common carriers providing long-haul toll services. When one considers the possibility of establishing a very powerful duopoly (NTT being one of the components) and its anti-competitive effect, the MPT is making an appropriate move by not allowing the electric utilities to form a nationwide telecommunications network.

References

Armstrong, M. (1997) 'Competition in Telecommunications', *Oxford Review of Economic Policy* 13(1): 64–82

Baumol, W., J. C. Panzar and Robert D. Willig (1982), *Contestable Markets and the Theory of Market Structure*, New York: Harcourt Brace Jovanovich

Beesley, M. E. (1997) *Privatisation, Regulation and Deregulation*, London: Routledge, 2nd edition, chaps 14–16

Callon, S. (1995) *Divided Sun: MITI and the Breakdown of Japanese High Tech Industrial Policy*, Stanford: Stanford University Press

Federal Communications Commission (FCC) (1986), Computer Inquiry III, Notice of Proposed Rulemaking, Washington, DC, mimeo

Financial Times (*FT*) (1999) 'EU challenges Japan over Telecoms Deregulation', 24 February, 4

Friedman, D. B. (1988) 'The Misunderstood Miracle: Industrial Development and Political Change in Japan', Ithaca, New York : Cornell University Press

InfoCom Research (1996), *Information & Communications in Japan 1996*, Tokyo, March

Ito, Y. (1986) 'Telecommunications and Industrial Policies in Japan: Recent Developments', in M. S. Snow (ed.), *Marketplace for Telecommunications; Regulation and Deregulation in Industrial Democracies*, New York: Longman

Johnson, C. A. (1989) 'MITI, MPT, and the Telecom Wars: How Japan Makes Policy for High Technology', in C. Johnson, L. Tyson, and J. Zysman (eds), *Politics and Productivity: How Japan's Development Strategy Works* 177–240, New York: Harper

Kahn, A. (1995) *Economics of Regulation*, Cambridge: MIT Press

Kawakita, T. (1985) *Tsusan Yusei Senso* (MITI–MPT War), Tokyo: Kyoikusha

Kira, M. (1987) 'Where to put the Smarts: Network or CPE?', Center for Information Policy Research, Harvard University, July

Maeno, K. (1993) 'Information Superhighway Japanese Style', *Journal of Japanese Trade and Industry* 4: 41–61

MPT, Ministry of Posts and Telecommunications (1996) 'Communications in Japan', White Paper, Tokyo

MPHPT, Ministry of Public Management, Home Affairs, Posts and Telecommunications (2001), White Paper, Tokyo

Nogami, Y. and C. Prestowitz (1992) *Competition and Cooperation in Telecommunications between Japan and the United States*, Center for International Studies, Cambridge, MA: MIT, MITJSTP 87–10

Noll, R. G. (1985) *Regulatory Policy and the Social Sciences*, Berkeley: Univ. of California Press

——and F. M. Rosenbluth (1995) 'Telecommunications Policy: Structure, Process, Outcomes', in P. Cowhey and M. McCubbins (eds), *Structure and Policy in Japan and the United States* 119–176, Cambridge: Cambridge University Press

NTT (1985) *Annual Report*, Tokyo: Government Printing Office

Shapiro, Carl and Hal R. Varian (1999), *Information Rules, A Strategic Guide to the Network Economy*, Boston: Harvard Business School Press

Takano, Yoshiro (1992), *Nippon Telegraph and Telephone Privatization Study*, World Bank Discussion Papers 179, World Bank, Washington, DC

Takashima, M., H. W. Gottinger and C. Umali (1997) *Economics of Global Telecommunication and the Internet*, Research Report, Nagasaki University, March

Vickers, J. and G. Yarrow (1997) *Privatization: An Economic Analysis*, Cambridge: MIT Press

Appendix B   Network size, value, and cycles

Introduction

One of the most striking economic aspects of networks is how they create externalities. Network externalities occur in both the demand and supply of the network. The textbook externality is a supply externality. For example, as a negative by-product of a factory's production, pollution spews into the air or water. Demand externalities, on the other hand, may exist for non-network goods, but they are not usually considered important enough to merit attention. For example, economists typically do not factor demand externalities into consumers' demand functions. Many models of consumer behaviour assume that the average consumer's demand for potatoes, lettuce, corn, etc., for example, are formed without any reference to how many other people are purchasing these products. Certainly the number of consumers in a given market affects demand and therefore price, but an individual's demand is independent – it does not depend directly on a product's popularity in most models. Such effects are assumed away as insignificant.

Besides the supply-side economies of scale the demand-side economies of scale are commonly seen in the communications and computer industries among others. For some goods and services, a person's demand depends on the demands of other people, or the number of other people who have purchased the same good may affect a person's demand. For example, the buyer of a telephone or fax machine would have not bought it if there were no one else who had purchased or would have purchased it. When more people have purchased it the more value of a telephone or fax machine the buyer would have obtained. This is a positive network externality based on an 'actual' or 'physical' network. Moreover, for some goods, such as Microsoft Office, the individual demand for that good inherently exists but enormously increases when other people buy the same good. In an actual network, products have very little or no value when alone, they generate value or more value when combined with others (example: fax machine). In a virtual network, hardware/software network products have value even if they exist alone. However, they are more valuable when there are more complementary goods, and also there will be more complementary goods when more people use the products. Application software developers are likely to write for the platform of the operating system that most people favour. Conversely, the operating system that more application software writes on are favoured by more people. The operating system with a larger market share will provide a bigger market for the application programs. At the same time, the availability of a broader array of application programs will reinforce the popularity of an operating system which in turn will make investment in application programs compatible with that operating system more desirable than investment in application programs compatible with other less-popular systems. As a result, the operating system with a larger installed base attracts more buyers whereas the small and later entrant with a smaller installed base with equal or even superior quality finds it difficult to compete. As more users are attracted to a network, the size of the network grows and confers greater value to the network users. Network effects directly challenge an important principle of classical economic theory, which posits decreasing (and eventually negative) returns to scale in most markets. Also this theory basically deals with increasing returns problems in case of supply-side economies of scale but ignores cases of demand-side economies of scale brought about by increasing value of existing users through increased demand, that is, through network externalities. That is, network markets offer increasing returns over a large portion of the demand curve or even the entire demand curve. Markets with increasing returns imply that bigger is better and consumers deriving more value as the number of users grows. The flip side of this situation in terms of market structure is that the strong grow stronger and the weak become weaker.

Hence, network markets provide potentially fruitful returns to firms that can make their own products as standards in markets or in aftermarkets for complementary goods. This presents the possibility of substantial first-mover advantages: being the first seller in a market may confer an important strategic advantage over later entrants because a first mover's technology may become locked in as a standard (Katz and Shapiro, 1986; Arthur, 1989). That is to say, the first technology that is introduced into the market may gain excess momentum when many early users join in anticipation of other users hopping on the bandwagon at a later date. This strong expectation is critical to network expansion (Choi, 1994). In the end consumers already belonging to an existing network will not likely switch to a new technology, even if it is better (Economides, 1996).

The switching costs associated with transferring to an incompatible but superior technology create 'excess inertia' to consumers. That means consumers will not adopt a new superior technology not only because of the sunk costs they have already put in but also because values from network externalities may be lost if they switch. Network effects, therefore, could stifle innovation.

In a traditional market, where network effects are negligible or non-existent, competition turns primarily upon price, quality, and service considerations. In contrast, in those markets in which network effects are significant, competition plays out in other dimensions as well: particularly in strategies to establish, maintain, and control standards for the industry. The computer industry hence suggests that network effects have played an important role in shaping the market structure and the margins on which competition occurs.

Also, increasing returns raise the possibility of leveraging a monopoly power from one market to another. Because users may be reluctant to commit to any given system unless they believe it will be adopted by many others, the 'network owner' may engage in a variety of strategies to discourage potential buyers from buying a smaller network regardless whether or not it is superior. Strategies include expanding the system to include complementary products offering a wide variety of complementary products at very attractive prices or through bundling. At the same time, leveraging is able to raise rivals' economic costs of competing in the marketplace.

For example, in its effort to be adopted as the next generation standard, the owner of one element of a system may enter complementary markets by engaging in alliances as part of a strategy of attracting users to its network. Consequently, rival operating systems need to ensure the provision of substantial complementary products in the market, otherwise very few buyers will try its system. As a result, the follow-on improved or complementary products markets become very difficult.

Strong network effects are therefore themselves barriers to entry, even though it is sometimes unclear whether entry into the market ought to be encouraged since increasing returns deter the incentive of new entrants and increase the costs of new entrants. Such a blunting of incentives can occur if the leveraging practice is undertaken, not primarily as part of a vigorous competitive strategy, but in part to decrease the likelihood of competitor entry, so that the dominant firm will continue to be dominant in competition for the next market. This has clearly been shown for the Japanese telecommunications market (Gottinger and Takashima, 2000). The unlikelihood of success for new entrants will reduce the incentives of other competitors to innovate to the extent that these competitors perceive that the opportunities to profit from their innovations are hindered. All of this is particularly significant because markets in which there is rapid technological progress are often markets in which switching costs are high, in which users find it costly to switch to a new technology that is not fully compatible with the older technology. The result is an increase in entry barriers.

From what follows the definition of a network externality is given by the value of a network created by the number of its nodes. Also, network externalities can exist both for the supply and demand side of the economic equation. And networks can generate negative, positive, or no externalities. Network externality networks are those that decrease in value when the number of nodes increases. More 'traditional' network industries fit into this category.

Perspectives on network externalities

We start with a useful distinction suggested by Economides (1996) in his survey of the literature. He divides the work on network externalities into what he calls macro and micro approaches. Macro investigations assume that externalities exist and then attempt to model their consequences. Micro investigations start with market and industry structures in an attempt to derive (theoretically) the source of network externalities. The later category is largely founded on case studies. Three of those are symptomatic. David's (1985) QWERTY study, Arthur's (1989) model, and the domination of VHS in the videotape recorder market combined, spurred theoretical and empirical interest in network externalities. The gist of

David's QWERTY study is that inferior technologies through network externalities may be subject to 'lock-ins'. This might apply to the keyboard QWERTY as well as to the adoption of the VHS against the Betamax standard though with specific technological advantages of Betamax over VHS. In empirical support of network externalities, Gandal (1994) finds that consumers pay a premium for spreadsheets which are compatible with Lotus 1-2-3 (an industry standard for spreadsheets). In other words, consumers are willing to pay for the ability to share spreadsheet information and analysis easily with other computer users. Thus he concludes that there is strong empirical support for the existence of network externalities in the computer spreadsheet market. In another paper, Saloner and Shepard (1995) test for the existence of network externalities in the network of Automated Teller Machines (ATMs), their results support existence.

Hypotheses on network externalities

Perhaps it is not surprising that little quantitative work on network externalities has been done. Many examples of network industries embody cutting-edge technologies, given that theoretical work on network externalities is still relatively new, data collection is fragmentary, and common-data sets upon which to test theories are severely limited. One particular important question emerging on network externalities is the functional relationship between the size of a network (its number of nodes) and the network's value.

Three key assumptions about the relationship between network size and network value underlie most analyses of network externalities and their effects. They relate to linear, logarithmic, and exponential assumptions.

The linear assumption postulates that, as networks grow, the marginal value of new nodes is constant. The logarithmic assumption postulates that, as a network grows, the marginal value of new nodes diminishes. Network externalities at the limit in this formulation must be either negative, zero, or of inconsequential magnitude in comparison to quantity effects on prices. In contrast, Katz and Shapiro (1986) make their assumptions explicit: network externalities are positive but diminish with development, at the limit they are zero. In any case, network effects diminish in importance in these models as a network grows. The third key assumption about the relationship between network size and value is the exponential assumption which in the popular business and technology press has been named 'Metcalfe's Law'. It embodies the idea of positive network externalities whose marginal value increases with network size. Robert Metcalfe (1995) states the 'law' in this way: 'In a network of N users, each sees a value proportional to the $N-1$ others, so the total value of the network grows as $N(N-1)$, or as N squared for large N'. The validity of Metcalfe's Law is crucial to the 'increasing returns' debate on the New Economy, facilitated by the aggregation of positive network externalities in high-tech industries. One could also consider a mixture of hypotheses such as a combination of Metcalfe's Law and the logarithmic assumption, that is early additions to the network add exponentially to the value of a network, yet later additions diminish in their marginal value. The result looks like an S curve, as illustrated (Figures B.1 and B.2). It is based on the idea that

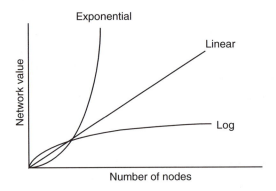

Figure B.1 Three assumptions of the network size/value relationship.

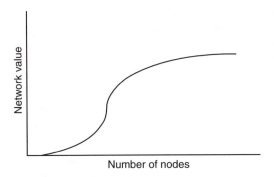

Figure B.2 The S-hypothesis.

early additions to a network are extremely valuable, but at some point 'network saturation' should take place and marginal value should fall.

In summary, the industry and hence aggregate (growth) benefits can be classified as follows:

(i)   industries that show an exponential growth (through strong complementarity)
(ii) industries that show linear growth (additive benefits)
(iii) industries that show a log relationship (stable benefits).

The mixtures of those economies create the features and the extent of the new economy. Such an economy is not immune to economic cycles, but to the extent that the network economy snowballs in an upswing period, by the same token it might also along the supply chain contract faster in a downswing period but with a better chance to stabilize quicker. As the *Wall Street Journal* worried about the state of the US economy by the end of 2000, it referred to timeless quotes by Allen Greenspan. 'Ultimately, Mr Greenspan contends, the aspects of new business technology that helped lift productivity and bring about the boom will also help the economy to bounce back more quickly. Now some fear the New Economy which fueled the boom could also deepen a bust' (Ip *et al.*, 2001). This emphasizes the strong cyclicity of the network economy reinforced by network size and value.

Technology adoption, network industries, and network effects

We look at the main hypotheses as how they are likely to affect the adoption process of particular network industries. The linear hypothesis is the assumption of Arthur's (1989) model subject to simulation. Given a very large number of trials, technology adoption leads (almost surely) to lock-ins. Given two technologies, *A* and *B*, further *R* and *S* agents that make adoption decisions, respectively, in Arthur's model each trial represents a random walk of an ever-increasing number of *R* and *S* agent decisions. As the number of trials increases, with symmetries in both technologies *A* and *B*, the split between *A* and *B* adoptions approach fifty-fifty. That is, either one of them will be adopted, and non-adoption will be most unlikely. In Arthur's analytical model, as the number of iteration goes to infinity, the possibility of non-adoption disappears.

Correspondingly, the average adoption time until lock-in will increase with decreasing probability (of non-adoption), in conformity with the linear hypothesis, in other words, more agents become (linearly) more convinced to adopt either way. This suggests that the network effect leaves only a neutral impact on the innovation process. Against this benchmark, when the value of network size grows logarithmically in relation to its size, the average time until lock-in occurs is extended. What appears surprising is how much the logarithmic assumption delays lock-in. That is, the logarithmic specification creates less growth prospects and greater instability by delaying (or preventing) adoption from occurring. In contrast to the logarithmic hypothesis, the exponential assumption shortens the average time until adoption occurs. The average adoption is affected just as drastically by the exponential assumption as by the logarithmic one. With the exponential assumption, however, the average adoption occurs much earlier than in the baseline case. No wonder, that on an aggregate scale across network industries, it is this network effect that lends support to 'increasing returns' by the proponents of the New Economy. It can even be reinforced by speed of transactions, for example, enabled through large-scale broadband internet technologies. This would support a scenario of a sustained realization of an exponential assumption as even more likely. If it can be established that the Internet triggers a technology adoption process in the form of a large and broad wave ('tsunami') across key industries, sectors, regions, and countries, then increasing returns will generate exceptional growth rates for many years to come. For this to happen there should be a critical mass of network industries being established in an economy. Then an innovation driven network economy feeds on itself with endogenous growth. It remains to be determined, empirically, which mix of sectors, given network effects with exponential, linear, and logarithmic relationships will have a sustained endogenous growth cycle.

From a slightly different perspective, it is interesting to note that the logarithmic assumption creates instability in the models. Metcalfe's Law, on the other hand, which leads to immediate adoption, creating a dynamics of its own, would prevent many contemporary models from reaching equilibrium.

Networked industrial organization

The development of the Internet and its use for business transactions, B2B or B2C, would make a good subject for the analysis of business cycles for several reasons. First, the Internet might constitute a formal mapping of business transactions for a networked economy, or major parts of their industries. Second, the Internet itself can be modelled and designed as a set of transactions among various agents, consumers, network suppliers, and services, that reflect the size and complexity of a distributed computing system (Chapter 8). That is, the Internet provides prototypical examples of a positive network externality industry. Unfortunately, the Internet is 'too recent' to make it an eligible candidate for a statistical study on the value of a network. Instead we use the US telecommunications network over the past fifty years. There are some intuitive reasons. In many industry studies, where positive network externalities are defined, Economides (1996) and the *The Economist* (1995), telecommunications is named as the signature network industry. The telecommunications industry is somehow described as a 'typical' network industry that makes it a logical place to begin a search for empirical evidence. Due to its structural similarity with other network industries like railroads, airlines, and the Internet, conclusions reached about network externalities in the communications system are arguably applicable to all of the rest.

In correspondence to the classifications (i) to (iii) in the section on 'Hypotheses on network externalities' we would venture the hypothesis that (i) exponential growth would likely be associated with an emerging, broadly based advanced technological, strongly growing network industry, (ii) a linear relationship would be tantamount to a maturing, structurally stable industry, while (iii) a logarithmic shape would go with a technologically mature, well-established industry.

The weighting of factors (i)–(iii) would characterize the scope and degree of a new economy, the higher the share of (i) and possibly (ii) the stronger the scope of a New Economy, though a sizable share of (i)–(iii) would form the basis of a New Economy.

We conjecture that the higher (i) and (ii) in a sizable share of (i)–(iii) the stronger the cyclicity of the economy and the higher the volatility of movements.

Regression specification

Regression analysis can test the three hypotheses about the relationship between network size and network value. Determining 'network value' is an obvious difficulty for empirical research done on network externalities. Gandal (1994) addresses the issue of network value by analysing prices: evidence of a price premium for products with a large network indicates that consumers value network externalities positively. The price approach, however, would be flawed if applied to the US telephone network due to its heavy regulation from the 1920s through the 1982 divestiture of AT&T. An alternative approach in such a regulated environment is to observe network usage as a proxy for network value, with greater network usage indicating greater network value.

Based upon conventional economic theory and ideas about network externalities, there are six variables which are likely to determine use of the US telephone network and which should therefore be considered in a regression analysis: (1) network size (number of nodes); (2) price of using the network; (3) the price of substitute services; (4) the population; (5) income; and (6) investment in the telephone network. Each of these variables can be quantified either through data that US telephone companies report or through standard statistical measures of the US population and economy: network size is recorded in the number of telephones active in a given year; average prices for the telephone and its major historical substitute (the telegraph or later the fax) can be derived from company operating revenues; telephone-system capital investment is tracked: and population and income are standard data kept by the US government. Moreover, network usage can be quantified as the number of telephone conversations per year.

Ad hoc conjecture, based upon standard economic logic, argues for the following predicted signs. Average price of a telephone call should be negatively correlated with network use. Population, income, capital investment, and average price of telephone substitutes should be positively correlated with telephone network use. These predictions are summarized in Table B.1.

The sign of the relationship between network size and usage, of course, is the primary focus. Two methods for specifying and testing the hypotheses regarding network size and usage could be used. The first method specifies a separate model for each hypothesis and then compares the fit of each model to the data. The second method uses a model general enough that any of the three hypotheses could be valid, and then uses the estimated beta coefficients to determine the most likely specification. We use the latter method because the model specifications necessary for the

Table B.1 Regression variables and predicted signs

Variable	Proxy	Data	Expected sign
Network value (dependent)	Network Usage	Number of phone conversations/year	
Network size		Number of 'telephone sets'	Positive[*]
Price of network use		Average cost of phone call	Negative
Substitute goods' price		Average cost of telegram	Positive
Income		Real GDP	Positive
Telephone system Investment		Capital Investment/year	Positive
Regulatory change	Dummy		

Note
* See text for more detail on the expected sign of the network size variable.

first method would be difficult to compare on the basis of fit (specifically, using a logarithmic transformation makes comparison to untransformed data problematic).

The second more general method requires that the variable's specification must be flexible enough to produce any of the functional forms of the hypotheses. Thus we use a polynomial equation to evaluate the relationship between network size and usage. Given a polynomial of sufficient degree, any functional form can be reproduced. Equation (1) shows the general form of the regression model, where y is the dependent variable and the bs represent the beta coefficients.

$$y = a + b_1 \text{ size} + b_2 \text{ size}^2 + b_3 \text{ size}^3 + b_4 P\text{phone} + b_5 \, P\text{tel} \\ + b_6 \text{GDP} + b_7 \text{ Dummy} + \cdots \tag{1}$$

Population does not appear as a separate variable in this formulation because all non-price variables have been transformed to per capita measures.

Estimation of the beta coefficients in equation (1) should yield evidence as to which of the hypotheses most accurately represents the relationship and value in the telephone network. For example, if b_1 is significantly while b_2 and b_3 are not significantly different from zero, this evidence would support the linear hypothesis (ii). In contrast, if b_2 were the only positive and significant coefficient, this would lend support to the assumptions of Metcalfe's Law.

The logarithmic and S-shape hypotheses could be simulated through several combinations of positive and negative coefficients among the polynomial terms, but a mixture of signs coupled with significant coefficients for the higher-order polynomial terms could argue for either the logarithmic or S-shape hypotheses. In any case, examining the signs of the variables will serve as both a check for consistency of the model specification against theoretical expectations and as an argument for which hypothesis best fits the data.

Econometric issues   One potential problem of working simultaneously with a dependent variable like network usage and the independent variables of network size, income, and network investment is that these variables are likely to trend upward together. The similar growth patterns of these four variables can then make it awkward to disentangle the effects of each independent variable on variation in the dependent variable. Such a situation may also tend towards the presence of heteroskedacity and serial correlation. Three measures are taken here to guard against the potential problems of working with these time series. First, we add a lagged dependent variable to the independent terms to remove significant time trends. Second, we perform the regression on both the untransformed dependent variable and its natural log to check for significant potential problems with residuals. And third, we use the Durbin–Watson and Cook–Weisberg tests to check for serial correlation and heteroskedasticity.

Regression results

The regression results overall support the linear assumption of (ii) although there is some evidence that the exponential assumption of (i) is valid for a group of new network industries. During the course of the analysis we tested several versions of the regression model. These versions varied primarily in the number of network-size polynomial terms (models with up to the fifth-order polynomials were tested), the inclusion of a lagged dependent variable, and in the inclusion of interaction terms. The need to correct for a strong time trend and the existence of serial correlation and/or heteroskedacity in early model specifications led to the inclusion of a lagged dependent variable and the use of the Cochrane–Orcutt procedure. Also the investment variable was dropped from the model because of multicollinearity problems as it correlated nearly perfectly with the variable measuring network size.

Table B.2 presents the full regression equation with estimated coefficients, standard errors of the coefficients, and *t*-statistics.

The full regression shows mixed results with two outstanding points. First, the linear, squared, and cubic terms of network size are significant at the respective confidence levels of 1, 5, and 10 per cent.

This indicates some non-linearity in the relationship between network size and value. Second, the other explanatory variables in this specification covering income and substitution effects are not significant.

These regression results are not especially convincing, given the lack of significance for all price variables, but this regression serves as a useful stepping stone in the econometric analysis. The important piece of information to glean from this full regression is the estimated relationship between network size and value derived from the network-size coefficients and the data. Forecasting a doubling

Table B.2 Full regression results

Predictor	Variable	Coefficient	Standard error	t-statistic
Dconvlag	Lagged dependent	0893283	0986104	0.906
Netsize (NS)	Number of telephone sets	1550.075	251.3466	6.167[*]
NS2	Net size squared	−1291.108	678.0486	−1.904[**]
NS3	Net size cubed	1471.154	727.8555	2.021[***]
Tgrafh	Average real price of telegram	10.35254	9.395631	1.102
GNPpc	Per capita real GNP	−0037915	0062658	−0.605
Avgcallp	Average real price of telephone call	−91.92725	149.9191	−0.613
Monop	Structural change dummy	−2.168961	6.681732	−0.325
Inter	Constant	3.082576	22.13733	0.139
Rho	Cochrane–Orcutt correction	0.8036	0.0732	10.973[*]
		No. of obs = 66		
		R-sq = 98.7%	Adj R-sq = 98.6%	

Notes
  * Denotes variable significant at the 1% level.
 ** Denotes variable significant at the 5% level.
*** Denotes variable significant at the 10% level.

in the density of telephones per capita in the US using the estimated coefficients displays an upward trend of a weak exponential relationship. Because the upward trend appears only in forecast, though, the evidence for the exponential hypothesis should be considered weak on average. Because the three network size terms essentially estimate a linear relationship between the number of telephones per capita and the number of domestic conversations per capita per year, a logical modification to the full regression specification given above is to eliminate the network size squared and cubic terms. Respecifying the regression in this manner results in an increase in the *t*-statistics for both the price variables, though the telephone-call price variable can still not be assumed to be non-zero. The full results of this final regression appear in Table B.3.

Two clear concerns in a model with significant time trends and a high adjusted *R*-squared measurement are heteroskedasticity and autocorrelation. Neither of the model specifications, however, displays signs of these problems. Fitted values versus residuals plots show no apparent problems with the residuals. Moreover, the Cook–Weisberg test for heteroskedasticity cannot reject the null hypothesis of constant variance and the Cochrane–Orcutt procedure for correcting autocorrelation has been employed. The subsequent Durbin–Watson *h*-statistic indicates no autocorrelation at a 1 per cent level of significance for each of the specifications.

Table B.3 Final regression results

Predictor	Variable	Coefficient	Standard error	t-statistic
DconvLag	Lagged dependent	−0969381	−0983045	0.986
Netsize (NS)	Number of telephone sets	1216.536	140.8213	8.639*
Tgraph	Average real price of telegram	16.05634	5.843993	2.747*
CNPpc	Per capita real GNP	−0036921	0063857	−0.578
Avgcallp	Average real price of telephone call	−151.5678	140.7213	−1.077
Monop	Structural dummy	−1.440889	6.617304	−0.218
Constant		18.70185	12.24442	1.527
Rho	Cochrane-Orcutt procedural variable	0.8442	0.0626	13.492*
		No. of obs = 66		
		R-sq = 98.1%	Adj R-sq = 97.9%	

Note
* Denotes variable significant at the 1% level.

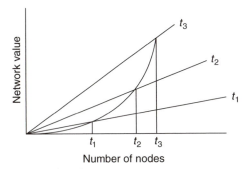

Figure B.3 Potential distortion over time.

Effects of technological change

In the present case one difficulty to observe variables that may affect the relationship between network size and network value and thus create problems in the results is technological change. Technological improvements, through better quality, value-added features, high-speed access and the like, could cause an upward shift in the relationship between network size and value. In other words, given a certain network size, technological improvements alone could lead to greater network usage. Figure B.3 shows the potential problems that shifts in the true relationship can cause for estimations. The straight lines t_1, t_2, t_3 show the true relationship as it shifts up; the curved line illustrates how sampling at different times can estimate an upward-curving relationship when it is really linear.

Conclusions

For various key technological sectors or industries we can identify a strong network economy with an exponential network value to size relation, as compared to one with a linear or logarithmic relationship. Such an economy is characterized by rapid growth and innovation trajectories reinforced by expectations on queueing constraints. As the dynamics unfolds lack of coordination through competitive pressures creates excess capacities which with a slackening demand supported by diminished expectations leads to swift, drastic, and steep-decline avalanching through the supply chain network. An exponential type network economy would trigger significantly more volatile business cycles than we would see in any network economies, or even in the rest of the 'old economy'. The level or extent to which a strong network economy affects the overall economy, such as the US economy recently, even less so physically than in perception, is tantamount to a serial negative queuing effect which is not supply but demand queueing.

References

Arthur, W. (1989) 'Competing Technologies, Increasing Returns, and Lock-in by Historical Events', *Economic Journal* 99: 116–131

Choi, J. P. (1994) 'Irreversible Choice of Uncertain Technologies with Network Externalities', *Rand Journal of Economics* 25(3): 382–401

David, P. (1985) 'CLIO and the Economics of QWERTY', *American Economic Review*, PP 75: 332–337

Economides, N. (1996) 'The Economics of Networks', *International Journal of Industrial Organization* 14: 673–699

Gandal, N. (1994) 'Hedonic Price Indexes for Spreadsheets and an Empirical Test for Network Externalities', *Rand Journal of Economics* 25(1): 160–170

Gottinger, H. W. and M. Takashima (2000) 'Japanese Telecommunications and NTT Corporation: a Case in Deregulation', *International Journal of Management and Decision Making* 1(1): 68–102

Ip, G., N. Kulish, and J. M. Schlesinger (2001) 'Capital Markets and Technology May Bring an even Deeper Decline', *Wall Street Journal*, 5 January

Katz, M. and C. Shapiro (1986) 'Technology Adoption in the Presence of Network Externalities', *Journal of Political Economy* 94: 822–841

Metcalfe, R. (1995) 'Metcalfe's Law: A Network Becomes More Valuable as it Reaches More Users', *InfoWorld* 17(40): 53

Saloner, G. and A. Shepard (1995) 'Adoption of Technologies with Network Externalities: An Empirical Examination of the Adoption of Automated Teller Machines', *Rand Journal of Economics* 26: 479–501

Studenmund, A. H. (1992) *Using Econometrics: A Practical Guide*, 2nd edn, Harper Collins, New York

The Economist (1995) *A Survey of Global Telecommunications*, September 1995

Statistical details: data sources

Data for regressions performed come partly from Historical Statistics of the United States (HSUS), from 1950 to 1970, for the remaining period up to 2000 annual FCC reports have been used. The time series have been constructed from various data sets over long periods of time, the notes on these data are extensive.

(i) *Elimination of duplicate figures.* In HSUS two separate figures exist for a number of years (see for example, data on the number of telephone instruments, the number of calls made, plant, revenue, and cost information). Usually, one figure is derived from FCC reports, and the other is culled from census data. These data do not always match. The yearly time series data were maintained, and the census material eliminated from the data set.

(ii) *Creation of the dependent variable.* Time series in HSUS give the average daily number of telephone calls in the US from 1950 to 1970. To eliminate international data that exist in these time series, but should not appear in the dependent variable time series, the new figures were obtained by subtracting overseas phone calls from total conversations per year.

(iii) *Per capita transformation.* The dependent variable (domestic conversations), the lagged dependent variable, and the independent variables network size, network size squared, network size cubed, and gross national product were transformed to per capita measurements using census figures.

(iv) *Creation of price variables.*   To create a figure for the average cost of telephone conversation, total telephone industry operating revenue was divided by the total number of conversations. Similarly, the average price of a telegram was calculated through the operating revenues of the entire domestic telegraph industry from 1950 to 1980. These operating revenues were divided by the total number of telegrams handled to arrive at the average figure. All price data and the time series for GNP were converted to real figures using historical consumer price index information. The base year is 1967.

(v) *Full regression specification.*   We present the full regression results for the three regression specifications discussed in the text.

(Cochrane–Orcutt regression)
Iteration 0: rho = 0.0000
Iteration 1: rho = 0.3183
Iteration 2: rho = 0.5303
Iteration 3: rho = 0.6652
Iteration 4: rho = 0.7374
Iteration 5: rho = 0.7748
Iteration 6: rho = 0.7922
Iteration 7: rho = 0.7994
Iteration 8: rho = 0.8022
Iteration 9: rho = 0.8032

Number of observ. 66
$F(8,58) = 563.52$

Source	SS	df	MS	
Model	156259.631	8	19532.4538	Prob $> F$ = 0.0000
Residual	2010.38066	58	34.6617355	R-sq. = 0.9873
				Adj R-sq. = 0.9855
Total	158270.011	66	2398.03047	Root MSE = 5.8874

DomConv	*Coef.*	*Std. err.*	*t*	*P > t*	*[95% Conf. interval]*	
DconvLag	−0893283	0.0986104	0.906		−0.1080619	0.2867185
NS	1550.075	251.3466	6.167	0.000	1046.95	2053.2
NS2	−1291.108	678.0486	−1.904	0.062	−2648.369	66.15401
NS3	1471.154	727.8555	2.021	0.048	14.19284	2928.115
Tgraph	10.35254	9.395631	1.102	0.275	−8.45486	29.15994
GNPpc	−0.0037915	0.0062658	−0.605	0.547	−0.0163339	0.0087509
AvgceLUp	−91.92725	149.9191	−0.613	0.542	−392.023	208,1685
Monop	−2.168961	6.681732	−0.325	0.747	−15.5439	11.20598
Inter	3.082576	22.13733	0.139	*0.890*	−41.2301	47.39525
rho	0.8036	0.0732	10.973	0.000	0.6573	0.9498

Sources
Durbin–Watson statistic (original) 1.360806.
Durbin–Watson statistic (transformed) 1.923850.

Final regression specification

(Cochrane–Orcutt regression)
Iteration 0: rho = 0.0000
Iteration 1: rho = 0.4283
Iteration 2: rho = 0.5829
Iteration 3: rho = 0.6910
Iteration 4: rho = 0.7650
Iteration 5: rho = 0.8077
Iteration 6: rho = 0.8288
Iteration 7: rho = 0.8381
Iteration 8: rho = 0.8420
Iteration 9: rho = 0.8436

Source	SS	df	MS	Number of obs. 66
				$F(6,60) = 504.79$
Model	108242.777	6	18040.4629	Prob > F = 0.0000
Residual	214444.31715	60	35.7386192	R-squared = 0.9806
				Adj R-squared = 0.9786
Total	110387.094	66	1672.53173	Root MSE = 5.9782

DomConv	Coef.	Std. err.	t	P > t	[95% Conf. interval]	
DconvLag	0.0969381	0.0983045	0.986	0.328	−0.0997001	0.2935763
NS	1216.536	140.8213	8.639	0.000	934.8516	1498.221
—		—		—	—	—
Tgraph	16.05634	5.843993	2.747	0.275	4.366612	27.74606
GNPpc	−0.0036921	0.0063857	−0.5785	0.547	−0.0164654	0.0090813
Avgcallp	−151.5678	140.7313	−1.077	0.542	−433.0523	129.9168
Monop	−1.440889	6.617304	−0.218	0.747		11.79569
					−14.6774	
Inter	0.132	−5.790629	43.19433			
rho	0.8442	0.0626	13.492	0.000	0.7193	0.9691

Sources
Durbin–Watson statistic (original) 1.142124.
Durbin–Watson statistic (transformed) 2.002030.

Durbin–Watson statistics

The transformed Durbin–Watson statistics for the two regression specifications
are: (full) 1.923850, and (final) 2.002030. Because a lagged dependent variable

is used in the regressions, the Durbin–Watson statistic cannot be used to judge the presence of autocorrelation (Studenmund, 1992), rather, the D–WQ statistic must be transformed into Durbin's *h*-statistic. Durbin's *h*-statistic for the two specifications are, respectively, 0.38611546 and -0.0103251, these statistics do not allow a rejection of the null hypothesis of no serial correlation at the 10 per cent confidence level.

Cook–Weisberg tests
The Cook–Weisberg tests for the models do not support the finding of heteroskedacity

Full specification
Cook–Weisberg test for heteroskedacity using fitted values of DomConv
    Ho: Constant Variance
    chi2(1) = 0.35
    Prob > chi2 = 0.5555

Final specification
Cook–Weisberg test for heteroskedasticity using fitted values of DomConv
    Ho: Constant Variance
    chi2(1) = 0.53
    Prob > chi2 = 0.4655

Appendix C Quality of service parameters in queueing networks for the Internet

In the context of congested networks the phenomenon of packet loss is due to two reasons: the first, packets arrive at a switch and find that the buffer is full (no space left), and therefore are dropped. The second is that packets arrive at a switch and are buffered, but they do not get transmitted (or scheduled) in time, then they are dropped. A formal way of saying this: for real-time applications, packets, if delayed considerably in the network, do not have value once they reach the destination. The sort and variety of delay can severely impact the operability and efficiency of a network and therefore is of eminent interest for economic analysis (Radner, 1993; van Zandt, 1998).

Loss probability requirement: utility function

In view of queueing discipline, we consider K agents, representing traffic classes of M/M/1/B type, competing for resources from the network provider. The utility function is packet loss probability (U_l) for the user classes. We choose the M/M/1/B model of traffic and queueing for the following reasons. The model is tractable, where steady-state packet loss probability is in closed form, and differentiable. This helps in demonstrating the economic models and concepts. Models such as M/M/1/B or M/D/1/B for multiplexed traffic (such as video) are appropriate where simple histogram-based traffic models capture the performance of queueing in networks.

For more complex traffic and queueing models (say, example of video traffic) we can use tail probability functions to represent QoS of the user class instead of loss probability. In the competitive economic model, each agent prefers less packet loss, the more packet loss the worse the quality of the video at the receiving end. Let each agent TC_k have wealth w_k which it uses to purchase resources from network providers.

Let each TC transmit packets at a rate λ (Poisson arrivals), and let the processing time of the packets be exponentially distributed with unit mean. Let c, b be allocations to a TC. The utility function U for each TC is given as follows:

$$
U = f(c,b,\lambda) = \begin{cases}
= \{(1- \lambda/c)(\lambda/c)^{b}/(1- (\lambda/c))^{1+b}, & \text{if } \lambda < c \\
\{1/(b+1), & \text{if } \lambda = c \quad (1) \\
= \{(-1 + \lambda/c)/(\lambda/c)(\lambda/c)^{b}/(-1+ (\lambda/c)^{1+b} & \text{if } \lambda > c.
\end{cases}
$$

The above function is continuous and differentiable for all $c \in [0,C]$, and for all $b \in [0,B]$. We assume $b \in \Re$ for continuity purposes of the utility function.

Theorem C.1   The utility function (packet-loss probability) for an M/M/1/B system is decreasingly convex in c for $c \in [0,C]$, and decreasingly convex in b, $\forall\, b \in [0,B]$. See Chapter 8.

Loss probability constraints

The loss constraint is defined as follows: it is the set of (bandwidth, buffer) allocations $\{x: x \in X, U(x) \le L^c\}$ where $U(x)$ is the utility function (loss probability function where lower loss is better) and L^c is the loss constraint. The preferences for loss probability are convex with respect to buffer and link capacity.

Computation of the QoS surface by supplier   Assume that the supplier knows the utility functions of the agents, which represent the QoS needs of the traffic classes, then the supplier can compute the Pareto surface and find out the set of Pareto allocations that satisfy the QoS constraints of the two agents.

This set could be a null set, depending on the constraints and available resources.

The QoS surface can be computed by computing the points A and B as shown in Figure 8.6. Point A is computed by keeping the utility of class 1 constant at its loss constraint and computing the Pareto-optimal allocation by maximizing the preference of class 2. Point B can be computed in the same way. The QoS surface is the set of allocations that lies in $[A, B]$. The same technique can be used to compute the QoS surface when multiple classes of traffic compete for resources. There are situations where the loss constraints of both the traffic classes cannot be met. In such cases, either the demand of the traffic classes must go down or the QoS constraints must be relaxed. This issue is treated as an admission-control problem, where new sessions are not admitted if the loss constraints of either class is violated.

Max and average delay requirements

A max delay constraint simply imposes a constraint on the buffer allocation, depending on the packet sizes. If the service time at each switch for each packet is fixed, the max delay is simply the buffer size or a linear function of buffer size. Once the QoS surface for loss probability constraints are computed, then the set of allocations that meet the buffer constraint will be computed. This new set will provide loss and max delay guarantees. A traffic class will select the appropriate set of allocations that meet the QoS requirements under the wealth constraint. An illustration is given in Figure 8.5.

A class of interesting applications would require average delay constraints on an end-to-end basis. Some of these applications include file transfers, image transfers, and lately Web-based retrieval of multimedia objects. Consider a traffic model such as M/M/1/B for each traffic class, and consider that several traffic classes (represented by agents) compete for link bandwidth and buffer resources at a link with QoS demands being average delay demands.

Let us now transform the average delay function into a normalized average delay function for the following reasons: average delay in a finite buffer is always less than the buffer size. If a user class has packet-loss probability and average delay requirements, then buffer becomes an important resource, as the two QoS parameters are conflicting with respect to the buffer. In addition, the switch buffer needs to be partitioned among the traffic classes. Another way to look at this: a user class can minimize the normalized average delay to a value that will be less than the average delay constraint. This normalized average delay function for an M/M/1/B performance model, for an agent, is shown below:

$$U_d = f(c,b,\lambda) = \begin{cases} [\lambda/c(1 - \lambda/c) - b(\lambda/c)^{1+b}/1 - (\lambda/c)^b]/\lambda b & \text{if } \lambda \to c \\ (b + 1)/2b\lambda & \text{if } \lambda \to c \quad (2) \end{cases}$$

This function is simply the average delay divided by the size of the finite buffer. This function has convexity properties. Therefore, an agent that prefers to minimize the normalized average delay, would prefer more buffers and bandwidth from the packet-switch supplier.

Theorem C.2   The utility function (2) (normalized average delay) for an M/M/1/B system is decreasing convex in c for $c \in [0, C]$, and decreasing convex in b for all $b \in [0, B]$.

Proof   Using standard techniques of differentiation one can show very easily that U' is positive.

$$U' = (c/\lambda)^b \lambda \log (c/\lambda)/c[(-1 + (c/\lambda))^b]^2$$

and

$$\lim_{c \to \lambda} U' = -1/2b^2\lambda.$$

The second derivative is also positive:

$$U'' = (1 + (c/\lambda)^b) \, (c/\lambda)^b \, \lambda \, \log \, (c/\lambda)^2/c[(1 + (c/\lambda)^b]^3$$

and

$$\lim_{c \to \lambda} U' = 1/b^3\lambda \,.$$

Consider that agents use such utility functions to obtain the required bandwidth and buffers for average delay requirements. Then competition exists among agents to buy resources. Due to convexity properties, the following theorem is stated:

Theorem C.3 Consider K agents competing for resources at a switch with finite buffer and finite bandwidth (link capacity) C. If the K agents have a utility function as shown in equation (2), then both Pareto optimal allocation s and equilibrium prices exist.

Proof An intuitive proof can be based on the fact that the traffic classes have, by assumption, smooth convex preferences in c_k, $\forall c_k \in [0,C]$ and b_k ($\forall b_k \in [0,B]$), and that the utility functions are decreasing convex in the allocation variables. The prices can be normalized such that $p_c + p_b = 1$. By normalizing the prices the budget set $B(p)$ does not change, therefore the demand function of the traffic classes (utility under the demand set) $\Phi(p)$ is homogeneous of degree zero in the prices. It is also well known that if the user (traffic class) has strictly convex preferences, then their demand functions will be well defined and continuous. Therefore, the aggregate demand function will be continuous, and under the resource constraints, the excess demand functions (which is simply the sum of the demands by the K traffic classes at each link minus the resource constraints at each link) will also be continuous.

The equilibrium point is defined as the point where the excess demand function is zero. Then using fixed-point theorems (Brouwer's fixed-point theorem), the existence of the equilibrium price for a given demand can be shown. Different sets of wealth inputs of the traffic classes will have different Pareto allocations and price equilibria.

If the user preferences are convex and smooth, then under the resource constraints, a Pareto surface exists. This can also be shown using fixed-point theorems in an exchange-economy type model, where each user (traffic class) is given an initial amount of resources. Each user then trades resources in the direction of increasing preference (or increasing benefit) until a point where no more exchanges can occur and the allocation is Pareto optimal. The proof is the same when using the unit price simplex property $p_c + p_b = 1$.

A graphical analysis of this surface is shown in Figure 8.6 for two traffic classes competing for resources on a single link with two resources.

Each traffic class prefers more of the resources and the preferences are shown via the contour function. For TC_1 and TC_2 a higher preference is attained when their contour functions are moving away from them. They touch at several points in the resource space as shown in Figure 8.6. All these points are Pareto optimal, therefore they form a Pareto surface. These points are obtained by choosing different initial allocations to the traffic classes.

An agent can use a utility function which is a combination of the packet-loss probability and normalized average delay function.

Tail-probability requirements: utility functions

Here we assume that agents representing traffic classes have tail-probability requirements. This is similar to loss probability. Some applications prefer to drop packets if they spend too much time in the network buffers. More formally, if a packet exceeds its deadline in a certain buffer, then it is dropped. Another way to formalize this is: if the number of packets in a buffer exceed a certain threshold, then the new incoming packets are dropped. The main goal of the network supplier is to minimize the probability that the number of packets in a buffer cross a threshold. In queueing terminology, if the packet-tail probability exceeds a certain threshold, then packets are dropped. The problem for the agent is to minimize packet-tail probability. The agents compete for resources in order to reduce the tail probability. First we discuss tail probability for the M/M/1 model, and then we consider agents which represent traffic classes with on–off models. which are of particular relevance to ATM networks. We assume all the traffic classes have the same requirement of minimizing tail probability which implies competing for resources from the supplier.

Tail probability with M/M/1 model

Consider agents representing traffic classes with tail-probability requirements, and consider an infinite buffer M/M/1 model, where the main goal is to minimize the tail probability of the queueing model beyond a certain threshold. Formally,

$$\text{Tail Prob.} = P(X > b) = (\lambda/c)^{b+1}. \tag{3}$$

The system assumes that $\lambda < c$. From the above equation the tail probability is decreasing convex with respect to c as long as $\lambda < c$, and is decreasing convex with respect to b as long as $\lambda < b$.

Consider agents using such a utility function for obtaining buffer and bandwidth resources, then using the convexity property and the regions of convexity being ($\lambda < c$). Using the equilibrium condition, as derived in Chapter 8, we obtain for Pareto optimal allocation and price equilibrium:

$$p_c/p_b = (b_1 + 1)/c_1 \log(\lambda_1/c_1) = (b_2 + 1)/c_2 \log(\lambda_2/c_2) = \cdots$$
$$= (b_n + 1)/c_n \log(\lambda_n/c_n). \tag{4}$$

We assume K agents competing for buffer and bandwidth resources, with tail probability requirements as shown in equation (3). For the case of two agents in competition, the equilibrium condition is as follows:

$$\log \rho_1/\log \rho_2 = [(b_1 + 1)/c_1] [c_2/(b_2 + 1)] \quad \text{with } \rho = \lambda/c. \tag{5}$$

For equilibrium in network economies we can interpret equation (5) as the ratio of the logs of the utilizations of the classes is proportional to the ratio of the time spent in clearing the buffer contents.

Tail probability with on–off models

In standard performance models the utility functions are derived using simple traffic models such as Poisson, with the mean arrival rate as the main parameter. Here we use on–off (bursty) traffic models in relation to the competitive economic model. The traffic parameters are mean and variance in arrival rate. We show how the traffic variability has an impact on the resource allocation, and in general the Pareto surface at a link. We assume an ATM type network where packet sizes are of fixed size (53 bytes).

On–off models are commonly used as traffic models in ATM networks (Sohraby, 1992; Kleinrock, 1996). These traffic sources transmit ATM cells at a constant rate when active and nothing when inactive. The traffic parameters are average burst length, average rate, peak rate, and variances in burst length. The traffic models for such sources are on–off Markov sources (Sohraby, 1992). A source in a time slot (assuming a discrete time model) is either 'off' or 'on'. In the on state it transmits one cell and in the off state it does not transmit any cell. When several such (homogeneous or heterogeneous) sources feed into an infinite buffer queue, the tail distribution of the queue is given by the following formula:

$$Pr(X > b) = h(c, b, \rho, C_v^2)g(c, b, \rho, C_v^2)^{-b}$$

where $h(c, b, \rho, C_v^2)$ and $g(c, b, \rho, C_v^2)$ are functions of traffic parameters and link capacity c.

Such functions are strictly convex functions in c and b. These functions are currently good approximations to packet-loss probability in finite buffer systems, where packet sizes are of fixed size. These approximations become very close to the actual cell (packet) loss for very large buffers. The utility function is as follows: A TC consists of S identical (homogeneous) on–off sources which are multiplexed to a buffer. Each source has the following traffic parameters: $\{T, r_p, \rho, C_v^2\}$ where T is the average on period, r_p is the peak rate of the source, C_v^2 is the squared coefficient of variation of the on period, and ρ is the mean rate. The conditions for a queue to form are: $Sr_p > c$ (peak rate of the TC is greater than the link capacity) and $Sr_p\rho < c$ (mean rate less than link capacity).

The packet-tail distribution of the queue when sources are multiplexed into an infinite buffer queue then has the form

$$U = Sr_p\rho/c \ [(1 + 2c - Sr_p\rho)/Sr_p\rho \ (1 - \rho)^2 \ (C_v^2 + 1)T]^{-b}. \tag{6}$$

Using a numerical example, we use two traffic classes (with the same values). There are $S_1 = S_2 = 10$ sessions in each traffic class, $T = 5, r_p = 1, \rho = 0.5$. Using the constraints $c_1 + c_2 = 60$ and $b_1 + b_2 = 100$, the Pareto surface is obtained. As C_v^2 increases from 1 to 20, the Pareto surface tends to show that buffer space and link capacity are becoming more and more valuable. The equilibrium price ratios $p(c)/p(b)$ vs C_v^2 increase as C_v^2 increases. A higher C_v^2 implies a higher cell-loss probability and therefore more resources are required, therefore a higher price ratio (link capacity is more valuable compared to buffer).

Specific cases

Now we consider some specific cases of agents with different QoS requirements.

(a) Loss and average delay

Consider the following case where two agents have different QoS requirements, one of them (agent 1) has a packet-loss probability requirement and the other (agent 2) has an average-delay requirement. We assume that the network supplier has finite resources, C for link bandwidth and B for buffer. Using the properties of loss probability and average delay with respect to bandwidth and buffer, the Pareto optimal solution is simply: all buffer to agent 1, as agent 2 does not compete for link buffer. The competition is for link bandwidth between agent 2 and agent 1. Let w_1 be the wealth of agent 1, and w_2 for agent 2, then the equilibrium prices of buffer and bandwidth are the following: $p_b = p_b^f$ and $p_c = (w_1 + w_2)/C$.

Since there is no competition for buffer space the cost of the buffer is simply the fixed cost p_b^f. The Pareto allocations are $\{B,C, w_1/(w_1 + w_2)\}$ for agent 1 and $\{0,C, w_2/(w_1 + w_2)\}$ for agent 2.

(b) Loss and normalized average delay

Consider the following case where agent 1 and agent 2 have preferences on loss probability and normalized average-delay requirements (transforming average-delay requirements into normalized average-delay requirements). In this case the two agents have different utility functions, however, their preferences are such that more buffer and more bandwidth is required and this causes the agents to compete for both resources.

The utility function for agent 1 is as follows:

$$U_1 = \gamma_1 U_{\text{loss}} + (1 - \gamma_1)\, U_{\text{delay}}, \quad \text{where } \gamma_1 \in [0,1].$$

The utility function for agent 2 is as follows:

$$U_2 = \gamma_2 U_{\text{loss}} + (1 - \gamma_2)\, U_{\text{delay}}, \quad \text{where } \gamma_2 \in [0,1].$$

For example, agent 1 might prefer more weight on loss probability than normalized average delay compared to agent 2 who weighs normalized average delay more than loss probability. Let agent 1 choose $\gamma_1 = 0.9$, and agent 2 choose $\gamma_2 = 0.1$. Due to the convexity properties of the loss-probability function and the normalized average-delay function, the resultant multi-objective utility function is decreasing convex with respect to bandwidth and buffer, respectively. Under the equilibrium condition the equilibrium prices for the resources have the familiar property that the ratio of prices is equal to the ratio of marginal utilities with respect to the resources, for each agent.

Using the resource constraints $c_1 + c_2 = C$ and $b_1 + b_2 = B$, we can obtain the Pareto surface. To compute a specific Pareto allocation one uses the following parameters: agent 1 and agent 2 have the same traffic arrival rate $\lambda_1 = \lambda_2 = 10$. The performance model is the M/M/1/B model for both agents. Using the tatonnement process, where agents negotiate with the link supplier to buy bandwidth and buffer resources, the process converges to a price equilibrium. The Pareto optimal allocation is split evenly with respect to buffer and bandwidth among the agents. The price of link bandwidth is higher than the price of buffer.

References

Kleinrock, L. (1996) *Queueing Networks*, Norton, New York 1996

Radner, R. (1993) 'The Organization of Decentralized Information Processing', *Econometrica* 61(5): 1109–1146

Sohraby, K. (1992) 'On the Asymptotic Behavior of Heterogeneous Statistical Multiplexer with Applications', Proceedings of the INFOCOM

Van Zandt, T. (1998) 'The Scheduling and Organization of Periodic Associate Computation: Efficient Networks', *Review of Economic Design* 3: 93–127

Index